Crisis and Resilience in the Bristol–West India Sugar Trade, 1783–1802

Eighteenth-Century Worlds

Series Editors:
Professor Eve Rosenhaft (Liverpool) and Mark Towsey (Liverpool)

Eighteenth-Century Worlds promotes innovative new research in the political, social, economic, intellectual and cultural life of the 'long' eighteenth century (c. 1650–c. 1850), from a variety of historical, theoretical and critical perspectives. Monographs published in the series adopt international, comparative and/or interdisciplinary approaches to the global eighteenth century, in volumes that make the results of specialist research accessible to an informed, but not discipline-specific, audience.

Crisis and Resilience in the Bristol–West India Sugar Trade, 1783–1802

Peter Buckles

LIVERPOOL UNIVERSITY PRESS

First published 2023 by
Liverpool University Press
4 Cambridge Street
Liverpool
L69 7ZU

This paperback edition published 2026

Copyright © 2026 Peter Buckles

Peter Buckles has asserted the right to be identified as the author of this book in accordance with the Copyright, Designs and Patents Act 1988.

All rights reserved. No part of this book may be reproduced, stored in a retrieval system, or transmitted, in any form or by any means, electronic, mechanical, photocopying, recording, or otherwise, without the prior written permission of the publisher.

British Library Cataloguing-in-Publication data
A British Library CIP record is available

ISBN 978-1-80207-883-1 (hardback)
ISBN 978-1-83624-473-8 (paperback)

Typeset by Carnegie Book Production, Lancaster

Contents

List of Figures and Tables — vii

Abbreviations — ix

Preface — xi

A Note on Methodology — xv

Introduction — 1

1 Knowledge, Networks, and the Crisis of Sugar Production in the West Indies — 17

2 Merchant-shipowners and the Crisis of Shipping in the Bristol–West India Trade — 49

3 Merchants, Brokers, and the Structure of the Bristol Sugar Market — 83

4 Crisis, Disruption, and Uncertainty in Bristol's Sugar Market — 123

5 Creditors, Debtors, and Caution in Times of Crisis — 157

Conclusion — 191

Bibliography — 195

Index — 209

Figures and Tables

Figure 1.1: John Pinney's Nevis–Bristol Network, 1783–1803   22

Figure 1.2: Network of Managers within John Pinney's Nevis–Bristol Network, 1783–1803   26

Figure 1.3: Size of John Pinney's Nevis–Bristol Network, with Pinney Removed, 1783–1801   28

Figure 2.1: Shipping Tonnage Entering Bristol, Yearly Totals, October 1784–September 1803 (tons)   51

Figure 2.2: Charles Maies' Network within John Pinney's Nevis–Bristol Network, 1783–1803   55

Figure 2.3: Average Monthly Shipping Tonnage Entering Bristol, 1784–1792 (tons)   67

Figure 2.4: Average Share of Shipping Tonnage Entering Bristol from the West Indies by Month, 1784–1801 (%)   69

Figure 2.5: Share of Shipping Tonnage Entering Bristol from the West Indies by Month, 1788/89 and 1797/98 (%)   70

Figure 3.1: Estimates of Sugar Imported into Bristol by Primary Source, by Year and Season, 1784–1801 (cwt)   88

Figure 3.2: Sugar Imports into England/Britain, Estimates by Elizabeth Schumpeter, by Year, 1783–1803 (cwt)   89

Figure 3.3: Bristol's Share of British Sugar Imports by Year, 1785–1801 (%)   90

Figure 3.4: Value of Sugar Imports into Bristol by Year, 1784–1800 (£)   90

Figure 3.5: Sugar Imports and Average Prices in Bristol by Month, December 1784–February 1786 (cwt and s/cwt)   112

Figure 3.6: Average Annual Price of Muscovado Sugar in Bristol and London, Inclusive of Duties, 1783–1800 (s/cwt)   115

Figure 4.1: Average Monthly Price of Sugar by Year, 1793–1798 (s/cwt)   137

Figure 4.2: Average Annual Price of Muscovado Sugar in London, Before Duties, 1783–1830 (s/cwt)   151

Figure 5.1: Network of Attorneys within John Pinney's Nevis–Bristol Network, 1783–1803   187

Table 3.1: Estimates of Sugar Imports into Bristol, by Primary Source, 1784–1801 (cwt)   87

Table 3.2: Top Twenty Largest Sugar Importers in Bristol, 1784–1801   92

Table 3.3: Summary Statistics for Bristol's Sugar Importers, 1784–1801   93

Abbreviations

BA	Bristol Archives
SHC	Somerset Heritage Centre
SMV	The Bristol Society of Merchant Venturers
UoBSC	University of Bristol Special Collections
WB	Wharfage Books
WIA	Bristol West India Association

Preface

OVER THE COURSE OF WRITING THIS BOOK, the world has seen a constant string of crises. Memories of the 2008 financial crash and the austerity that followed in its wake are conscious influences on its author. Its material form was conceived at the point when Britain decided it would leave the European Union. As it has evolved over the years from postgraduate research project to monograph, the experience of trade disputes, the worsening of climate change and inequality, the coronavirus pandemic, energy crises and spiralling inflation, and geopolitical conflicts between nuclear powers have followed. I am ashamed to say that, in a fit of scientific disinterest, I was intrigued to see that a key theoretical observation of this book—that in preparing for one crisis a business can unwittingly save itself from another—seemed to ring true when businesses that had been stockpiling for Brexit were able to draw on such stockpiles during the first lockdowns of the coronavirus pandemic. This satisfaction in being 'right', of course, gives way to a much more melancholy realisation: such crises, and the tragedies they portend, continue to happen, and they won't stop happening. Indeed, such is the nature of our contemporary moment that, in 2022, 'permacrisis' was declared word of the year by *Collins Dictionary*.[1]

The inevitability of crises only strengthens the need to study them. We are taught as we train to be historians that to change the present we must first

---

1 David Shariatmadari, 'A year of "permacrisis"', *Collins Language Lovers Blog* (1 November 2022) <https://blog.collinsdictionary.com/language-lovers/a-year-of-permacrisis/> [accessed 22 February 2023].

understand the past; we are taught, too, that our understanding of the past is coloured by our present. Against this, the optimist looks not at the crisis, but at the response to it. And there one finds a good deal to be inspired by. The response of numerous societies to the coronavirus pandemic, for one; the seeming realisation by businesses and governments that they bear responsibility for addressing climate change, perhaps another.

This book is, therefore, a product of the times in which it was written. It is a product, too, that was guided by numerous individuals. I am grateful, first, to the ESRC NWSSDTP, whose funding provided me with the opportunity to conduct much of the research that forms the bedrock of this text. I am grateful, too, to William Ashworth, Siobhan Talbott, and Aashish Velkar, whose insightful comments, suggestions, critiques, and directions for reading have been invaluable, and to the late Kate Marsh, whose help and support at the beginning of my time as a postgraduate student at the University of Liverpool were instrumental in shaping this project. My sincerest thanks also to Sheryllynne Haggerty, who has helped me in numerous ways, not least by acting as the external examiner for the thesis upon which this book is based, and to Laura Sandy, who was the internal examiner. I am grateful to Robert Lee for his guidance and interest in this research. Thanks also to several anonymous reviewers, who have taken great care in their reading of both the proposal and the manuscript. Their feedback has greatly informed this book.

Numerous others have offered me advice and pointed me in the right direction during my time in academia, including, but not limited to, Mark Towsey, Elaine Chalus, Stephen Kenny, Sophie Jones, Chris Pearson, Harald Braun, Anna Bocking-Welch, Christienna Fryar, Andrew Davies, Roland Clark, Graeme Milne, Shalini Sharma, and Ian Atherton. Special thanks are due to the archivists at the University of Bristol Special Collections, at the Somerset Heritage Centre, and at Bristol Archives, whose support and suggestions in the gathering of the primary material were especially valuable. Thank you to Tom and Emma for allowing me to stay with them on my trips to Bristol. My thanks also to the Economic History Society, the Association of Business Historians, and to the British Commission for Maritime History for allowing me to speak at their events, and for the valuable feedback I have received in discussion with their members. My thanks, too, to Ally Lee and the team at Liverpool University Press for guiding me through the publication process.

This project would also not have been possible without the love and support of my friends and family, especially Liz, Jeff, Julia, and Emily.

The following has benefited from the critical feedback given by many of these individuals. Any mistakes remain my own.

Stylistic conventions

The firm at the centre of this thesis went through several name changes. It began as Pinney & Tobin, then changed to Tobin & Pinney, finally becoming Tobin, Pinney & Tobin until the end of the period. For the sake of simplicity, it is referred to as Tobin & Pinney throughout. The firm's name at the time is mentioned in the footnotes when its letters are referenced. Ampersands are used to indicate partnerships: 'Tobin & Pinney' refers to the firm, while 'Tobin and Pinney' refers to the two individuals, James Tobin and John Pinney. To avoid repetition, Tobin & Pinney is also referred to as 'the firm' or 'the partners' where appropriate.

The term 'merchant' is used to refer to individuals who bought and sold goods, moved them around, dealt in money and credit, and were typically of high status. 'Factor' refers to individuals who acted as agents for others, selling goods on their behalf for a commission. These roles were not mutually exclusive: merchants could be—and very frequently were—factors. 'Broker' refers to intermediaries who linked buyers and sellers. 'Trader' refers to people who bought and sold goods more broadly, regardless of social status.[2] 'Enslaved people' is preferred instead of 'slaves' to refer to the men, women, and children who were forcibly taken from Africa to the West Indies to work on the plantations. The word 'slave' is still used when referring to concepts or acts, for example, the slave trade or slave trader, or in the network graphs, where 'enslaved person' proves too long.[3] 'Abolition' is used to refer to the abolition of the slave trade in 1807, and the movement leading up to it; this is not to be confused with 'Emancipation', which is used to refer to the abolition of slavery in 1833. These terms also reflect the British context.[4]

Contemporary quotations are styled in their original forms. This includes spellings, emphasis (e.g. underlining), sub- and superscripts, and punctuation. Note that some quotations include language that is today considered to be

---

2 These distinctions follow Sheryllynne Haggerty, *The British-Atlantic Trading Community, 1760–1810: Men, Women, and the Distribution of Goods* (Leiden: Brill, 2006), pp. 4–7, 41–46.

3 Eickelmann argues that this terminology is 'cumbersome and sometimes downright unwieldy', and this sometimes can be the case. Where space allows, I still prefer to use 'enslaved people' over 'slaves', however. See Christine Eickelmann, *The Mountravers Plantation Community, 1734–1834* (2020), p. 20 <https://seis.bristol.ac.uk/~emceee/mountraversplantationcommunity.html> [accessed 23 September 2020].

4 This follows, for example, Walter E. Minchinton, 'Abolition and Emancipation: Williams, Drescher and the Continuing Debate', in *West Indies Accounts: Essays on the History of the British Caribbean and the Atlantic Economy in Honour of Richard Sheridan*, ed. by Roderick A. McDonald (Kingston, Jamaica: University of West India Press, 1996), pp. 253–73.

offensive and derogatory, especially with regard to race. This is unavoidable, especially if we want to understand historical figures as they were, and the repetition of this language in these quotations is in no way an endorsement of its use in any present discourse.[5]

Periods styled as '1789–1791' refer to the span of those years, while periods styled as '1789/90' indicate a season or defined period, depending on the context. Currency is styled as '£ s d', for example, £7 6s 2d. If simply represented as such, this refers to pounds sterling—where colonial currencies are referred to, this is specified (e.g. £200 Nevis currency). 'Cwt' is used generally as the long hundredweight (112 lb), unless stated otherwise.[6] Sugar was priced at shillings per hundredweight, which is written as 's/cwt', or sometimes just 's' if referenced in the context of sugar prices.

Finally, network graphs are used in this book to showcase interconnections within the trading community I analyse; Liverpool University Press have made versions of these graphs available online, with links present beneath the relevant figure.

---

5 Eickelmann, *Mountravers*, pp. 19–21.
6 John J. McCusker, *Essays in the Economic History of the Atlantic World* (London: Routledge, 1997), p. 53.

A Note on Methodology

Much of the analysis in this book is based on traditional qualitative and quantitative methods that will be familiar to most readers. However, integrated amid this are some methods that readers may not have come across before. Significantly, this includes social network analysis, a tool for understanding the interrelations between people that has been growing in popularity for the past two decades. This is a technique borrowed from the social sciences, which has since become embedded in the field of social and economic history. In essence, social network analysis is used to measure the number of actors (people, firms, countries, etc.) in a group and the relationships between them. Using Graph Theory, actors are represented as 'nodes' (points on a graph), and their relationships (these might include marriage links, trading arrangements, and so on) are represented as 'edges' (the lines connecting the points on the graph). This study uses John Pinney's account books to identify actors within the Nevis trading community: it includes anyone who had a transacting relationship with any other actor, with evidence of a transacting relationship provided by an entry in John Pinney's accounts. In the context of this study, it is important to note where particular actors are interacting with lots of different people, as this demonstrates their 'popularity', so to speak. For a full explanation of how these graphs have been put together, and for an in-depth analysis, see my article in *Enterprise & Society*.[1] There are also more resources available for understanding network

---

1 Peter Buckles, 'A Historical Social Network Analysis of John Pinney's Nevis–Bristol Network: Change over Time, the "Network Memory," and Reading Against the Grain of Historical Sources', *Enterprise & Society* (2022), doi:10.1017/eso.2022.19.

analysis. Several historians, including myself, have written overviews of the literature on this methodology in historical studies, and I would recommend starting with that of Kate Davison.[2] I also recommend that the reader refer to the bibliography compiled by the Historical Network Research Community.[3] These are useful starting points for finding out more about this methodology.

In Chapter 3, the reader will note that I use the Herfindahl–Hirschman Index (HHI) as a measure of competition and concentration. This is calculated by multiplying the percentage market share of each firm by itself, and then adding these together (HHI = $X^2 + Y^2 + Z^2$, where X, Y, and Z are the percentage shares of each firm). A perfect monopoly is indicated by a score of 10,000. It is not a perfect measure, but it is useful as a yardstick.[4] The US Department of Justice uses it to gauge the impact of mergers on the market, determining that unconcentrated markets have HHI scores below 1,500, moderately concentrated markets have scores between 1,500 and 2,500, while highly concentrated markets have scores above 2,500.[5] So, if firms X, Y, and Z had shares of 30%, 30%, and 40%, respectively, this would be calculated as $30^2 + 30^2 + 40^2$, which equals 3,400, which would indicate a high level of concentration.

---

[2] Kate Davison, 'Early Modern Social Networks: Antecedents, Opportunities, and Challenges', *The American Historical Review*, 124:2 (2019), 456–82. For my own perspective on the topic, see Peter Buckles, 'Spreading Information in Eighteenth-Century Mercantile Networks: Experiments in Historical Social Network Analysis', in *Business News in the Early Modern Atlantic World*, ed. by Sophie Jones and Siobhan Talbott (Leiden: Brill, forthcoming).

[3] 'HNR Bibliography', *Historical Network Research: Network Analysis in the Historical Disciplines*, <http://historicalnetworkresearch.org/bibliography/> [accessed 12 February 2023].

[4] For contestation on its use, see recently Jaap W. B. Bos and others, 'Competition, Concentration and Critical Mass: Why the Herfindahl–Hirschman Index is a Biased Competition Measure', in *Handbook of Competition in Banking and Finance*, ed. by Jacob A. Bikker and Laura Spierdijk (Cheltenham: Edward Elgar, 2019), pp. 58–88.

[5] See US Department of Justice and the Federal Trade Commission, 'Horizontal Merger Guidelines' (2010), <https://www.justice.gov/atr/horizontal-merger-guidelines-08192010> [accessed 12 February 2023].

Introduction

> War, so fatal to some states, has ever been the best friend of this town, by augmenting the consumption and demand of merchandizes; by filling it with new accessions of people and wealth; and by laying open that profitable traffic in these seas which in time of peace is too strictly watched. From the earliest settlement of this island, its trade was ever most flourishing while war subsisted with the Spaniards; which has administered such constant opportunities of sharing in their gold and silver, as well by private commerce as by open hostility. For this reason, their proverbial saying of, "Peace with England, and war with the rest of the world," was not ill-founded.
>
> Edward Long, *The History of Jamaica*, 1774[1]

CRISIS. THE WORD ITSELF IS ENOUGH TO EVOKE IMAGERY of a particularly perilous kind. One imagines a crisis as something terrible and unexpected; something unforeseen, generating uncertainty as lightness turns to dark, as the future becomes difficult to predict, with no one sure of what path to take because no one can see clearly where any path leads. Indeed, such a definition has formed the basis for theoretical examinations of the subject. This is not uncontested, however: some scholars see a crisis not as some great event that people did not see coming, but as any event

---

1 Edward Long, *The History of Jamaica; Or, General Survey of the Antient and Modern State of That Island, With Reflections on Its Situation, Settlements, Inhabitants, Climate, Products, Commerce, Laws, and Government*, Vol. II (London: T. Lowndes, 1774), p. 120.

which, if not responded to, could result in 'reputational, operational, or financial harm'.[2] A crisis, then, is some event which requires action to prevent harm; it is a catalyst for change, perhaps, or a threat to the established order, a challenge of deep significance that we must face. Yet crises can occur at multiple levels, affecting individuals, communities, nations, or humanity at large. In other words, a particular crisis might be out of the blue or extraordinary, or something familiar yet damaging; a crisis in itself is not normal. A crisis is never a crisis alone, however; one or more can easily become a feature of everyday life. A crisis is an abnormality. *Crises*, though, are normal.

The interrelation of crisis and trade in the eighteenth century has been an object of interest for some time. Historians have examined the impact of crises on shippers, merchants, smugglers, financiers, contractors, and a host of other economic actors.[3] This is of interest not just to historians of the Anglo-American Atlantic, but in European contexts too, and for earlier periods.[4] A significant number of historians see warfare as one of the worst crises that merchants could face. Indeed, this is something of an unspoken assumption within the literature, perhaps born of our understanding of 'total war', a feature of conflict in the nineteenth and twentieth centuries that has coloured our understanding of warfare in the eighteenth century. Pierre Gervais, for example, in a passage that is representative of how this assumption manifests, states bluntly that

> for an eighteenth-century merchant, the ultimate crisis was war; armed conflicts disrupted trade both practically, by subjecting the goods transported to confiscation by the enemy, and financially, by threatening the national and international credit networks and compensation systems on which merchants relied to clear their transactions.[5]

---

2 Sheryllynne Haggerty, *'Merely for Money'? Business Culture in the British Atlantic, 1750–1815* (Liverpool: Liverpool University Press, 2012), pp. 199–206.

3 A recent example is Margarette Lincoln, *Trading in War: London's Maritime World in the Age of Cook and Nelson* (New Haven, CT: Yale University Press, 2018).

4 See recently Jeremy Baskes, *Staying Afloat: Risk and Uncertainty in Spanish Atlantic World Trade, 1760–1820* (Stanford, CA: Stanford University Press, 2013); Siobhan Talbott, *Conflict, Commerce and Franco-Scottish Relations, 1560–1713* (London: Pickering and Chatto, 2014); Edmond Smith, *Merchants: The Community That Shaped England's Trade and Empire* (New Haven, CT: Yale University Press, 2021).

5 Pierre Gervais, 'Facing and Surviving War: Merchant Strategies, Market Management and Transnational Merchant Rings', in *Merchants in Times of Crisis (16th to Mid-19th Century)*, ed. by Andrea Bonoldi and others (Stuttgart: Franz Steiner, 2015), pp. 79–95 (p. 79).

Similarly, Kenneth Morgan argues that, with war, 'trade was often interrupted; freight and insurance rates increased; and convoy protection was needed for commerce with the Caribbean'. Disruption was limited by a strong navy (which had to be paid for with higher taxes) and privateering.[6] In his seminal work on Bristol, however, Morgan argues that during wartime, 'attention to privateering coupled with a marked cutback in normal trading voyages meant ... that Bristol's transatlantic shipping lost vital ground in the 1740s to that of Liverpool, whose geographical location was more distant from the sea passages frequented by enemy men-of-war'.[7] Wartime, for the port, was 'a severe ordeal', especially during the American Revolution. Indeed, Morgan argues that war was a key factor in Bristol's relative decline.[8]

Similar sentiments appear elsewhere in the historiography. Historians tend to emphasise that convoys caused disruption, delays, and gluts as ships arrived at markets all at once, and that insurance and freight rates became expensive.[9] Silvia Marzagalli argues further that 'the French Wars intensified the uncertainty surrounding business choices and forced merchants' to revert to 'traditional forms of risk management'.[10] War is, therefore, portrayed as particularly disruptive. Merchants' peacetime operations were thrown into disarray as they were forced to cope with periods of conflict that threatened their mercantile operations. Their focus on short-term gains from privateering led to neglect of long-term investment. War was damaging. The ultimate crisis.

And yet with crisis comes resilience, the ability to cope, adapt, even thrive, despite difficult circumstances. In this vein, some historians have placed renewed focus on the merchants who benefited from war, and significantly those who had access to government contracts. David Hancock's seminal *Citizens of the World* is focused on such men. As Hancock observes, 'war and slavery had enabled them to build fortunes ... they were called on to fill government contracts, underwrite government bonds, lend much-needed

---

6 Kenneth Morgan, *Slavery, Atlantic Trade and the British Economy, 1660–1800* (Cambridge: Cambridge University Press, 2000), pp. 16–17.
7 Kenneth Morgan, *Bristol and the Atlantic Trade in the Eighteenth Century* (Cambridge: Cambridge University Press, 1993), p. 20.
8 Morgan, *Bristol*, pp. 25–29, 213.
9 Recent examples are Kenneth Morgan, ed., *The Bright-Meyler Papers: A Bristol–West India Connection, 1732–1837* (Oxford: Oxford University Press, 2007), pp. 96–98; Christer Petley, *White Fury: A Jamaican Slaveholder and the Age of Revolution* (Oxford: Oxford University Press, 2018), p. 178.
10 Silvia Marzagalli, 'Establishing Transatlantic Trade Networks in Time of War: Bordeaux and the United States, 1793–1815', *Business History Review*, 79:4 (2005), 811–44 (p. 812).

capital' and advise the government on its imperial expansion.[11] Indeed, just as the merchants in Britain benefited from government contracts, so too did the British government benefit from 'well-developed markets and an abundance of potential contractors in most fields', as Roger Knight and Martin Wilcox conclude.[12] Similarly, Tom Cutterham has shown how merchants who were well placed inside in the emerging US government benefited from contracts and spikes in demand for food and materials during the American Revolution.[13] War provided these merchants, who had government connections and victualling contracts, with an avenue for profit.

A recent movement in the historiography shows how even merchants outside government circles and victualling trades could maintain their everyday operations despite conflict. War, far from being an unusual and destructive event, was part of the familiar trading environment within which merchants operated. No matter how one frames the period, there were a lot of wars over the eighteenth century, especially involving Britain: over 1688–1802, for example, Britain was at war for 51 of the 114 years.[14] As Sheryllynne Haggerty argues, 'many merchants were used to, and comfortable with, coping in a war economy'. Indeed, some merchants 'positively thrived on these situations or involved themselves in speculation'. Furthermore, 'wars, and indeed other crises' could be perceived as positive events that swept away weaker firms and forced 'merchants to adapt their mercantile habits'.[15] Similarly, Marzagalli argues that the rapid reaction of French shippers and traders to the war in 1793 demonstrated their experience and familiarity with warfare. Further still, Marzagalli posits that warfare was actually necessary to balance out the imbalances of peace, especially for the French system, because it lowered the mercantilist restrictions that biased trade in their favour and, thus, helped perpetuate the system.[16] Merchants operating during

---

11 David Hancock, *Citizens of the World: London Merchants and the Integration of the British Atlantic Community, 1735–1785* (Cambridge: Cambridge University Press, 1997), p. 279.

12 Roger Knight and Martin Wilcox, 'War, Government and the Market: The Direction of the Debate on the British Contractor State, c. 1740–1815', in *The Contractor State and Its Implications, 1659–1815*, ed. by Richard Harding and Sergio Solbes Ferri (Las Palmas: Universidad de Las Palmas de Gran Canaria, 2012), pp. 169–92.

13 Tom Cutterham, 'The Revolutionary Transformation of American Merchant Networks: Carter and Wadsworth and their World, 1775–1800', *Enterprise & Society*, 18:1 (2017), 1–31.

14 Morgan, *Slavery, Atlantic Trade*, p. 16.

15 Haggerty, 'Merely for Money'?, pp. 198, 204.

16 Silvia Marzagalli, 'Was Warfare Necessary for the Functioning of Eighteenth-Century Colonial Systems? Some Reflections of the Necessity of Cross-Imperial and Foreign Trade in the French Case', in *Beyond Empires: Global, Self-Organising,*

the eighteenth century were, therefore, almost guaranteed to have operated, in one way or another, through a period of warfare. A renewed focus on how merchants coped with war shows us that it was not as bad as one might assume and, indeed, that it could be a source of opportunity. By 1793, then, when war broke out again in Europe, were merchants not well placed to cope?

There was much about the French Revolutionary Wars that made them unlike earlier conflicts. Where the Seven Years War had set the stage for expansive, global warfare, the motivations for war changed in 1793.[17] While war between Britain and France was very familiar, the French had emerged from the Revolution in a new guise. As James Davey observes, Revolutionary France was 'a novel and threatening adversary', and the conflict was 'sharply ideological'.[18] The revolutionary element to the war gave it a 'real difference', as Margarette Lincoln shows: 'the revolutionary principles that had ignited France had also found fertile ground in Britain ... it was not simply that, as usual, war had its opponents: some had a nagging anxiety that the patriotism of key workers ... could not be trusted'.[19] Contemporaries were also well aware of the differences. Merchants observed that the French were likely to engage in warfare in 'the most desperate and piratical manner'; they believed that the war was bound to be 'very obstinate and destructive'.[20] A contemporary pamphlet argued that the French were 'an Enemy of a new kind ... who fights not to subdue States, but to dissolve society – not to extend Empire, but to subvert Government'.[21] William Pitt the Younger, in a state of political posturing, argued of the French that 'their ambition was unbounded, so the anarchy, which they hoped to establish, was universal'.[22] The war with Revolutionary France was, thus, to be one of the most threatening to mercantile operations. It would seem that the assumptions reflected by Gervais are probably right. War may have offered benefits for some, but it became more intense over the course of the eighteenth century,

---

Cross-imperial Networks, 1500–1800, ed. by Catia Antunes and Amelia Polonia (Leiden: Brill, 2016), pp. 253–77.

17 Linda Colley, *The Gun, the Ship and the Pen: Warfare, Constitutions and the Making of the Modern World* (London: Profile Books, 2021), p. 26.

18 James Davey, *In Nelson's Wake: How the Royal Navy Ruled the Waves after Trafalgar* (New Haven, CT: Yale University Press, 2017), pp. 2–3.

19 Lincoln, *Trading in War*, p. 185.

20 Tobin & Pinney to John Hendrickson, 30 April 1793, and Tobin & Pinney to William Delaroche, 14 February 1793, Bristol, University of Bristol Special Collections (UoBSC), MS DM58/Letter Book/39.

21 Davey, *In Nelson's Wake*, p. 2.

22 Roger Knight, *Britain Against Napoleon: The Organization of Victory, 1793–1815* (London: Penguin, 2014), p. 61.

more encompassing, more pernicious; warfare, as this great conflict between European powers, was surely the ultimate crisis.

Not necessarily. While, on the one hand, merchants were witness to the intensification of warfare, on the other, they became ever more experienced with it. If the 'ultimate crisis' is a measure of the harm that a crisis can cause, bound up in this, too, must be the response, the resilience, the ability to weather the storm: and by 1793, merchants knew how to respond to warfare. Indeed, for British merchants, it was not just their familiarity with warfare that prepared them, for they were experienced in dealing with a range of crises. They had faced financial crises, such as those in 1772 and 1793, which led to a significant number of bankruptcies; even the boom-and-bust cycle of the eighteenth-century economy drove waves of financial failures that could cause intense challenges.[23] Embargoes, trade disputes, and political disruption could all potentially frustrate mercantile operations.[24] These the sugar merchants of Bristol endured, and more. They faced natural hazards, including hurricanes, and other crises in sugar production. The plantation economy, based as it was on the labour of enslaved Africans, faced crises in the form of uprisings and other forms of resistance as the enslaved people fought back against the violence of their captors. The abolitionist movement was similarly problematic for those who benefited from the system of slavery. Indeed, given that there was such a variety of problems that could befall a business—some less foreseeable, some more uncertain—can warfare really be considered the 'ultimate crisis', as Gervais suggests?

This book uses a case study of merchants in Bristol—two in particular, set against the context of their peers more broadly—to show how the problems of warfare could be overcome and to explore the impact of and warfare's interrelation with other crises. The argument central to this book is that the sugar merchants of Bristol were able to overcome the crises that they faced by using their knowledge of production and their networks in the West Indies, by taking necessary steps to safeguard and control their shipping, by using their understanding and power in the market, and by cautiously using credit. As such, I show that warfare was not the 'ultimate crisis' as many historians

---

23 While government regulation following the South Sea Bubble in 1720 may have seen off booms and busts as a result of asset price inflation (see William Quinn and John D. Turner, *Boom and Bust: A Global History of Financial Bubbles* [Cambridge: Cambridge University Press, 2020]), stocks were not the only cause of rise and ruin.

24 There are numerous works on this subject. For some significant recent publications in this context, see Haggerty, *'Merely for Money'?*, pp. 198–234; Petley, *White Fury*; Trevor Burnard and John Garrigus, *The Plantation Machine: Atlantic Capitalism in French Saint-Domingue and British Jamaica* (Philadelphia: University of Pennsylvania Press, 2016).

assume. The undercurrent to this argument is the notion that crises were normal, and that 'peacetime' was not necessarily peaceful. The absence of warfare did not mean the absence of conflict—there was conflict between merchant and planter, buyer and seller, enslaved and oppressor. Indeed, during the 1783–1793 period of 'peace', West India merchants and planters faced the challenges of a new trading relationship with the United States, a series of hurricanes and bad harvests (along with continued problems with soil degradation), the threat of war with France and Spain in 1787 and 1790, the strengthening of the abolitionist movement, and the revolution in Saint Domingue (now Haiti). These posed a threat to production and shipping, and disrupted markets, credit, and networks just as the war did from 1793. Though different in their nature, they were each a crisis just as war was, and as such necessitated a response. And even if sugar merchants were perhaps among the most directly affected by these challenges, the plantation economy was foundational to the economy of the North Atlantic and the emerging systems of capitalism. The sugar merchants examined here are not part of some special class of merchant to be considered separate to all others: they are central and important figures in this broader story.

Sugar and Bristol in 1783

> We see frequently societies of merchants in London and other trading towns, purchase waste lands in our sugar colonies, which they expect to improve and cultivate with profit by means of factors and agents; notwithstanding the great distance and the uncertain returns
>
> Adam Smith, *Wealth of Nations*, 1776[25]

Sugar was at one point the world's most valuable commodity, and the men who cultivated it and traded it were wealthy men indeed. Its function in society shifted dramatically from medicine to spice, to preservative, to sweetener, and then to drug over the centuries. It was, until the abolition of slavery, the product of forced labour. Today it is still consumed across the globe as an additive and sweetener; humanity's toxic relationship with the substance is responsible for a range of health crises from obesity to diabetes.[26] In 1799, £10.3 million worth of sugar was imported into Britain. To put this

---

25 Adam Smith, *An Inquiry into the Nature and Causes of the Wealth of Nations*, Vol. I (London: Cadell and Davies, 1812 [1776]), p. 245.

26 See James Walvin, *Sugar: The World Corrupted, from Slavery to Obesity* (London: Robinson, 2017); Sidney Mintz, *Sweetness and Power: The Place of Sugar in Modern History* (New York: Penguin, 1985).

into context, the Exchequer's average tax receipt per annum for 1796–1800, by Patrick O'Brien's estimate, was £28.5 million.[27] As a result, leading West India planters were obscenely wealthy. Poor men could go out to the West Indies, establish their fortune, and a century later their dynasty—and their wealth—would live on.[28] Stereotypes of these men abounded. At one end, planters complained of being portrayed as 'as a herd of criminals and convicts' owing to the lowly beginnings of the Caribbean's buccaneers and deportees, and at the other of being 'too much addicted to expensive living, costly entertainment, dress and equipage', given their reputation for extravagance.[29]

Yet as Adam Smith suggests, this is not just a story of the planters, but also a story of the 'merchants' working alongside their 'factors and agents' to produce sugar and transport it over a 'great distance' to markets in Britain. At the market, it became a story of 'profit' and 'uncertain returns'. And it was not just London to which merchants, factors, and agents transported sugar, but 'other trading towns'; foremost among these in Adam Smith's mind may have been Bristol.

Despite losing its place as Britain's 'Second City' to Liverpool over the eighteenth century, Bristol still retained significance and influence. Importantly, it was the second largest sugar-importing centre in Britain after London until it was surpassed by Liverpool in 1799.[30] It remained intimately connected to the West Indies, both socially and economically, into the nineteenth century. It also remained a significant regional distribution centre, serving the south-west and Wales with manufactures and colonial produce, including glassware, metalware, alcohol, refined sugar, tobacco, and chocolate.[31] There is a long literature that examines Bristol's relative decline

---

27 Patrick K. O'Brien, 'The Political Economy of Taxation, 1660–1815', *Economic History Review*, 41:1 (1988), 1–32 (p. 3).

28 Eric Williams, *Capitalism & Slavery* (Chapel Hill: University of South Carolina Press, 1994), pp. 85–97.

29 Bryan Edwards and Edward Long, quoted in P. J. Marshall, 'A Polite and Commercial People in the Caribbean', in *Revisiting the Polite and Commercial People: Essays in Georgian Politics, Society, and Culture in Honour of Professor Paul Langford*, ed. by Elaine Chalus and Perry Gauci (Oxford: Oxford University Press, 2019), pp. 173–90 (pp. 175–76).

30 Morgan, *Bristol*, pp. 23–28; Jacob M. Price and Paul G. E. Clemens, 'A Revolution of Scale in Overseas Trade: British Firms in the Chesapeake Trade, 1675–1775', *The Journal of Economic History*, 47:1 (1987), 1–43 (p. 28).

31 See Kenneth Morgan, 'The Economic Development of Bristol, 1700–1850', in *The Making of Modern Bristol*, ed. by Madge Dresser and Philip Ollerenshaw (Tiverton: Redcliffe, 1996), pp. 48–75 (pp. 54–63); Walter E. Minchinton, 'The Port of Bristol in the Eighteenth Century', in *Bristol in the Eighteenth Century*, ed. by Patrick McGrath (Newton Abbot: David and Charles, 1972), pp. 127–60 (pp. 132–34).

over the eighteenth century. Several historians have observed how its port had become overly dependent on the West India trade, and that its merchant elite, more interested in social cohesion than competition, failed to improve the port quickly enough.[32] Others have cited external factors, in particular the superior geography of Liverpool, with its canal connections to the West Midlands metal and pottery industries, the salt of Cheshire, Manchester cotton textiles, Leeds woollen cloth, and Lancashire coal.[33] Kenneth Morgan has synthesised these views. In addition to the above, Morgan argues that the lack of industrial development in the hinterland from the 1760s that stemmed from the import-led nature of Bristol's economy, alongside its expensive port dues, were the key factors for its decline.[34]

Concerns about relative decline are considered by others to be overblown. Charles Harvey and Jon Press, looking more broadly at the city and not just the port, argue that the diverse range of industries that emerged and survived throughout the eighteenth and nineteenth centuries, in particular tobacco and chocolate manufacturing, show that Bristol prospered in a 'robust fashion'.[35] Other research has shown that the port system remained profitable into the nineteenth century, and attracted increasing shipping: the city's merchants 'were operating a system that brought in profits and were content to continue as they were'. The largest problem the port faced was its tidal range, which no amount of improvement in the port itself could overcome.[36] Indeed, the tidal range, at 45 feet along the seven-mile stretch of winding river, made the Avon particularly difficult for ships to navigate. Yet Bristol's overseas trade kept expanding. Before the American Revolution, tonnage peaked in 1774/75 at around 60,000 tons, which was surpassed in 1787/88 at 68,226 tons, with

---

32 C. M. MacInnes, *A Gateway of Empire* (Bristol: Arrowsmith, 1939), pp. 358–71; Richard Pares, *A West-India Fortune* (Bristol: Longmans, Green, 1950), p. 212. See discussion in Morgan, 'Economic Development'.

33 See Alan F. Williams, 'Bristol Port Plans and Improvement Schemes of the Eighteenth Century', *Transactions of the Bristol and Gloucestershire Archaeological Society*, 81 (1962), 138–88 (p. 180); Brian J. Atkinson, 'An Early Example of the Decline of the Industrial Spirit? Bristol Enterprise in the First Half of the Nineteenth Century', *Southern History*, 9 (1987), 71–89.

34 Morgan, *Bristol*, pp. 3–4; Morgan, 'Economic Development', p. 68.

35 Charles Harvey and Jon Press, 'Industrial Change and the Economic Life of Bristol Since 1800', in *Studies in the Business History of Bristol*, ed. by Charles Harvey and Jon Press (Bristol: Bristol Academic Press, 1988), pp. 1–32.

36 John Gilbert MacMillan, 'The Port of Bristol in the Second Half of the Eighteenth Century: An Examination of the Organisational Structure of the Port Pertaining to the Management and Operation of its Shipping with Special Reference to Ships Trading with the West Indies and America', unpublished PhD thesis, University of Exeter, 2015, pp. 314–18.

a peak in 1791/92 of 84,131 tons. Despite the congestion in the port and the few major improvements made until the floating harbour was finished in 1809, its sustained growth meant that Bristol remained a significant and substantial shipping centre up to the nineteenth century.[37]

As Bristol was reaching its peak for overseas shipping in the West India trade, James Tobin and John Pinney, the two figures who are the focus of this book, began their careers as sugar merchants. Both had been planters in Nevis. John Pinney, born John Pretor, had left Britain after the Seven Years War to take up the inheritance of a family estate in Nevis—he adopted the Pinney name as a condition of his inheritance (the estate was founded by his forebear, Azariah Pinney, who was condemned to transportation to the island following his involvement in the 1685 Monmouth Rebellion). Until 1783, John Pinney worked the plantation himself, and he left his cousin Joseph Gill in charge when he moved to Bristol.[38] Pinney had seven children: John Frederick, Elizabeth, Azariah, Alicia (who died as a baby), Pretor, Mary, and Charles. Pinney's daughters married into banking, significantly Elizabeth to Peter Baillie, son of Evan Baillie (an old associate of Pinney's).[39] James Tobin and his wife, Elizabeth, themselves had eight children, including the naval officer George Tobin, the playwright John Tobin, and, ironically, the abolitionist James Webbe Tobin.[40] The firm went through several iterations as Pinney and Tobin both drafted their children into service. Azariah joined the firm in 1789—it was first styled Pinney & Tobin, but after Azariah's arrival became Tobin & Pinney. One of Tobin's sons, Henry Hope, joined in 1796, and the firm became Tobin, Pinney & Tobin. Azariah left in 1802 to begin working with brother John Frederick, though he died shortly after in 1803, as did Henry Hope in the same year. The firm continued thereafter with more of John Pinney's children becoming involved. The firm was wound up in 1850, and Charles, the youngest, sold the family counting house in 1861.[41]

Tobin & Pinney began with a start-up capital of £12,000, most of this advanced by John Pinney, despite nominally sharing half the firm with Tobin. Over his lifetime, Pinney reinvested over £200,000 into the firm; at the time of his death in 1818, Richard Pares calculates that Pinney's fortune,

---

37 Morgan, *Bristol*, pp. 28–29; Morgan, 'Economic Development', pp. 51–53; Minchinton, 'The Port of Bristol in the Eighteenth Century', pp. 135–41.
38 MacInnes, *Gateway*, pp. 307–21; Pares, *West-India Fortune*, pp. 36–39, 52–54.
39 Pares, *West-India Fortune*, pp. 164–71.
40 See biographies of these individuals composed by David Small in the *Oxford Dictionary of National Biography* (2004).
41 Pares, *West-India Fortune*, pp. 171–74.

on paper, stood at £340,000, which equates to £22.2 million at 2022 rates.[42] Tobin & Pinney was not even the largest sugar-importing firm in Bristol: William Miles, Protheroe & Claxton, Thomas Daniel, Evan Baillie, Thomas Harris, and John Fisher Weare were more substantial. These were men with whom Tobin and Pinney were in contact, mostly through Bristol's West India Association.[43] They probably met at the coffee houses and the quays, and visited each other's counting houses. Tobin & Pinney shared ownership of its vessels with Protheroe & Claxton, so the two firms likely met for business. Tobin and Pinney cannot, of course, be taken as wholly representative of Bristol, but their engagement with the community, and their willingness to adopt and conform to the prevailing sentiments, means that their experience can—and does—speak to the experience of Bristol's mercantile community. Alongside the letters of their peers, including Thomas Harris, John Fisher Weare, and Lowbridge & Richard Bright, the experience of Tobin & Pinney can help us understand how the merchants who were engaged in Bristol's sugar trade responded to the crises and challenges that they faced in this period.

The main primary sources used in this case study are the letters of the firm Tobin & Pinney alongside the account books of John Pinney. These are held in the University of Bristol Special Collections, having been reunited there after their dispersal among the Pinney family homes.[44] Their letter books record much of their outgoing correspondence. Within the firm, comparatively less is known about James Tobin, whose physical records, aside from his letters as part of the firm, consist of a series of pamphlets contesting James Ramsay's attack on the slave trade.[45] By contrast, we know much more about John Pinney. He kept extensive records which have been consulted by a number of historians. One of the most important of these works is Richard Pares' *A West-India Fortune*.[46] This work makes use of much of the Pinney papers, examining the family business as it related to the plantation in Nevis and the firm in Bristol. Every historian who has written on the

---

42 Pares, *West-India Fortune*, pp. 175, 178, 320–21, 330–31. Conversion from 1818 to 2022; see Bank of England, *Inflation Calculator* (2023), <https://www.bankofengland.co.uk/monetary-policy/inflation/inflation-calculator> [accessed 1 February 2023].

43 BA, MS SMV/8/3/2/1 West India Association Minute Book, 1782–1804 (WIA).

44 UoBSC, MS DM58/Letter Book/37–40 and 42, and MS DM58 UoBSC, MS DM58/Account Books/30–41, 43, 45, 47, 52, 54, 57, and 59; Pares, *West-India Fortune*, pp. 333–35.

45 See David Beck Ryden, *West Indian Slavery and British Abolition, 1783–1807* (Cambridge: Cambridge University Press, 2010), pp. 189–91.

46 Pares, *West-India Fortune*. Pares was preceded by Charles MacInnes, who included a case study on John Pinney in his work on Bristol, entitled *A Gateway to Empire*.

Pinney family since, myself included, is indebted to Pares' scholarship. Others include Kenneth Morgan, whose seminal work on Bristol was published in 1993, and more recently Albane Forestier, whose thesis used the Pinney papers as part of a comparative case study comparing the French and British sugar trades. Forestier has also published on the role of family in Tobin & Pinney's business network.[47] Notable work has been conducted by Christine Eickelmann and David Small on the enslaved population of John Pinney's Mountravers Plantation, which has also resulted in the publication of a book on Pero Jones, an enslaved man who acted as Pinney's personal servant.[48] As important and insightful as these contributions are, the following chapters show that there is much more about the nuts and bolts of the sugar trade to understand that these sources can show us. By synthesising analyses of these and other primary sources, this book contributes new levels of depth and detail, demonstrating how these merchants developed their resilience to crises as they cultivated, processed, shipped, and sold sugar.

Other family papers have been used, such as those of the Dickinson family of Kingweston kept at Somerset Heritage Centre.[49] The Dickinsons were absentee plantation owners, with income from estates in Jamaica. William Dickinson was an MP, and corresponded about plantation business with family members Ezekiel, Caleb, and Barnard Dickinson. William was also connected to Stephen Fuller, one of the West India interest's most famous and notorious merchants and agents, through his marriage to Stephen's daughter, Phillipa.[50] The Dickinsons were also connected to the Pinneys through marriage: John Frederick, son of John Pinney, married Frances Dickinson, William's daughter.[51] The sources are of value to this study for their references to the plantations on Jamaica, and significantly for the

---

47 Morgan, *Bristol*; Albane Forestier, 'Commercial Organisation in the Late Eighteenth Century Atlantic World: A Comparative Analysis of the British and French West Indian Trades', unpublished PhD thesis, London School of Economics, 2009; Albane Forestier, 'Risk, Kinship and Personal Relationships in Late Eighteenth-Century West Indian Trade: The Commercial Network of Tobin & Pinney', *Business History*, 52:6 (2010), 912–31.

48 Eickelmann, *Mountravers*; Christine Eickelmann and David Small, *Pero: The Life of a Slave in Eighteenth-Century Bristol* (Bristol: Redcliffe, 2004).

49 Taunton, Somerset Heritage Centre (SHC), MS DD/DN/4/2, correspondence of William Dickinson.

50 Walter E. Minchinton, *Jamaica Plantation Records from the Dickinson Papers 1675–1849 in Somerset Record Office and Wiltshire & Swindon Record Office: Introduction to the Microfilm Collection* (Wakefield: Microform Academic Publishers, 1978); Kenneth Morgan, *Slavery and the British Empire: From Africa to America* (Oxford: Oxford University Press, 2007), p. 50.

51 Pares, *West-India Fortune*, p. 167.

incoming correspondence from sugar factors, including Bristol merchants James Sutton, Thomas Harris, and John Fisher Weare, who sold sugar for the Dickinsons at various points over this period. There are also letters from Stephen and Rose Fuller, who acted as William Dickinson's sugar factors in London, and from Edward Shiercliff, Dickinson's Bristol agent, who gave him detailed news updates.[52] These business letters are at their most complete over this period for 1782–1795, after which there is a gap until the mid-1800s. Despite their importance, they have been under-utilised by historians thus far. Printed primary sources, including the records of the Bright family compiled by Morgan, and collections published by the Bristol Records Society, have also been consulted.[53] These sources help broaden the analysis, and provide useful comparisons to the Pinney papers that help substantiate the observations and experiences of Tobin & Pinney.

Other records used include the wharfage books kept by the Society of Merchant Venturers, which provide useful statistical data. They have been used by Morgan to examine broader trends over the eighteenth century, though, much like the Pinney papers, their detail allows for a much more granular use over a shorter period. They list the arrival times, tonnage, port of origin, place of owner, and dues paid for ships, alongside goods imported and by which firm or individual.[54] The records of Bristol's West India Association have also been consulted, which list the members of what was, in effect, Bristol's West India lobby. These records capture their meetings (social and political) and resolutions, and include copies of letters and petitions. The association's members included John Pinney and James Tobin.[55] Both of these records can be used in conjunction with the records of merchant firms to help place them in their broader context, as well as provide analytical insights of their own that help understand Bristol's sugar trade over this period.

Much secondary research has also been consulted. Foundational to our understanding of the sugar-slave economy is Eric Williams's *Capitalism &*

---

52 Edward Shiercliff was also the author of *The Bristol and Hotwell Guide* (Bristol: Bulgin and Rosser, 1789).

53 Morgan, *Bright-Meyler Papers*; Walter E. Minchinton, ed., *Politics and the Port of Bristol in the Eighteenth Century: The Petitions of the Society of Merchant Venturers, 1698–1803* (Bristol: Bristol Records Society, 1963); Nicholas Rogers, ed., *Manning the Royal Navy in Bristol: Liberty, Impressment and the State, 1739–1815* (Bristol: Bristol Records Society, 2014).

54 Bristol, Bristol Archives (BA), MS SMV/7/1/1/72–83 Wharfage Books, 1784–1803 (WB).

55 BA, MS SMV/8/3/2/1 WIA. Pinney was admitted in November 1784, Tobin in April 1786.

Slavery, published in 1944. Significantly, Williams argues that the abolition of the slave trade was driven principally, not by humanistic or moral concerns, but by economic factors, in particular the decline of the mercantilist plantation system and the rise of industry. Further, he argues that profits from the slave trade contributed to the growth of this industry.[56] These two arguments have been the subject of substantial debate and revision since Williams's original work, not least by Joseph Inikori.[57] Inikori's work has broadened the analysis beyond the profits of the slave trade to the systems upon which slavery and the slave-related trades were built. This includes much of the financial system, and is not just concerned with the West Indies, but with the wider Atlantic.[58] This literature is important for the study of sugar and for the analysis I conduct in this book.

THE STRUCTURE OF THIS BOOK

This book has five chapters, each examining the crises that Bristol's sugar merchants faced and their means of resilience to such crises. The first is centred on the production of sugar in the West Indies. It explores what the merchants in Bristol needed to know to act effectively as cogs in the plantation machine to overcome the challenges that they faced: the aftermath of war with the newly formed United States, devastating hurricanes, and, significantly, the movement to abolish the slave trade. I show that they relied on networks of knowledge, with these networks explored using social network analysis. This social infrastructure was supported by the physical infrastructure of the time: shipping. Chapter 2 focuses on the ships that carried goods, people, and letters, showing how merchants used the tried-and-tested convoy system to maintain their connection to the islands during wartime. Moreover, they had systems for reducing moral hazards and natural hazards, not least of which was insurance. Making use of convoys and insurance during wartime (and complaining about their drawbacks) was as natural to merchants as managing shipping during peace.

---

56 Williams, *Capitalism & Slavery*.
57 See survey in Ryden, *West Indian Slavery*.
58 Joseph Inikori, *Africans and the Industrial Revolution in England: A Study in International Trade and Economic Development* (Cambridge: Cambridge University Press, 2002). The debate, and public interest in it, is still alive; recent contributions to the literature that have gained popular appeal include Padraic X. Scanlan, *Slave Empire: How Slavery Build Modern Britain* (London: Robinson, 2020) and Michael Taylor, *The Interest: How the British Establishment Resisted the Abolition of Slavery* (London: Bodley Head, 2020).

Just as the supporting shipping contributed to the flow of people and information, so too did it ensure the safe delivery of sugar. Chapter 3 dives deep into Bristol's sugar market, outlining its mechanisms and identifying the people involved in the trade of sugar, from captains and their crew to brokers and coopers. It explores the means by which prices moved (or did not), showing that production, above all, remained the key determinant of prices. Chapter 4 takes this further, showing how price uncertainty came from transitional periods between states of war and peace, rather than from war and peace themselves. Against this, production remained the single most important cause for alterations in price, while the Saint Domingue Revolution, a conflict between oppressor and oppressed on the island that was to become Haiti, unveiled the power of an altogether different kind of conflict, one different to the typical battle between European hegemons. The conflict raised the price of sugar in Britain and gave merchants considerable power in the market; overproduction and the subsequent fall in prices in 1799 ended their period of good fortune.

Throughout this—movements in markets, crises in shipping, and the perils of production—merchants were managing their credit. Chapter 5 shows how, using caution as their guiding principle, these merchants in Bristol were able to retain their investments in production in the face of crisis and uncertainty. Indeed, given the number of crises that they faced in this period, including significantly the movement to abolish the slave trade, the sugar merchants examined here became particularly adept at surviving crisis, staying afloat into the 1800s even as others floundered.

Broader movements took hold, of course, and sugar soon lost its significance to Britain's economy as cotton became king; the Caribbean islands became a relic as Britain's imperial ambitions turned east instead of west. Against the rolling tides of history, however, are the day-to-day operations of businesses and their means of resilience in the face of crisis.

1

Knowledge, Networks, and the Crisis of Sugar Production in the West Indies

> When a Clergyman of learning and abilities introduces himself to the notice of the world in the amiable character of a friend to humanity, and stands forth a volunteer in the noble cause of universal liberty, he is undoubtedly intitled to the applause, and reverence of mankind. But when such an author endeavours to attain so desirable an end, by means which would, if possible, tend to its disgrace; when he deals in rash assertions, gross misrepresentations, and virulent invectives; when he lavishly sacrifices to the absurdest prejudices of the vulgar ... the true motives of his zeal, and the immaculate purity of his intentions, may become justly liable to suspicion.
>
> James Tobin, *Cursory Remarks*, 1785[1]

JAMES TOBIN'S RESPONSE TO THE REVD JAMES RAMSAY'S pamphlets decrying the immoralities of the slave trade reveals a key truth about the merchant's role in the plantation system. It was the duty of the sugar merchant, not just to ship and insure the sugar bound to him in consignment, not just to sell the sugar for the best price possible, nor just to advance credit and smooth the finances of their planter clients; it was a merchant's duty, too, to take any steps the planter client required, from their vantage point on Britain's temperate soil, to ensure that the production of sugar, in the tropical climate of the Caribbean so remote to them, continued unabated. One might

---

1 James Tobin, *Cursory Remarks upon the Reverend Mr Ramsay's Essay on the Treatment and Conversion of African Slaves in the Sugar Colonies* (London: G. and T. Wilkie, 1785).

be forgiven for believing that the plantation machine was a product only of the Caribbean islands and the southern regions of the American mainland. This impression is, of course, not without a sound evidential basis. The machine—a concept proposed by Sidney Mintz and developed by Trevor Burnard and John Garrigus—is a fitting metaphor. Such explanations of sugar production typically focus on the combination of 'farm and factory' that plantations embodied.[2] Fields of sugar cane were harvested by the enslaved African labourers, who carted the cane from fields to mills, to boiling houses, and the semi-refined product to curing houses and the liquid by-product to distilleries. The machine was powered by enslaved human and animal labour; it was run by the white planters who sat atop the hierarchy of management.[3] The machine was not just the planter-management and the enslaved contingent they purported to own, however: the merchants were themselves cogs within this machine, sitting not, as the resident planters and managers did, in the lordly homes that were juxtaposed against the deprivation to which the enslaved people were subjected, but in counting houses and lordly estates in London, Bristol, Liverpool, Glasgow, and elsewhere in Britain. With its merchant contingent, the plantation machine was truly transatlantic.

Were the West Indies free of crisis, the merchant cog might well have been made redundant; the horrors of the plantation system might well have been confined to the Caribbean, remote from Britain. Yet a West Indies free of crisis was a fantasy. Crisis drew those who were resident in the metropole close to the colonies, if not physically then figuratively, with colonial matters occupying the minds of merchants, insurers, politicians, activists, and others with a stake, in one way or another, in colonial events. In the 1780s alone there were at least three crises that we can point to that disturbed, perturbed, and disrupted production—the American Revolution and its aftermath, natural disasters that devastated the islands, and the movement to abolish the slave trade. Barely a year went by in this decade when the islands were unaffected by one or a combination of these events. Being a well-oiled cog in the plantation machine, for the merchant class, meant helping planters navigate the new regulatory environment that they faced in the aftermath of the formation of the United States of America. It meant sending vital supplies across from Britain to keep enslaved Africans fed well enough to continue their forced labour. It also meant, for the merchants in Bristol upon whom this book is focused, supporting the planters financially as they purchased enslaved labourers, and defending the trade from the abolitionists

---

2 See recently Scanlan, *Slave Empire*, pp. 67–74.

3 Burnard and Garrigus, *Plantation Machine*, pp. 4–8; Mintz, *Sweetness and Power*, ch. 2.

who would dare to challenge their authority and threaten their prosperity. It meant, finally, intervening in plantation operations by offering advice, altering orders, and otherwise ensuring that the production process carried on smoothly. Thanks to merchants on the opposite side of the Atlantic, the production of sugar was resilient to the crises it faced.

New challenges

In the 1780s, three major crises presented themselves to West India planters and merchants, threatening to disrupt production. They would not be the last, as later chapters show. At this point, however, as we focus our attention on sugar production in the islands, limiting the analysis to these three is instructive. Later chapters will build on the foundations laid down here. As the effects of these crises show, in the West Indies, with production focused significantly on sugar (as well as other colonial cash crops), and despite attempts to achieve self-sufficiency, plantations were heavily dependent on the outside world for food, materials, and consumer goods, as well as tools and capital goods. Indeed, the plantation system could not exist independently of Britain, Europe, and North America.

Events from 1775 disrupted this delicate framework. By then, the North American mainland had become the principal source of grain, livestock, and lumber for the West Indies. Planters funded the purchase of these goods through the sale of rum and molasses, for which there was little demand in Britain.[4] Nevis, the island which Tobin & Pinney served, was no exception.[5] Access to these vital inputs was impeded by the war that followed the American Declaration of Independence, a situation exacerbated by Spanish and French involvement in the conflict. Though the islands survived the war—indeed, the fact that they did not join the thirteen colonies in rebellion is a matter of deep scholarly interest[6]—there was no guarantee that they would survive the peace. While Britain had retained parts of North America, the plantations had been especially reliant on the thirteen colonies for vital supplies of provisions to sustain both themselves and the enslaved labourers

---

4 Lowell Joseph Ragatz, *The Fall of the Planter Class in the British Caribbean, 1763–1833* (New York: Octagon Books, 1971), pp. 88–92.

5 Marco G. Meniketti, *Sugar Cane Capitalism and Environmental Transformation: An Archaeology of Colonial Nevis, West Indies* (Tuscaloosa: University of Alabama Press, 2015), p. 105.

6 Andrew Jackson O'Shaughnessy, *An Empire Divided: The American Revolution and the British Caribbean* (Philadelphia: University of Pennsylvania Press, 2000); Taylor, *The Interest*, p. 69.

they purported to own. From 1783, trade between the British Empire and its former colonies, which had once been free, was regulated by a series of orders-in-council. To favour Britain's remaining colonies (Ireland and British North America), imports from the United States into the West Indies of meat, dairy, and salted provisions were prohibited. To support the West Indies, imports of lumber, grain, vegetables, and livestock from the United States were allowed, as were exports of colonial produce. Yet for the benefit of British shipowners, trade was restricted to British ships, which came annually and would make perhaps one trip for provisions from North America, if at all. Allowances were eventually made for single-decked American vessels under 100 tons to enter with provisions, but trade failed to reach levels seen before the war. These orders-in-council were repeated annually from 1783 until they became permanent by Act of Parliament from 1788.[7]

Worse than warfare were the series of hurricanes that devastated the islands almost annually from 1780. Indeed, as Burnard and Garrigus argue, 'hurricanes were the principal difficulty Jamaica faced in the 1780s, not the conflict between Britain and North America'. Together, these factors resulted in a devastating scale of death, estimated by contemporaries to be in the tens of thousands, mostly among the enslaved population.[8] Some 2,000–5,000 people died in Barbados, their deaths attributed directly to a hurricane in 1780, and 15,000–21,000 people died in Jamaica, deaths which were attributed by contemporaries to the hurricanes that hit Jamaica from 1780, and the ensuing famine, exacerbated as it was by the lack of imports from America. The war and hurricanes that hit the West Indies at the same time presented a significant challenge for the planters: their access to provisions was cut off and the populations of enslaved labourers were devastated.

Repopulating the plantations with enslaved labourers was, therefore, of paramount concern for those who profited from this violent system. The ability of planters and merchants to continue this vile traffic was threatened by the abolitionist movement, however, which picked up pace from the

---

7 Selwyn H. H. Carrington, 'The United States and the British West Indian Trade, 1783–1807', in *West Indies Accounts: Essays on the History of the British Caribbean and the Atlantic Economy in Honour of Richard Sheridan*, ed. by Roderick A. McDonald (Kingston, Jamaica: University of West India Press, 1996), pp. 149–68; Herbert C. Bell, 'British Commercial Policy in the West Indies, 1783–93', *The English Historical Review*, 31:123 (1916), 429–41; S. Basdeo and H. Robertson, 'The Nova Scotia-British West Indies Commercial Experiment in the Aftermath of the American Revolution, 1783–1802', in *Canada and the Commonwealth Caribbean*, ed. by Brian Douglas Tennyson (Lanham, MD: University Press of America, 1987), pp. 25–49 (pp. 25–26).

8 Burnard and Garrigus, *Plantation Machine*, pp. 220, 226–29.

mid-1780s, with the Society for Effecting the Abolition of the Slave Trade formed in 1787. The genesis of anti-slavery was much earlier, forming notably in communities of Dissenters, and in particular the Quakers, who were early opponents of the slave trade. A series of significant court cases, along with growing public awareness of slavery as a political issue, gave the cause impetus in the 1780s.[9] The threat of abolition was perceived by contemporaries to be greater than that of warfare or hurricanes: colonies taken could be recaptured, buildings destroyed could be rebuilt. Abolition, however, threatened the very underpinnings of the plantation system. Merchants and planters connected to the West Indies, including those in Bristol, did all they could to prevent any advances being made in the name of abolition.

Networks of Knowledge

Key to overcoming the new challenges that West India merchants and planters faced in the 1780s was knowledge about production in the West Indies, and connections between individuals in the islands and at home along which information could travel. Vital for merchants was understanding the precise ways in which the production process worked. The foundations of their knowledge were built, for many, on experience of working in the islands themselves. Many merchants were also plantation owners, especially so in Bristol, as Kenneth Morgan has shown.[10] Personal experience, which gave the merchants an appreciation of the intricacies and nuances of the plantation system—a form of tacit knowledge, untaught and not learned from books—was augmented by the passage of information across the Atlantic Ocean. Information exchange was built on the information technologies of the time—ink and paper, and the associated systems of accounting and letter writing[11]—and the infrastructure upon which it depended—merchant vessels and packet ships.

Central to this system were the individuals at the heart of the plantation community. To identify these individuals, and to help us quantify their influence, we can use social network analysis.[12] The network I present here is based on John Pinney's account books. The dots (nodes) on the graph represent individuals, and the lines (edges) connecting them indicate

---

9 Scanlan, *Slave Empire*, p. 162.
10 Kenneth Morgan, 'Bristol West India Merchants in the Eighteenth Century', *Transactions of the Royal Historical Society*, 3 (1993), 185–208 (pp. 193–94).
11 See Caitlin Rosenthal, *Accounting for Slavery: Masters and Management* (Cambridge, MA: Harvard University Press, 2018).
12 See A Note on Methodology, above.

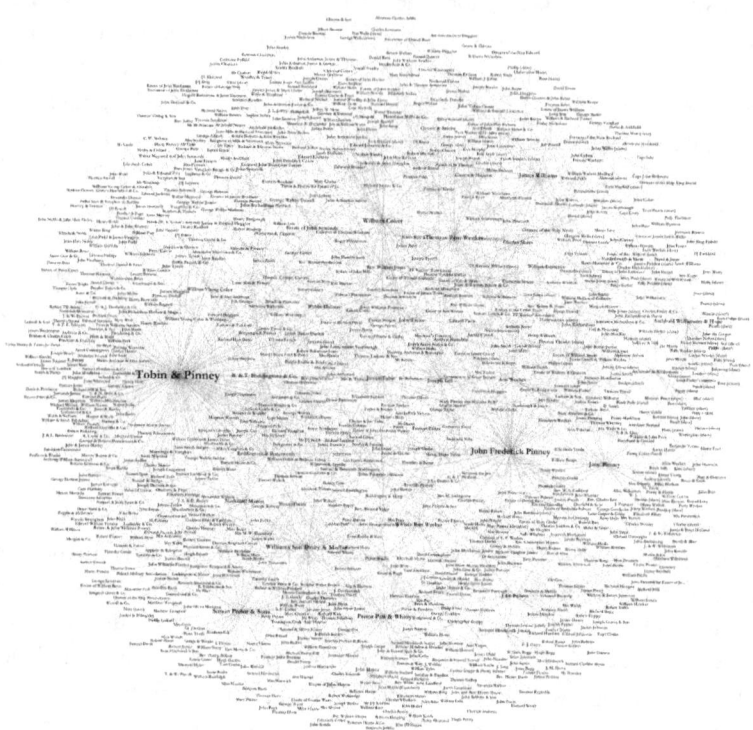

Figure 1.1: John Pinney's Nevis–Bristol Network, 1783–1803
Note: John Pinney has been removed.
Rendered in Gephi <https://gephi.org/>.

Source: UoBSC, DM58 Pinney Family Papers, 1538–1948, Account Books 30, 31, 33, 34, 35, 36, 39, 41, 43, 45, 47, 52, 54, 57, and 59.

https://liverpooluniversitypress.manifoldapp.org/projects/crisis-and-resilience/resource/crisis-and-resilience-figure-1-1

the presence of a transacting relationship between the two. Transacting relationships are evidenced by the instance of one or more transactions recorded in Pinney's account books. Individuals are considered to be influential if they are connected to many nodes.[13] While the network thus recreated is based on transacting relationships, it serves as a useful proxy for interaction and communication more broadly. Indeed, as Chapter 5 shows, the centrality of credit to the West Indies economy makes a network recreated

---

13 Buckles, 'A Historical Social Network Analysis'.

around this element perfectly suitable for explaining and understanding the trading community. For the purposes of this chapter, however, it is useful for bringing particular individuals to our attention whom we can begin to investigate further.

Figure 1.1 shows the network in its entirety. High among those who can be identified as influential are the managers of John Pinney's plantation. I will refer to these individuals, and their role in the plantation network, over the following sections as I develop the argument that these networks of knowledge were central to the organisational solutions that merchants in Bristol relied upon in the face of the crises outlined above. The next section will explore the relationship between the merchants in Bristol and the system of plantation labour. The section that follows will explore the relationship between the merchants and the production process. Throughout, I show the ways in which merchants across the Atlantic drew on their knowledge and experience to intervene in plantation operations and support the plantation system, helping planters—resident and absentee—navigate crises.

Merchants and plantation labour

In order to safeguard the plantation against crisis—indeed, to help it maintain its normal operation—merchants needed to know several key things about the plantation system. They would need to know, in general terms, the size and composition of the labour force of the plantations they served. They would understand the different roles that enslaved people, alongside free whites and free people of colour, had on the plantations. Finally, they would understand the levers of control that were central to the violence that dominated plantation life. They needed to know these things for several reasons. First, because it was their responsibility, especially in the wake of the American Revolution, to keep the labour force fed. Moreover, given that they advanced these provisions (and other goods) on credit, this amounted to an investment, a decision which itself had to take into account the plantation's productive capacity, based as it was on these factors. Secondly, with the exceptionally high death rates that followed the hurricanes (further to the typically high death rates that resulted from the violence inherent in the system), the merchants in Bristol were responsible for ensuring the forceable transportation of enslaved Africans across the Atlantic. Even though they were not themselves typically involved directly in the slave trade, as only a few merchants in Bristol still were by this stage, many still supported the slave trade financially by providing credit to planters, helping them to buy enslaved people. Moreover, even for those who had no direct financial connection to the slave trade (their financial interest in the plantations themselves notwithstanding), almost all of Bristol's West India merchants—all of note and standing—joined together, with their compatriots in London and Liverpool, to defend the slave trade politically.

The plantation system in the late eighteenth century was rigidly hierarchical and divided along distinct and highly defined racial lines. Atop the hierarchy was the white planter or, if the owner were an absentee, the white manager. Below him (and the planter or manager in the West Indies was typically male) were the white overseers, while the majority of the service positions—physicians, lawyers, etc.—were also held by whites. At this stage, in contrast to the situation a century or so earlier, many, if not all, of the skilled labourers on the plantations were likely to be enslaved or free Blacks and people of colour. These skilled positions were filled by enslaved people 'promoted' from field work. It was mostly men who were drafted into the crafts as they became older, or boys of particular status (including children born as a result of sexual relations between the planters or managers and enslaved women) who were apprenticed. These tradesmen could be hired out of the plantation for the financial benefit of the planter. Some, however, might perform extra work for money and earn enough to buy their own freedom. Women, often 'promoted' at an older age than men after their bodies had been fully exploited in the fields, or women of mixed race, would become cooks, nurses, and domestic servants.

The majority of enslaved people worked in the fields, however. The field labour was separated into gangs, allocated based on age and ability in order to improve efficiency. The first gang had the heaviest work, which included planting and tending to the sugar canes. A second gang, made up of the older and weaker labourers, weeded and carted, while the third, made up of children, collected the 'trash' (the offcuts of the cane intended for fuel), and performed other lighter tasks, such as picking grass to feed the cattle. The children would enter the second gang from about the age of ten. The work was torturous and, as a consequence, this system was supported by violence. Whipping was common, as were other means of punishment, up to and including execution. To prevent suicides, bodies were mutilated so that enslaved people would fear not just for their earthly bodies, but their spirits too. Death rates, because of the violent exploitation of their bodies, as well as disease and poor nutrition, were high.[14] Indeed, as Kenneth Morgan emphasises,

---

14 Ragatz, *Planter Class*, pp. 16–18; Rosenthal, *Accounting*, pp. 23–41; Ryden, *West Indian Slavery*, pp. 129–45; Pares, *West-India Fortune*, pp. 129–33; Matthew Mulcahy, *Hubs of Empire: The Southeastern Lowcountry and British Caribbean* (Baltimore, MD:

There were examples, of course, of humane masters and relatively cordial relations between the white personnel on plantations and the enslaved. But even where benevolence appeared to hold sway, it was always a matter of an iron fist lying behind the velvet glove because slavery ultimately rested on physical coercion.[15]

Merchants were thoroughly complicit in this system. Many understood it so well because, especially those in Bristol, they owned plantations themselves. Even if merchants were not themselves plantation owners, it was not unusual for them to travel to the West Indies, as sons of merchants or junior partners in firms, for training or business.[16] John Pinney was among their number. He owned a plantation which, as of 1788, comprised 190 acres of cane land and 202 enslaved labourers. He understood well the violence of the system, and the need for a rigid racial hierarchy. Despite his objections to 'excessive cruelty', he believed wholeheartedly in the virtue of the whip. The white managers were well compensated for their labours. William Coker, one of the earliest managers on the Pinney plantation, earned £200 in Nevis currency per annum, while his successor, Thomas Pym Weekes, earned £150. Overseers earned around £100, and their subordinates around £60.[17] For perspective, this translated to roughly £114, £86, £57, and £34 sterling, respectively, with average family incomes for the mid-eighteenth century at around £46 per annum—an income of over £100 sterling a year would put someone in the top 6 per cent of the population.[18]

Being a manager meant being embedded in plantation life. Unsurprisingly, these managers were some of the most heavily connected individuals in John Pinney's plantation network. Figure 1.2 shows their networks and the number of connections each manager had. Joseph Gill (manager from 1783 to

---

Johns Hopkins University Press, 2014), pp. 120–21; S. D. Smith, *Slavery, Family, and Gentry Capitalism in the British Atlantic: The World of the Lascelles, 1648–1834* (Cambridge: Cambridge University Press, 2006), pp. 299–300.

15 Morgan, *Slavery and the British Empire*, p. 111.
16 Morgan, 'Bristol West India Merchants', pp. 193–94; Morgan, *Bright-Meyler Papers*, p. 83.
17 See UoBSC, MS DM58/Account Books/35, fols. 35–37 and UoBSC, MS DM58/Account Books/39, fols. 15, 74, 137; Pares, *West-India Fortune*, pp. 103, 130, 135–36.
18 The Nevis to sterling exchange rate in the 1780s was approximately £175 (Nevis) to £100 (sterling), though it did fluctuate, with Nevis reaching as low as £160 in 1780 and as high as £187.5 in 1784. See UoBSC, MS DM58/Account Books/30 and 39. For pre-1775 rates, see John J. McCusker, *Money and Exchange in Europe and America, 1600–1775: A Handbook* (London: Macmillan, 1978), p. 271. For information on average incomes, see Robert D. Hume, 'The Value of Money in Eighteenth-Century England: Incomes, Prices, Buying Power—and Some Problems in Cultural Economics', *Huntington Library Quarterly*, 77:4 (2015), pp. 373–416.

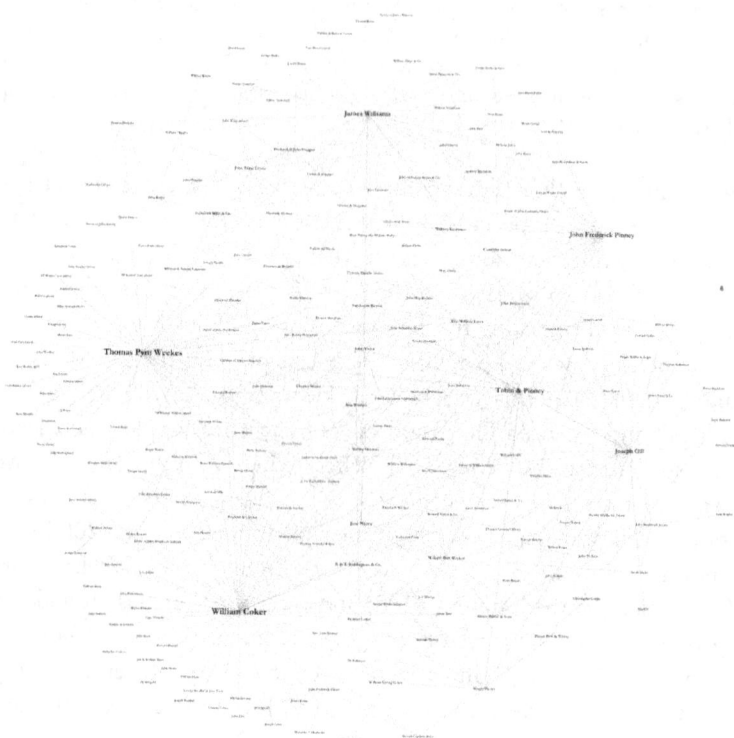

Figure 1.2: Network of Managers within John Pinney's Nevis–Bristol Network, 1783–1803
Note: John Pinney has been removed. Rendered in Gephi <https://gephi.org/>.

Source: UoBSC, DM58 Pinney Family Papers, 1538–1948, Account Books 30, 31, 33, 34, 35, 36, 39, 41, 43, 45, 47, 52, 54, 57, and 59.

https://liverpooluniversitypress.manifoldapp.org/projects/crisis-and-resilience/resource/crisis-and-resilience-figure-1-2

1785), William Coker (1786–1790), Thomas Pym Weekes (1790–1794), and James Williams (1794–1803) were all influential members of the plantation community, for better or worse.[19]

---

19 See also Eickelmann, *Mountravers*, chs 5 and 6.

Issues with management

Such was their influence that Pinney needed to keep a close eye on plantation affairs. Indeed, though his body was removed from the islands, his mind was still there. His greatest concern was the management of his plantation. Spikes in the growth of Pinney's plantation network, shown in Figure 1.3, were driven by his visits to the West Indies in 1790 and 1794. Indeed, he might have visited more often, such were his concerns with his managers. His first, Joseph Gill, had worked alongside Pinney since 1768, and was entrusted with the estate after Pinney's departure in 1784. Alas, the temptation of rum was too great, and the quality of his management—and with it the quality of Pinney's sugar—degraded. Gill, the sugar, and the accounting were in various states of ill-health.[20] Pinney was saved from returning to Nevis at this point by William Coker, who had been the manager of the plantation when Pinney had inherited it. Coker travelled out to replace Gill late in 1785, taking the reins in January 1786. However, his management also fell far below Pinney's high standards. Coker speculated in strains of sugar cane that failed to produce the quality of sugar Pinney had himself achieved. Further, he bought supplies in Nevis at higher rates (a symptom of the restrictions on trade with the United States that had raised the price of provisions), rather than sending orders for stores from Bristol. During his tenure, the enslaved people also became more restless, indicating a harsher work environment.

This time, Pinney had to go out himself.[21] When he arrived, he found his plantation in an unsavoury state. Pinney recorded his outrage in his accounts, referring to Coker's management as 'disgraceful'. He took particular issue with Coker's appointment of his son, John Frederick Coker, as overseer of the boiling house. This was a critical position, usually held by an enslaved man who had served the plantation for years, that required considerable skill. John Frederick Coker's inexperience in this position therefore turned out to be 'manifestly injurious' to Pinney's interests. Pinney appointed Thomas Pym Weekes, Jane Pinney's half-brother and the plantation's doctor, as manager instead.[22]

Yet Weekes turned out to be just as damaging to Pinney's interests as his predecessors. His list of transgressions was long. He 'disregarded the instructions' of Pinney, and further attempted to buy an estate on Pinney's behalf without his knowledge. Weekes's power of attorney was thus revoked, and though this may have limited his ability to make outrageous decisions at Pinney's expense, it did not improve his management style. Pinney complained

---

20 Eickelmann, *Mountravers*, pp. 600, 604–05.
21 Eickelmann, *Mountravers*, pp. 607–08; Pares, *West-India Fortune*, pp. 142–44.
22 UoBSC, MS DM58/Account Books/39, fol. 55.

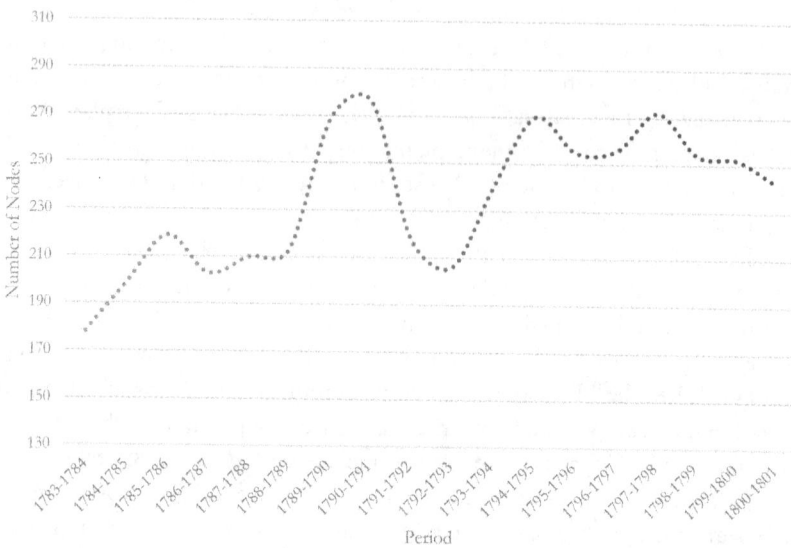

Figure 1.3: Size of John Pinney's Nevis–Bristol Network, with Pinney Removed, 1783–1801

Source: UoBSC, DM58 Pinney Family Papers, 1538–1948, Account Books 30, 31, 33, 34, 35, 36, 39, 41, 43, 45, 47, 52, 54, 57, and 59.

of Weekes's attempts to rebuild various structures, without Pinney's consent, that incurred unnecessary costs. Weekes engaged in masonry projects that Pinney had no desire of, and, like Coker, purchased unnecessary goods, among other things. He was replaced, in the end, by James Williams, who was promoted from overseer of the estate. Williams did not seem to cause Pinney any significant problems, at least until the early 1800s.[23]

As the network measures show, these managers were influential members of the plantation community. Figure 1.2 shows the scope of their networks within the community that was formed around Pinney's plantation. In many ways, that they were influential is not surprising. They were, after all, at the top of the plantation hierarchy. What makes this interesting is that, because of their mismanagement, their position of influence did not make them a force for good, especially not in Pinney's eyes. That half of the managers in this period—namely Gill and Weekes—were Pinney's own family did not

---

23 UoBSC, MS DM58/Account Books/45, fols. 12–14; Eickelmann, *Mountravers*, p. 633; Pares, *West-India Fortune*, pp. 145–47.

help, and may well have exacerbated the issues.[24] Gill, his cousin, was told by Pinney that he should not 'buoy himself up with expectations from me merely because he is my relation'.[25] When reflecting on his choice of Weekes, his brother-in-law, as Coker's replacement, Pinney was persuaded by the idea that Weekes's 'Gratitude alone, independent of the family connection between them'—Pinney had funded Weekes's medical training—'would always prove a sufficient spur to induce him to attend to the interest of Mr P'. Weekes was entrusted with command of one of Pinney's attorneys, an 'indulgence Mr P would not have granted to any other Person existing, except his own Sons'.[26] The failure of family in this instance meant that Pinney had to keep a watchful eye over his own plantation, even as he acted as an agent for other planters in Bristol. His experience is exemplary of the kind of situations merchant-planters were exposed to, and this understanding—and especially the lived experience of knowing just how problematic plantation managers could be—allowed them to deal more effectively with the plantations of their clients.

Food and scarcity in the islands

The need for active intervention kept Pinney, like the other merchants and merchant-planters who together rubbed shoulders in the coffee houses and at the local West India Association, up to date with the latest developments in plantation needs and methods. Pinney and his partner, fellow merchant-planter James Tobin, were well positioned to keep plantations stocked with supplies that the labourers needed to subsist, an especially important role following the limited access to provisions that followed the peace with the US and the spate of hurricanes that affected the crops grown in the West Indies. At times of severe scarcity, the regulations on trade with the United States allowed governors to temporarily open their ports to American ships. Yet these regulations were often insufficient and reactionary, and even if they could alleviate scarcity, were not enough to prevent it. Tobin & Pinney in Bristol received frequent reports from clients about the 'scarcity of Negroe provisions'.[27] Provisions were 'much wanted', and every shipment from Bristol, and especially of oats and grain (one of the key exports of the former thirteen colonies) was felt to be 'a very seasonable and critical supply'.[28]

---

24 For more on issues with family members, see Haggerty, *'Merely for Money'?*, pp. 165–66; David Hancock, 'The Trouble with Networks: Managing the Scots' Early-Modern Madeira Trade', *The Business History Review*, 79:3 (2005), 467–91 (pp. 474–82).
25 Pares, *West-India Fortune*, p. 142.
26 UoBSC, MS DM58/Account Books/45, fol. 12; Pares, *West-India Fortune*, p. 144.
27 Pinney & Tobin to Jeffery Shaw, 28 July 1787, UoBSC, MS DM58/Letter Book/37.
28 Pinney & Tobin to William Colhoun, 8 November 1786, and Pinney & Tobin to John

Compounding food pressures, flour at times proved scarce in Britain, making it unreliable as a food source. Poor harvests in 1788 and 1789, for example, pressured the British government to lift a ban on the importation of flour into Britain from the United States, while its export from Britain was strictly controlled.[29] Herrings were also increasingly shipped from Bristol, a commercial enterprise that was supported by a number of Bristol's merchants.[30] Though considered not 'quite so large and fat as the scotch', they were cheaper, and Tobin & Pinney had 'reason to believe they will keep better'.[31] Appreciation of the scarcity spurred merchant firms such as Tobin & Pinney to send goods out quickly and promote their local fishing industry in order to keep the labourers fed.

It was not just the enslaved labourers who merchants had to keep fed, but also the white planters, managers, and other employees. Understanding tastes in the islands, and shaping tastes in line with emerging trends at home, was therefore of the utmost importance, with merchants acting as key bridges in this transatlantic exchange. Tobin & Pinney frequently sent out cheese, salt, tripe, ale, beef, ham, and butter, as well as Madeira wine and French claret. Salted and meat goods were also sent from Ireland, which was opened up to trade with the United States in 1778 (despite the protestations of Bristol's merchants, who had profited from the re-export of Irish goods).[32] Ships frequently called at Cork on the way to the West Indies to pick these goods up. Orders also included many of the manufactures that stimulated British industry, and for Bristol sustained its hinterland, such as soap, candles, leatherware, metalware, tobacco, and refined sugar. Cloth goods were also ordered from Britain, including bedding, shoes, stays, and millinery, alongside fabrics such as the coarse woollen penistones and linen osnaburgs that served as clothing for the enslaved labourers.[33] It was not just the men of the firm who had to understand tastes in the West Indies. The women associated with the firm—Jane Pinney and Elizabeth

---

Budgen, 7 September 1789, UoBSC, MS DM58/Letter Book/37.

29 Paul Sharp and Jacob Weisdorf, 'Globalization Revisited: Market Integration and the Wheat Trade between North America and Britain from the Eighteenth Century', *Explorations in Economic History*, 50:1 (2013), 88–98 (p. 92).

30 There are numerous references to Bristol's budding herring trade of the 1780s in the correspondence of Tobin & Pinney, John Fisher Weare, and Thomas Harris.

31 Pinney & Tobin to John Richardson Herbert, 16 January 1787, UoBSC, MS DM58/Letter Book/37.

32 See Minchinton, *Politics*, pp. 153–54.

33 Tobin & Pinney's correspondence is filled with numerous discussions of orders that reveal the array of goods sent across the Atlantic. See also Morgan, *Slavery, Atlantic Trade*, pp. 6–9.

Tobin—were responsible for sending across items for their counterparts in the West Indies. Reflecting a still highly gendered role, they sourced a range of textiles and homeware, goods about which Tobin & Pinney professed to know little. Such proxy shopping bound their clients ever closer to the firm, making them reliant not just on the expertise of John and James, but of Jane and Elizabeth too.[34]

Slavery and the Threat of Abolition

Merchants were not always successful in relieving scarcity, while the increase in already high death rates that accompanied the hurricanes devastated enslaved populations. A steady stream of new labour therefore had to be forced across the Atlantic. The Trans-Atlantic Slave Trade Database shows that ships flying the British flag forcibly removed at least 2.9 million Africans from their homeland over 1660–1807. Slave traders took 378,624 people (13.1%) in the 1783–1793 decade alone.[35] Bristol's share, though comparatively smaller during this decade than in previous decades, was still high at 15.3% of total voyages from Great Britain (compared with 20.4% for the period as a whole; Liverpool's share was 68.7% for 1783–1793 and 47% for 1660–1807).[36] There were still a few merchants in Bristol engaged almost entirely in the slave trade, such as James Rogers, who spent a decade organising and financing slaving voyages.[37] Others, such as Evan Baillie, financed a few slaving voyages, but concentrated predominantly on sugar importing.[38] Profits were still high, averaging at around 8–10% after outfitting costs and overheads.[39] Incentives were, therefore, still present for the slave traders to carry on this traffic. They continued to purchase Africans from the west coast, transporting them across

---

34 Buckles, 'A Historical Social Network Analysis'.
35 See *The Trans-Atlantic Slave Trade Database*, <https://www.slavevoyages.org/> [accessed 1 March 2023]. Variables selected: Flag = Great Britain. Year arrived with slaves = 1660–1807; 1783–1793.
36 Sources as above. Variables selected: Place of departure = Bristol; Liverpool; Great Britain, England, Scotland. Year arrived with slaves = 1660–1807; 1783–1793. Overall, 184 slaving vessels left Bristol out of a total of 1,203 from Britain in 1783–1793, and 2,035 out of 9,971 for 1660–1807. For Liverpool, the figure was 827 for 1783–1793 and 4,682 for 1660–1807.
37 Kenneth Morgan, 'James Rogers and the Bristol Slave Trade', *Historical Research*, 76:192 (2003), 189–216.
38 Douglas Hamilton, 'Local Connections, Global Ambitions: Creating a Transoceanic Network in the Eighteenth-Century British Atlantic Empire', *The International Journal of Maritime History*, 23:2 (2011), 283–300 (p. 293).
39 Morgan, *Bright-Meyler Papers*, pp. 115–18.

the Atlantic—the notorious middle passage—during which they were poorly fed, kept in cramped conditions, and thereby exposed to a range of diseases.

While merchants were extremely knowledgeable about how plantations functioned, slave traders were guided by a crude understanding of African people as they structured their slaving voyages. As Eric Williams has observed,

> an Angolan Negro was a proverb of worthlessness; Coromantines (Ashantis), from the Gold Coast, were good workers but too rebellious; Mandingoes (Senegal) were too prone to theft; the Eboes (Nigeria) were timid and despondent; the Pawpaws or Whydahs (Dahomey) were the most docile and best-disposed.[40]

These stereotypes were meaningless given that many Africans were brought from interior regions of Africa which slave traders knew little about, and were captured through raids, or were prisoners from wars that were started and perpetuated with the aim of capturing people. Yet these fantasies, though not the only factor (another being the availability of enslaved people given the nature of the internal slave trade), contributed to the direction of British slaving ventures, leading British slave traders to show a preference for the Bight of Biafra, Central Africa, the Gold Coast, and Senegambia. They understood, for example, that, due in part to the influence of these stereotypes, New Calabar and Bonny Africans sold better than Angolans. These enslaved people were sold to planters in the West Indies, their price dependent on the season, supply and demand, and their region of origin, sex, age, and physical condition.[41] Knowledge of the labour needs of the plantations, with labour allocated by gender, age, and fitness, helped slave traders use these factors, alongside the regional stereotypes, to navigate this market for people, and ensure that an increasing supply of enslaved Africans reached the West Indies.

While Bristol was no longer the hub of slave traders it once was, in the 1780s merchants were still financially interested in the slave trade, even if they were not directly investing in slaving ventures. These were often the wealthiest merchants, such as William Miles, who was one of the Bristol's most prolific sugar importers. Support was given through the 'guarantee

---

40 Williams, *Capitalism & Slavery*, pp. 37–38.
41 Morgan, 'James Rogers', pp. 193–94; David Richardson, 'The British Empire and the Atlantic Slave Trade, 1660–1807', in *The Oxford History of the British Empire, Vol. II: The Eighteenth Century*, ed. by P. J. Marshall (Oxford: Oxford University Press, 2001), pp. 440–64 (pp. 450–53); Robin Pearson and David Richardson, 'Insuring the Transatlantic Slave Trade', *The Journal of Economic History*, 79:2 (2019), 417–46 (p. 439).

system', whereby wealthy merchants supported planters with long credit terms and slave traders with regular returns. Bills of exchange drawn by planters were becoming longer towards the end of the century—sets of three would have repayment dates of 18, 24, and 30 months after sight. These guarantors specialised in handling the risks associated with long drafts, paying bills when due if the planter had not already, and then seeking compensation from the planter himself.[42]

Above all, merchants in Bristol used their knowledge and position to defend the slave trade politically when it came under threat from the abolitionist movement. In response to the growing calls for abolition in the latter half of the 1780s, various meetings were held by Bristol's West India Association (WIA) in 1788 and 1789. These meetings involved the creation of various petitions in April 1789 that were to be sent to the House of Commons in opposition to the bills for the abolition of the slave trade that were thereby proposed. Fifty-four merchants, slave traders, absentee planters, and others connected with the sugar trade and manufactures of Bristol attended the 13 April 1789 meeting to help organise their defence. They agreed to write three separate petitions, one for West India merchants, planters, sugar bakers, annuitants, and creditors; one for African merchants (i.e., slave traders); and one for the manufacturers of Bristol and the surrounding areas. These petitions were sent round Bristol, Gloucester, Bath, and Somerset to be signed by affected parties. The attendees also pledged to donate 6 pence per hogshead of sugar or puncheon of rum to the West India Society to help fund the defence of the slave trade.[43] The WIA of Bristol coordinated with counterparts in London and Liverpool, and even took lengths to emphasise that the petitioners of Bristol were independent of both the WIA and the Society of Merchant Venturers, the other powerful lobby of the city. These petitions were read aloud in the House on 12 May 1789.[44]

The petitions reveal the scale of the threat that these merchants and planters perceived. The main argument in defence of the slave trade was that it was foundational to the economic prosperity of the West Indies, and therefore, by extension, to the prosperity of Britain. Bristol's defence here

---

42 Kenneth Morgan, 'Remittance Procedures in the Eighteenth-Century British Slave Trade', *The Business History Review*, 79:4 (2005), 715–49; Kenneth Morgan, 'Merchant Networks, the Guarantee System and the British Slave Trade to Jamaica in the 1790s', *Slavery & Abolition*, 37:2 (2016), 334–52.
43 Slave Trade – 1789, BA SMV/8/3/2/5.
44 See *Papers against Abolition of the Slave Trade – 1788–1789*, BA SMV/7/2/1/15. The following analysis of the arguments made by the planters are drawn from the letters and petitions held in this volume. General assertions of arguments made are drawn predominantly from these.

differed from Liverpool's in that it made less effort to defend the slave trade itself, but rather defended it through its connection to the West Indies, with the need for West Indian prosperity defended by the connection between the West Indies and the rest of the economy. The petitioners relied on a racialised understanding of labour, whereby Europeans were unfit to work in the heat of the West Indies, arguing that only Black Africans were suited to the kind of work that engendered sugar production. Despite their supposed fitness for work there, enslaved communities were still subject to 'common accidents', as the torturous conditions were euphemistically called, which led to high death rates that necessitated a constant stream of labour from Africa. Without the fresh importation of enslaved Africans, sugar production would inevitably decline, and thus so would imports of plantation produce into Britain. Various parties, in their connection to the West Indies, would be harmed by this decline. These included creditors and mortgagees, who were estimated by the petitioners of London and Liverpool to have around £70 million of capital tied to West India property; sugar refiners, a key branch of Bristol's manufactures and a large regional employer with a supposed £500,000 tied up there; and Bristol's other sundry manufacturers, both in the city's broader hinterland and in the Midlands, who relied on selling iron goods, clothes, cutlery, crockery, and so on to the islands.[45]

Moreover, they claimed, what affected Britain's economy affected its national security. Justifying the press gangs about which they would later complain, they argued that the shipping and fishing industries that were supported by the trade in slaves and sugar were 'considered as the nursery of our Seamen' and shipwrights, and were, thus, vital to Britain's maritime prowess. Conversely, whatever Britain gave up would simply be engrossed by her rivals. France, Spain, and the newly formed United States would outcompete Britain with their fertile lands and unrestricted access to enslaved Africans. This would bring them sugar, wealth, and power, with a larger merchant navy and, thus, superior naval power. This argument was echoed in Liverpool.[46] This line of reasoning played on the issue of Britain's rivalry with other European nations. After having been so recently scarred by defeat at the hands of France and Spain in the American Revolution, could Britain really afford to abolish a trade that brought it vital maritime strength?[47]

---

45 See the various petitions drafted by Bristol's West Indians in *Papers against Abolition of the Slave Trade*. See also Haggerty, *'Merely for Money'?*, pp. 216–17; Ryden, *West Indian Slavery*, pp. 197–207.

46 Haggerty, *'Merely for Money'?*, pp. 219–20.

47 That Britain had only recently mobilised its navies again in 1787 gave the argument added potency. See Knight, *Britain Against Napoleon*, p. 10.

A decline in economic prosperity would further lead to a loss of revenue for the state. Taxes were paid on the manufactures made for export to the African and West Indian markets, and taxes were paid on sugar imported and refined in Britain. Thus, in both exports and imports, the system of West Indian trade, to which the slave trade was central, contributed significantly to the public purse. Were the slave trade to be abolished, expenses would increase, naturally, because the government would have to pay for the relief of those negatively affected by abolition—this was a commitment that the government later took seriously, with the controversial payment of £20 million to slave holders following the abolition of slavery. Moreover, the petitioners in 1789 argued, sugar bakers, if they did not leave the country, would 'with their families become Burdensome' to their local communities, which were already 'oppressed with Parochial Taxes'.[48] Therefore, not only would abolition lead to a decline in the revenues of the state, but it would also increase its expenditure.

The claim to compensation was a natural consequence of the historical and continued support that the government had given to the slave trade, as the petitioners studiously pointed out. In this line of argument, the Bristol petitioners clearly echo their London counterparts, who placed the constitutional issue at the heart of their argument. The argument that Parliament was betraying its merchant citizens was similarly made in Liverpool.[49] The petitioners declared that the colonists had a right to the property that they had legally acquired, property that was founded on grants and sales of the Crown and on charters and Acts of Parliament. With Parliament sanctioning the trade in African people, the petitioners had invested their capital in property in the West Indies. Furthermore, Parliament had been sanctioning the trade for over 150 years, over which time such property had been accumulated. A note in the Society of Merchant Venturers' papers on abolition lists the key acts and proclamations passed and issued by Crown and Parliament dating back to 1618, showing their process in gathering these data and keeping it close to hand in the formation of their arguments.[50] The most recent of Parliament's actions came after the Seven Years War. Then,

---

48 Quoted in 'The humble Petition of the West India Planters residing in the City of Bristol & its Vicinity, The West India Merchants, Sugar Refiners & others within the said city who have advanced their Property in West India Securities either by Mortgage, Bond, Annuity or otherwise [n.d. c. April 1789]', *Papers against Abolition of the Slave Trade*.
49 Ryden, *West Indian Slavery*, pp. 195–97; Haggerty, *'Merely for Money'?*, pp. 220–21.
50 'Resolutions of 13th April 1788', *Papers against Abolition of the Slave Trade*; Cf. the London lobby: Ryden, *West Indian Slavery*, p. 207; Haggerty, *'Merely for Money'?*, pp. 220–21.

they emphasised, 'on the Cession of the Island of St Vincents Domincia & Tobago ... the Lands were sold at public auction ... & the money arising therefrom paid into the Treasury'. The petitioners had, 'at great Expense', purchased the lands under the 'implied Terms of cultivating & improving them by Negroe Slaves'.[51] Turning on their commitment to property would not just harm the petitioners in the present, but would harm the government's long-term credibility.

A final argument, unconnected to economics and offered seemingly as an afterthought, was a retort to the powerful moral argument presented by the abolitionists. The terms of this ranged from dismissively claiming that the abolitionists were simply mistaken about the nature of the slave trade, to claiming perversely that abolition itself would be 'destructive to liberty & the welfare of the human species'.[52] To the claim that slavery promoted war and slowed the progress of civilisation in Africa—the latter being a key concern of liberal abolitionists[53]—the London West India lobby claimed that slavery was good for the enslaved Africans, as they were prisoners of war who would otherwise be massacred, or convicts, whose sentences were commuted from death to slavery. The lobbyists from across Britain further argued, despite evidence to the contrary, that no slave trader nor slave owner would want to harm their own property, since it was against their financial interest to do so. Moreover, any attempt to prohibit the slave trade was self-defeating, for in their economic worldview, whichever enslaved people Britain did not traffic would be trafficked by France or Spain.[54]

Before and while the merchants joined together to lobby as a group, individuals played their own part in preventing or stalling abolition. Notable among these was James Tobin, partner to John Pinney as a sugar importer, and, like Pinney, a slave owner himself. Tobin made his mark on the history of abolition by engaging the Revd James Ramsay in a pamphleteering duel. Over three essays that attempted to deconstruct, respond to, and dismiss Ramsay's claims, Tobin established himself as an authority on the pro-slavery side, even being invited to give evidence in Parliament.[55] While it is not

---

51 'The Humble Petition of the West India Planters, West India Merchants & others residing within the City of Bristol & its Vicinity [n.d. c. April 1789]', *Papers against Abolition of the Slave Trade*.
52 Samuel Green to James Jones, 18th February 1789, *Papers against Abolition of the Slave Trade*.
53 See Scanlan, *Slave Empire*.
54 As well as the petitions found in *Papers against Abolition of the Slave Trade*, see also Ryden, *West Indian Slavery*, pp. 195–96, 201–02; Haggerty, 'Merely for Money'?, p. 222; Smith, *Slavery*, p. 271.
55 Ryden, *West Indian Slavery*, pp. 189–91.

necessary to analyse Tobin's arguments in detail, it is worth noting the extent to which they appeal to episodes of history and abstract legal concepts, as well as drawing on personal and other observations of the 'reality' in the colonies, as he saw it. Tobin attempts at each stage to downplay the horrors of slavery. Discussing the use of the whip, for example, Tobin observes that in the colonies, 'twenty strokes with a whip is reckoned a pretty smart infliction', and this compared to the military, where 'two, three, or five hundred lashes' might be given 'to a poor culprit'. The ethics of military punishments notwithstanding, Tobin makes a point of justifying slavery with reference to practices both commonplace and tolerated within British society. Most perversely, Tobin positions himself—as slave holder and plantation owner—as an opponent to 'unnatural slavery', and as someone who considers slavery to be an 'evil', sitting beside 'pain, sickness, poverty, &c', with the hope that 'the blessings of freedom will in due time, be equally diffused over the face of the whole globe'.[56] West Indian slavery was, somehow, simply a step towards this greater liberty.

The defence of slavery and the slave trade, was, then, many-pronged. The lobby had a range of arguments at its disposal, and diffused them into the public sphere through petitions and pamphlets. Their arguments supported and nourished the plantation system, just as the merchant contingent played their role in the plantation machine by shipping supplies that nourished—poorly—the enslaved people, the traffic of whom the merchants and planters resident in the metropole sought to justify and maintain. Just as they supported the use of enslaved labour on the plantation, so too did these merchants support the production of sugar itself.

Merchants and the production process

Merchants in the West India trade were not simply factors, selling sugar on behalf of planters at the best price possible (though this was perhaps the most significant aspect of their role). Rather, they acted as cogs in the plantation machine by supporting production, timing shipments to arrive at particular points in the production process and making interventions in the activities of planters and managers in the form of recommendations of new technologies. They were also required to interpret and, at times, intervene in the orders made by planters for manufactures, as well as negotiate with the

---

56 Tobin, *Cursory Remarks*, pp. 5, 7, 48; James Ramsay, *A Letter to James Tobin, Esq., Late Member of His Majesty's Council in the Island of Nevis* (London: James Phillips, 1787), p. iii.

manufacturers on behalf of their clients. To do this, they needed an intimate knowledge of the production process. This knowledge, as we shall see, helped them comment on the quality of the sugar and make investment decisions as they acted as financiers and creditors to planters. Significantly, it helped them safeguard the islands against the crises that they faced in this period.

It was their understanding of the production process itself that bound them so closely to the plantations; this knowledge oiled the cogs. They knew that planting occurred over around eight weeks, typically in the autumn and early winter. Trenches with holes about six inches deep were dug for the canes, on 15- to 20-acre plots. This was done predominantly by the enslaved men and women, using hoes rather than with the plough. The canes would take 12–18 months to reach heights of about eight feet, and over that time would require constant weeding. This backbreaking work was lessened if the ratoon—the bottom of the stalk that was left after harvesting—was left in to regrow. The yield of ratoon crops was less than that of freshly planted canes, though they took only two-thirds of the time to grow. Because of the poor yield, Pinney did not use ratoons, preferring a fresh crop each time. The harvest was timed to occur during the dry season from January to April, and lasted for around 11–13 weeks. The cane had to be crushed and boiled within 24 hours of being cut to prevent souring, meaning that the mill and boiling house had to be operated day and night. It was intense work for the labourers working 18-hour days. The harvested cane was transferred to the mill by ox- or mule-drawn carts. The mill, a set of three vertical rollers made of wood and iron, or entirely from cast iron, was powered by wind, animal, or water. It was incredibly dangerous, with canes passing through several times. The sleep-deprived, malnourished workers who were feeding and re-feeding the mill risked losing limbs.[57] One particular innovation, a 'dumb-returner' that automatically re-fed the cane, alleviated some of the danger. This consisted of 'a curved plate installed along one side of the cylinders to guide the cane back between the cylinders for the second crushing'.[58]

The crushed canes produced juice that was piped from the mill to the boiling house into a large pan of around 300–400 gallons. The pan was heated to reduce the liquid, while temper lime (known more commonly now as slaked lime), imported from Britain, was added to prevent souring and aid crystallisation. The rule of thumb was a pint of temper lime for every 100

---

[57] See, among others, Pares, *West-India Fortune*, pp. 109–18; Ryden, *West Indian Slavery*, pp. 84–91; Ragatz, *Planter Class*, p. 57; Mulcahy, *Hubs of Empire*, pp. 47n50; Mintz, *Sweetness and Power*, pp. 21–22, 46–52.

[58] J. H. Galloway, 'Tradition and Innovation in the American Sugar Industry, c. 1500–1800: An Explanation', *Annals of the Association of American Geographers*, 75:3 (1985), 334–51 (p. 346).

gallons, but it was added based on the judgement of the head boiler, typically a skilled enslaved man, promoted to the position after years of service on the plantation. Waste cane was used as fuel for the furnaces that heated the pans. Such was the intensity of the heat that water had to be splashed on to the ceiling to prevent the roof from catching fire. As the mixture was heated, impurities rose to the surface that were skimmed off by the enslaved labourers, who risked severe burns. As the liquid was reduced, it was transferred into a succession of five or six smaller pans. The combination of the heat and reduction of the liquid left a crystallised sucrose supersaturated in a pool of molasses. The head boiler, with his skill and experience, judged when to take the sugar off the heat. He might dip his thumb and forefinger into the liquid, and then pull them apart to see if it formed a thread between the two. When ready, the sucrose mixture was transferred into pots or hogsheads to cool in the curing house, from which the molasses would be drained, collected, and transferred to the distillery to make rum.

The merchants who understood this process, often because of experience as planters themselves, could offer advice to planters. In this way, they become important repositories of information. Tobin & Pinney remarked of one new planter's intention to use the plough and some other 'new kind of Husbandry', for example, that

> experience and observation emboldens us to remark that you will most probably find yourself materially injured by any such attempts at innovation – A Sugar Estate must be cultivated more like a Garden, than like a Farm[59]

They could offer advice on the early refinement process, too. According to Pinney's experience, adding too much temper lime would make the sugar 'rocky', though it would preserve it better. Too little made it soft. Striking the sugar at a lower heat was better than striking it too high, and the sugar cured better if it was potted when warm. An improper application of heat would lead to too much molasses. Where the cane was grown mattered: on Nevis, low ground sugars were 'more liable to waste by draining'.[60] A practice of 'claying'—common early on in Barbados and in the French West Indies, but not in Jamaica and the Leeward Islands—was also used to improve the quality. Claying involved the application of wet clay to the top of the sugar.

---

59 Tobin, Pinney & Tobin to Henry Keyworth, 19 August 1796, UoBSC, MS DM58/Letter Book/40.

60 Pares, *West-India Fortune*, pp. 117–18; Pinney & Tobin to Edward Brazier, 2 December 1786, and 26 January 1788, and Pinney & Tobin to John Scarbrough, 25 January 1788, UoBSC, MS DM58/Letter Book/37; Tobin & Pinney to Alexander Houstoun & Co., 16 August 1792, UoBSC, MS DM58/Letter Book/38.

This slowly released water through the cooling sugar, further cleansing it of molasses.[61] Without claying, the end result would be a crystallised sugar that was somewhere between very dark brown and very light in colour, very wet, almost treacle-like, to very hard in consistency, and usually sweet in taste. The quality—whether good or bad—was judged by merchants and their sugar brokers in Britain. Their understanding of production helped them not just to inform clients about how well it sold, but to give qualitative information on quality that could guide their production. They would, for example, be able to tell if the sugars had been burnt in the boiling process. Their knowledge of the production process was, therefore, vital to their ability to give advice and provide feedback on the quality of the sugar.

Merchants knew well also, for the sake of understanding quality, the impact of natural hazards and the environment on production. Hurricanes, bringing wet weather and heavy winds, were especially destructive. Forming when north-easterly and south-easterly winds converged, they destroyed lives, property, infrastructure, and plantations.[62] A hurricane in 1790 caused planter William Dickinson's crop to fall by half, for example.[63] Heavy rains independent of hurricanes also negatively affected the quality of the crop.[64] Such weather out of season was particularly alarming. As Tobin & Pinney recounted to an absentee, there were 'heavy rains in the beginning of April, as has done very considerable damage at St. Kitt's, Nevis, St. Eustatia &c by <u>washing away</u> Land, Buildings, Canes, Negroes &c as was never before known at that season of the year'.[65] Floods drowned crops, and frequently reduced yields and ruined planters' hopes of clearing their accounts with their merchant financiers. Conversely, dry weather and droughts could be as damaging for cane yields as wet weather. Tobin & Pinney noted on several occasions when dry weather seemed likely to lead to a reduced crop. In the 1790 planting season, 'the weather still continued so dry that not a Cane has been planted even for the Crop after next'. Rains came eventually, meaning 'the Crop for 1792, is well put in, though late'.[66] In 1794, with 'the

---

61 Mulcahy, *Hubs of Empire*, pp. 47–50.
62 Ragatz, *Planter Class*, p. 191; Morgan, *Bright-Meyler Papers*, pp. 90–91; Ryden, *West Indian Slavery*, pp. 83–84; Mulcahy, *Hubs of Empire*, pp. 125–26.
63 Stephen & Rose Fuller to William Dickinson, 8 and 11 November 1790, SHC, MS DD/DN/4/2/33(2).
64 Pinney & Tobin to Edward Brazier, 3 July 1787, and Pinney & Tobin to Mrs Arthurton, 29 July 1787, UoBSC, MS DM58/Letter Book/37.
65 Tobin & Pinney to William Colhoun, 21 May 1792, UoBSC, MS DM58/Letter Book/38.
66 Pinney & Tobin to William Colhoun, 31 March 1786, UoBSC, MS DM58/Letter

weather continuing extremely dry ... not half a Crop is expected'.[67] Indeed, drought conditions could be so bad that even hurricanes would be welcomed. A hurricane that hit St Kitts on 23 August 1793 did 'little damage there further than driving ashore a few small Craft and has been followed by fine rains which were much wanted'.[68] The Dickinsons' estates in Jamaica were similarly harmed by droughts, especially their cotton crop.[69]

Crops were further afflicted by pests and weeds. Rats were common (having travelled to the Caribbean with the colonists), as were cane-eating ants. Knotgrass, devil's grass, and vassal's grass were common weeds, which the enslaved labourers were expected to remove.[70] Nevis had a particular problem with the borer worm in 1787 and 1788. The worm—actually the larva of a moth, *Diatraea saccharalis*—burrowed into the cane, compounding with bad weather to reduce sugar yields.[71] Knowing whether a poor crop was the fault of poor management or of natural hazards that affected all helped merchants to distinguish between better and worse investment opportunities, and helped them identify the planters to whom advice was best given.

Knowledge and understanding of the ways in which production could be disrupted allowed merchants and absentee planters to intervene in the running of estates from afar, whereby they could suggest various innovations and improvements. Absentee planters and merchants, with their proximity to Britain's manufacturers and knowledge of Britain's West Indies communities at their disposal, were able to offer suggestions and send items across to the Caribbean. William Dickinson, an absentee planter, engaged in a long-distance discussion with his manager over the prospect of damming one of his Jamaican estates to prevent flooding.[72] John Pinney, intervening from Bristol, requested that the manager of his Nevis plantation try soot as a manure, rather than dung, which was relatively scarce. It proved effective, and the trend soon caught on, the information travelling along networks that no doubt extended further than recreated in Figure 1.1. The rise in demand led to an increase in price, along with an increase in adulteration. Soot

---

Book/37; Tobin & Pinney to Edward Brazier, 3 January 1791, UoBSC, MS DM58/Letter Book/38.
67 Tobin & Pinney to John Budgen, 5 April 1794, and Tobin & Pinney to John Hendrickson, 25 November 1794, UoBSC, MS DM58/Letter Book/39.
68 Tobin & Pinney to George Webbe, 12 October 1793, UoBSC, MS DM58/Letter Book/39.
69 Barnard Dickinson to William Dickinson, 12 June 1791, SHC, MS DD/DN/4/2/36(1).
70 Ragatz, *Planter Class*, pp. 58n61; Scanlan, *Slave Empire*, p. 70.
71 Pinney & Tobin to Edward Brazier, 26 January 1788, and Pinney & Tobin to John Budgen, 22 July 1788, UoBSC, MS DM58/Letter Book/37.
72 William Dickinson to John White, 4 August 1794, SHC, MS DD/DN/4/2/40(1).

suppliers were adding 'Cork-dust, fine ashes, and Charcoal ... which it will be very difficult to detect', reducing its quality and effectiveness. When freight prices rose with wartime, it became less cost-effective to ship compared to other products, and the craze died down.[73] Merchants could also use their proximity to manufacturers to make suggestions for improvements. Tobin & Pinney suggested that clients install John Garnett's newly developed mill rollers. This involved adding 'a Set of patent friction-rollers, in which the Gudgeons move instead of the old brasses'. This was such an improvement 'that 18 or 20 Mills have been made, and are making here on this principle'.[74] Merchant firms and absentees, anxious that these plantations were operating as effectively as possible, informed planters and managers about technological developments and made suggestions for improvements.

This kind of intervention was facilitated, not just by the experience of merchants in handling their own plantations, but in the detailed communication between planters and merchants, or between managers and absentee owners. The information, as I have emphasised, travelled along the networks of people and relied on the communication technologies of the time. This demonstrates just how important these key relationships were—the relationships that acted as vectors of information—between absentees and managers. When Dickinson discussed the damming of his estates, for example, plans were drawn up, annotated, and shared, with letters sent back and forth referencing the annotations.[75] As S. D. Smith has shown, Edward Lascelles' overhaul of his plantations was performed by ensuring that his managers and overseers were consistently completing journals and ledgers, which were returned to the absentee. Much of Lascelles' decision making was based on the information he received.[76] This reflects what Caitlin Rosenthal sees as the beginnings of the modern separation of ownership and management. Developments in written instruction and knowledge exchange allowed absentees, who received accounts and updates from their managers, to guide investment from afar.[77] Absentees such as the Pinney and Dickinson families and several clients of Tobin &

---

73 Tobin & Pinney to Edward Brazier, 19 February and 7 December 1793, and Tobin & Pinney to John Budgen, 7 April 1795, UoBSC, MS DM58/Letter Book/39; Pares, *West-India Fortune*, pp. 112–13.

74 Tobin & Pinney to Jeffery Shaw, 29 December 1791, UoBSC, MS DM58/Letter Book/38; Owen Ward, 'The House of Pinney and Garnett's Patent Rollers', *Transactions of the Bristol and Gloucestershire Archaeological Society*, 128 (2010), 189–205 (pp. 196–97).

75 William Dickinson to John White, 4 August 1794 SHC, MS DD/DN/4/2/40(1); Caleb Dickinson to William Dickinson, 4 June 1792, SHC, MS DD/DN/4/2/37.

76 Smith, *Slavery*, ch. 8, quote on p. 235.

77 Rosenthal, *Accounting*, pp. 41–48.

Pinney, on whose behalf the firm operated, were, therefore, on the cutting edge of business organisation, using account books and letters to direct investments and delegate responsibility to knowledgeable men on the ground.

Other innovations, of course, came from within the West Indies. One such innovation was the adoption of new varieties of sugar cane, significantly the Otaheite cane (also known as the Bourbon or Tahiti cane), which was introduced into the British West Indies from Martinique in 1793, and which originated from the Pacific Islands. A double-edged sword, this new variety produced a greater yield of a poorer quality sugar and exhausted the soil much more quickly, exacerbating a problem that had been plaguing Britain's colonies for the previous century. Pinney was among those who rejected it after comparing its quality to the old cane.[78] The introduction of this new cane variety contributed to the dramatic increase in production from the 1790s and into the 1800s, which was more rapid than at any other time. This increase was driven predominantly by the extension of land under cultivation in the larger islands, but also by the adoption of this new high-yield variety of cane.[79] Other innovations, such as the steam engine, did not become common until the nineteenth century. Steam was adopted more rapidly in the newer colonies with abundant, untouched land, such as Cuba, Berbice, and Demerara, whose larger estates could be designed around the new technology.[80]

Importantly, knowledge of the plantations' needs helped merchants interpret and fulfil the orders that clients sent out to them in their letters. Merchants were responsible for shipping out livestock from Britain, which was especially important in the aftermath of the American Revolution. Cattle were used for milk; horses, bulls, and mules were used to power mills and move the carts that carried canes and sugar; all were valued for their dung.

---

78 Galloway, 'Tradition and Innovation', pp. 340–42; Lucy Frances Horsfall, 'The West Indian Trade', in *The Trade Winds: A Study of British Overseas Trade during the French Wars, 1793–1815*, ed. by C. Northcote Parkinson (London: George Allen and Unwin, 1948), pp. 157–93 (p. 166); McCusker, *Essays*, pp. 213–15; Richard B. Sheridan, 'The Formation of Caribbean Plantation Society, 1689–1748', in *The Oxford History of the British Empire, Vol. II: The Eighteenth Century*, ed. by P. J. Marshall (Oxford: Oxford University Press, 2001), pp. 394–414 (p. 396); Pares, *West-India Fortune*, pp. 110–11.

79 Dale Tomich, 'Commodity Frontiers, Spatial Economy, and Technological Innovation in the Caribbean Sugar Industry, 1783–1878', in *The Caribbean and the Atlantic World Economy: Circuits of Trade, Money and Knowledge, 1650–1914*, ed. by Adrian B. Leonard and D. Pretel (London: Palgrave Macmillan, 2015), pp. 184–216 (pp. 186, 190); Ahmed Reid, 'Sugar, Slavery and Productivity in Jamaica, 1750–1807', *Slavery & Abolition*, 37:1 (2016), 159–82.

80 Tomich, 'Commodity Frontiers'; Burnard and Garrigus, *Plantation Machine*, pp. 4–5; Morgan, *Bright-Meyler Papers*, pp. 130–31.

They were difficult and expensive to ship, and often resisted being coaxed on board.[81] Pinney's plantation inventory for 1787 listed 25 mules, four horses, and two camels (intended as a substitute for horses). The work for animals was gruelling. Pinney's accounts record the death of ten mules in 1787 alone. More were bought to replace them, five of which were shipped in from Bristol.[82] Lime, used for tempering the sugar as well as for building, was ordered specially from Bristol, which had local, good-quality supplies. Merchants had to take special care when sending this out. Temper lime was shipped as a dry powder, and planters frequently complained of their lime getting wet and losing its potency.[83] An understanding of the needs of the plantation helped merchants to identify livestock and goods that they knew would be of appropriate quality, and to ensure they were shipped with care.

This knowledge further enabled merchants to fill in the gaps in vague orders. Tobin and Pinney certainly benefited from their experience in this regard. Indeed, as they emphasised, 'From our own experience as <u>Planters we</u> luckily have it in our power to correct' mistakes in clients' orders, while 'Merchants in common would consider themselves as bound to abide strictly to the <u>Letter</u> of your order though much at your expense'.[84] John Richardson, for example, made 'a mistake in the <u>length</u> of two of the setts of Gudeons, which we [Tobin & Pinney] have taken the liberty to rectify'.[85] An order made by Ulysses Lynch was particularly vague: to fulfil an order for stationery, Tobin & Pinney sent 'such as we should ourselves think necessary'; for a floor cloth, ordered without dimensions, the firm sent a 'middling sized one'; an order of tinware was small, so they assumed it was for personal use and sent 'the best Sort'.[86] When James Tobin noticed that George Webbe had omitted boiling lime from his order, he added it, as it was 'an Article

---

81 Thomas Harris to William Dickinson, 24 October 1788, SHC, MS DD/DN/4/2/26(1); Ezekiel Dickinson to William Dickinson, 14 November 1783, SHC, MS DD/DN/4/2/17(1).
82 UoBSC, MS DM58/Account Books/35, fol. 38, MS DM58/Account Books/36, fol. 40; Pares, *West-India Fortune*, pp. 119–20; Mulcahy, *Hubs of Empire*, p. 52; Meniketti, *Sugar Cane Capitalism*, p. 95.
83 Bryan Edwards, 'History of the British West-Indies, 1819', in *Papers Respecting the Culture and Manufacture of Sugar in British India* (London: Cox, 1822), Third Appendix, pp. 106–19 (p. 113); See Tobin & Pinney to Jedediah Kerrie, 1 November 1790, UoBSC, MS DM58/Letter Book/38.
84 Tobin & Pinney to Edward Brazier, 25 October 1794, UoBSC, MS DM58/Letter Book/39.
85 Pinney & Tobin to John Richardson, 14 April 1786, UoBSC, MS DM58/Letter Book/37.
86 Tobin & Pinney to Ulysses Lynch, 1 October 1789, UoBSC, MS DM58/Letter Book/38.

of such material consequence ... such omission might have proved of great injury to your Crop'.[87] There were limits to their ability to interpret orders. For complex orders such as mill parts and furnaces, planters had to send exact measurements, which would save 'much trouble and often needless expence'.[88] Merchants would pass these on to the manufacturers to ensure that such items arrived as expected. Otherwise, it was their knowledge of the production process that helped the firm intervene in the orders of planters and ensure that they were well stocked.

Furthermore, an intimate knowledge of the plantations' needs meant that these merchants were in a position to negotiate with manufacturers, ensuring that the capital goods and tools were of sufficiently high quality. Tobin and Pinney were always 'glad to receive an account of how the Goods we send are approved of with such remarks as may see that we may be better enabled to remedy any improper or negligent conduct in our tradesmen'.[89] It was their responsibility to check the equipment and challenge the tradesmen on any imperfections. In one case, a furnace cracked in cooling owing to the contraction of the metal. It was reinforced with an iron loop until the crack appeared to be 'perfectly closed and tight', and was expected by the manufacturer to 'bear the fire as well if not better'.[90] Hoes were frequently an object of complaint.[91] Complaints were brought to manufacturers, and 'through this kind of dialogue, the product was amended and refined'. Hoes were eventually designed for particular parts of the Caribbean: those intended for Nevis differed to those intended for Barbados. They were, as Chris Evans argues, and as Tobin & Pinney's correspondence suggests, a bespoke article, made for 'different crops and different regions ... for individual islands, even for individual plantations'.[92] Complaints extended even to the minutiae of planters' orders. Planters complained about cheap clothing, poorly packaged goods, or broken coals that fell through the fireplace grating.[93] Tobin &

---

87 Tobin & Pinney to George Webbe, 15 October 1795, UoBSC, MS DM58/Letter Book/39.
88 See Pinney & Tobin to William Ferrier, 13 October 1788, UoBSC, MS DM58/Letter Book/37.
89 Pinney & Tobin to John Richardson, 14 September 1786, UoBSC, MS DM58/Letter Book/37.
90 Tobin & Pinney to George Webbe Junior, 9 November 1791, UoBSC, MS DM58/Letter Book/38.
91 See Pinney & Tobin to Edward Huggins, 13 October 1788, UoBSC, MS DM58/Letter Book/37.
92 Chris Evans, 'The Plantation Hoe: The Rise and Fall of an Atlantic Commodity, 1650–1850', *The William and Mary Quarterly*, 69:1 (2012), 71–100 (pp. 85–88).
93 See Pinney & Tobin to Edward Huggins, 18 May 1787, and Pinney & Tobin to Francis Canham, 24 May 1788, UoBSC, MS DM58/Letter Book/37.

Pinney noted that things would go wrong, for it was 'impossible for us to see every article which we send out'.[94] Indeed, for any 'Cargo consisting of Such a variety of Articles we cannot always get it done entirely to our Satisfaction'.[95] Yet despite such limitations, Tobin and Pinney's understanding of the plantations' needs enabled them to take complaints to the manufacturers and negotiate on behalf of their demanding clients.

Conclusion

Knowledge and networks therefore bound West India merchants to the islands that they served and made them integral cogs in a plantation machine that was resilient to crisis. Using their understanding of plantation labour and the sugar production process, merchants in Bristol and beyond supported the islands following the American Revolution and the devastating spate of hurricanes by shipping provisions and lobbying incessantly against the abolition of the slave trade, crises that together threatened the very foundations of the plantation system. The concept of the plantation machine devised by Mintz, Burnard, and Garrigus is not complete without the merchants in the metropole who, though distant in space from the islands, were still present in mind.

Using the communications infrastructure of the time, they wrote frequently to their connections in the islands, maintaining and supporting their networks. Many merchants, having worked as planters themselves, kept their understanding of the violent system of slavery up to date through such contact. Indeed, Pinney, still a plantation owner, made two trips to Nevis to deal with issues of plantation mismanagement. Being there not only helped him maintain his personal business, but also let him see the state of the islands. Frequent communication also impressed on the minds of Bristol's merchants the importance of the scarcities facing the islands in the 1780s, and they made every effort to ensure the smooth supply of provisions as a response. Significantly, they used their position as cogs in the machine to act on behalf of their own and their clients' interests to defend the slave trade against the abolitionist movement. Their carefully crafted arguments, despite their inherent contradictions, were launched to stay the threat and maintain the plantation machine of which they were a part.

---

94 Tobin & Pinney to Edward Huggins, 23 October 1793, UoBSC, MS DM58/Letter Book/39.
95 Tobin & Pinney to Ulysses Lynch, 21 January 1790, UoBSC, MS DM58/Letter Book/38.

Moreover, their understanding of the production process ran deep. Merchant firms such as Tobin & Pinney offered advice to planters old and new, and took pains to ensure that their clients were sending them the best-quality sugar, the first step of which was understanding just how the quality of sugar could be affected. They recommended technologies, from new mill rollers to manure, and discussed the benefits of new varieties of cane. Importantly, they used their understanding to fill the gaps in vague orders which, should they have been followed to the letter, would have seriously harmed their clients' productivity. Finally, they negotiated with manufacturers on their clients' behalf to ensure that the tools they received were fit for purpose.

Such knowledge and networks rested on the communications infrastructure of the time, namely, shipping. Yet the shipping that bound the cogs of the plantation machine together, and which carried the knowledge that lubricated the machine, faced its own threats that merchant-shipowners had to work to overcome.

2

Merchant-shipowners and the Crisis of Shipping in the Bristol–West India Trade

> Friday a very hot press broke out at Bristol, which has continued ever since; they have stripped all the outward-bound vessels in Kingroad of their hands, and the men of war's boats are stationed down the Channel, waiting the arrival of the ships from the West Indies, &c. It is computed they have already procured 700 sailors.
>
> *English Chronicle*, 27–29 July 1790

> Monday last one Thomas Mills, who arrived that day in Kingroad, on board the *Hope* from Jamaica, took the sad resolution of jumping overboard with intent to swim to shore in order to evade the press-gang; but the tide running out very strongly, he was drowned.
>
> *World*, 3 September 1790[1]

THE NETWORKS OF PEOPLE, and the knowledge they passed between them, formed the social infrastructure that supported plantation operations. The physical infrastructure—the ships that carried goods, people, and letters—was equally as important for the continuation of trade, however. This infrastructure, connecting the islands across the Atlantic to the port cities in Britain, much like the plantations in the West Indies themselves, suffered shocks in the 1780s and 1790s. Just as the merchants and merchant-planters worked tirelessly to sustain plantation operations,

---

1 Rogers, ed., *Manning the Royal Navy*, p. 131.

they also worked—as shipowners, which many merchants were, to greater or lesser degrees—to sustain the wood and sails that linked them physically to the colonies, and which connected the sugar to the markets in Britain. These merchants would face a range of challenges and crises in this period. There were environmental dangers—at all times, shipping could be disrupted or overwhelmed by the harsh and unforgiving Atlantic Ocean. They also experienced interpersonal challenges, or 'moral hazards', facing what economists refer to as the 'principal–agent problem'. As such, merchants had to trust their captains to act as effective agents on their behalf in the West Indies as they collected sugar. Most significantly of all, however, with war in 1793 came the risk of commerce raiding as French privateers, much like their English counterparts, captured ships flying belligerent flags.

Yet the merchants of Bristol demonstrated resilience in the face of these difficulties. Insurance provided a layer of protection from natural hazards. Moral hazards were overcome through a variety of measures: captains with strong reputations were sought out, paid comparatively well, and had their behaviour limited with strict sets of instructions, while failure would be punished with dismissal. The problems of war were dealt with effectively, too. Surviving port data, represented in Figure 2.1, shows that the overall tonnage entering Bristol's port remained remarkably stable, growing in the interwar period (1783–1793), and recovering later in the 1800s as the war progressed. Much of the decline during the war was driven, understandably, by a decline in trade with Europe. The transatlantic trades—a key target of privateers, given the value of the ships and their cargo—and the West India trade especially were comparatively stable. Indeed, the mean tonnage entering Bristol for the peacetime period (14,788 tons) was only negligibly higher than the tonnage entering during the wartime period (14,212 tons).

This comparative stability was the result of the merchant-led organisation of convoys. Bristol's West India merchants, using their combined influence as part of the city's West India Association, resurrected the tried-and-tested system, lobbying the government incessantly. There were drawbacks to using convoys, as there are drawbacks to every system, and convoys have been much maligned as a result. They did, indeed, worsen congestion in the port, while their strict schedules limited the independence of merchants. The concentration of shipping into particular dates limited opportunities to send letters on merchant vessels. Convoys were delayed by bad weather. We should not go too far, however. A loss of independence was a trade-off for protection, while packet ships offered merchants other opportunities to send urgent communications; poor weather was a constant of shipping, and would delay ships regardless of convoys. Moreover, using convoys made insurance—itself an extra layer of defence for merchant-shipowners—considerably cheaper.

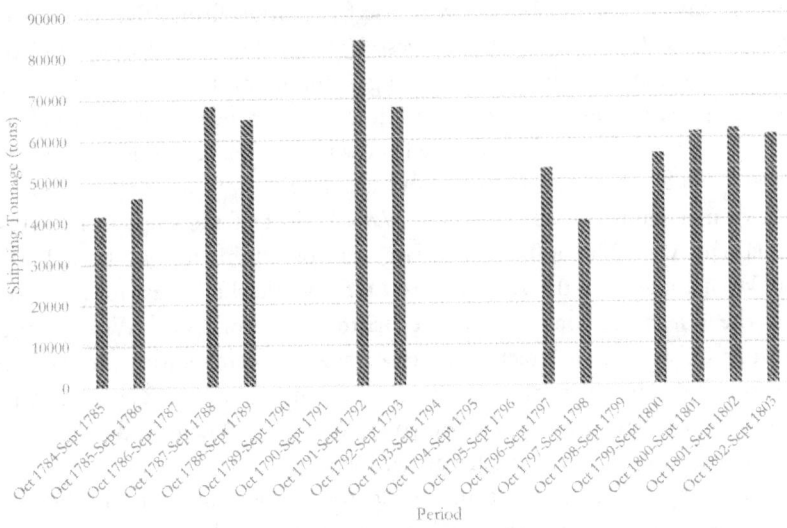

Figure 2.1: Shipping Tonnage Entering Bristol, Yearly Totals, October 1784–September 1803 (tons)

Source: BA, MS SMV/7/1/1/72-83 Wharfage Books, 1784–1803.

This chapter explores these issues in turn. We start, however, by examining the challenges facing merchant-shipowners.

The challenges facing merchant-shipowners

Many of Bristol's leading sugar merchants were shipowners. They stood in contrast to London where, in the words of Tobin & Pinney, 'the first houses there are hardly interested in Shipping'.[2] London was unusual in this regard, and it was still common in the Atlantic world for the lines between merchant and shipowner to be blurred.[3] While London might have been world-leading with respect to this increasing specialisation of roles, merchant-shipowners in other major economic centres were making the most of cheaper and more readily available marine insurance, and the larger shares in ships that they could purchase as a consequence. Tobin & Pinney was not unusual in owning

---

2 Tobin & Pinney to Edward Brazier, 11 May 1787, UoBSC, MS DM58/Letter Book/38.
3 See recently Emma Hart and Cathy Matson, 'Situating Merchants in Late Eighteenth-Century British Atlantic Port Cities', *Early American Studies*, 15:4 (2017), 660–82 (p. 670).

several ships in partnership between itself and other firms. The firm owned the *Nevis* (a 277-ton, two-decked vessel), the *Edward* (259 tons), and the *Rachel* (270 tons) jointly with fellow sugar importers, Protheroe & Claxton. The *King David*, owned singly by Tobin & Pinney, was the firm's smallest, at 227 tons. Protheroe & Claxton also owned the *Fame*, while John Fisher Weare owned the *Tobago Planter* and the *Industry*; Samuel Span, another Bristol merchant, owned the *Union Island*.[4] Most of the ships in the West India trade were 200–500 tons. The largest recorded ship to enter Bristol from the West Indies was the *Hector*, at 540 tons, while the largest for any trade was the *Trio*, a 561-ton vessel on the Bristol–New York line.[5] With tonnage serving only as an abstract measure of size, contemporaries preferred to measure ships by their practical capacity. Tobin & Pinney's *King David*, for example, was estimated to have a capacity of 400–500 hogsheads for its 227 tons (or around 1.75–2.2 hogsheads per ton).[6]

Protecting these ships against risks was important, not just because they were the means by which these hogsheads, filled with sugar, reached the market, but because they themselves were a considerable investment. Tobin & Pinney valued *King David* at £4,000, and *Rachel* at £5,000. The investment could be recovered through chartering—when offering the *King David* to other merchants, the firm asked for £2,000 to charter it outright, boasting that it earned them £1,792 in freight revenue on its return voyage, and £850 to £1,100 on its outward journey.[7] More importantly, having ownership over the shipping between the islands gave merchants control over the infrastructure that supported the trade. Though it was considered to be unbecoming for them to do so, merchant-shipowners could use their control as a tool for gaining consignments, with captains instructed only to allow sugars on board that were consigned to the ship's owner. Tobin and Pinney outwardly expressed their disdain for this 'narrow policy too often adopted by masters of Ships from this Port (which we fear generally originates in their Owners)'. This was especially true early on in their career, when it prevented them from receiving consignments from a new client. When others did it,

---

4 Thomas Harris to William Dickinson, 21 October 1783, SHC, MS DD/DN/4/2/17(1); Thomas Harris to William Dickinson, 22 November 1787, SHC, MS DD/DN/4/2/25; Edward Shiercliff to William Dickinson, 1 October 1787, SHC, MS DD/DN/4/2/22(2).
5 BA, MS SMV/7/1/1/72-83 WB.
6 Tobin, Pinney & Tobin to Edward Brazier, 9 April 1799, and Tobin, Pinney & Tobin to John Hendrickson, 20 June 1799, UoBSC, MS DM58/Letter Book/40. See also McCusker, *Essays*, pp. 26–46.
7 Tobin, Pinney & Tobin to Samuel Turner, 22 September 1800, UoBSC, MS DM58/Letter Book/42.

such as rival Samuel Span, Tobin and Pinney decried that it would cause 'injury to the whole body of Merchants', inducing everyone to act only in their self-interest. Yet, as shipowners, they themselves sent captains out with instructions to call on particular planters first and give them preference for freight, especially when their inventory of ships grew.[8] Having their ships full was a constant concern, given that the freight costs (paid by the planters) were needed to cover the running costs, and a full load on both legs of the voyage, but especially the return journey, was needed to turn a profit.[9] Yet as Richard Pares contends, even running a ship at a loss was worth it for the advantage that it gave merchants in obtaining consignments.[10] Safeguarding these vessels against a variety of moral and natural hazards was therefore crucial.

One of the key risks that merchant-shipowners faced came from the very people who they employed to run the vessels. A trustworthy and experienced captain was as valuable as the ship itself, and those with reputations for ability, sobriety, care, and industriousness were much sought after. Captains were responsible for maintaining the ship's paperwork and accounts, and dealing with Customs officials.[11] They might also find themselves acting as debt collectors on behalf of their employers, or entertaining passengers on board their ships. Yet they were well compensated for their hard work and experience. Charles Maies, captain of the *Nevis* and a key part of Tobin & Pinney's business network, was given a range of benefits: as well as £6 a month in wages, he was given £15 worth of freight for the home cargo, whatever he could charge after the first £6 per passenger, 5% commission for articles sold on the ship's account, 5s a day in the West Indies (local currency) and 2s 6d in Britain for expenses while waiting for convoy, charges of 2.5% on the amount of freight for primage when loading the ship outward, and £10 with which to purchase stores.[12]

---

8 Pinney & Tobin to John Julius, 12 October 1787, and Pinney & Tobin to Charles Maies, 20 January 1787, UoBSC, MS DM58/Letter Book/37; Tobin, Pinney & Tobin to John Taylor, 1 July 1799, and Tobin, Pinney & Tobin to Rowland Burton, 12 August 1799 and 29 October, UoBSC, MS DM58/Letter Book/40.

9 See, for example, Tobin, Pinney & Tobin to George Webbe Junior, 16 December 1799, UoBSC, MS DM58/Letter Book/40; See also Jacob M. Price, 'What Did Merchants Do? Reflections on British Overseas Trade, 1660–1790', *The Journal of Economic History*, 49:2 (1989), 267–84 (p. 273).

10 Pares, *West-India Fortune*, pp. 210–11, 222–23.

11 For examples of the type of records they kept, see BA, MS 39654/3 Voyage Accounts for the *Triton*, 1770–1790, and MS 39654/4 Voyage Accounts for the *Druid*, 1790–1792.

12 Tobin, Pinney & Tobin to George Webbe Junior, 16 December 1799, UoBSC, MS DM58/Letter Book/40.

As well as giving captains additional perks and benefits on top of their wages, merchant-shipowners gave them strict sets of instructions. The intention was to limit their behaviour, giving them as little room as possible for using their initiative (which would risk introducing their own self-interest) in the face of uncertainty. The orders defined the destination and the means of loading and unloading the cargo. Captains were given a list of planters' names to call on for sugars and of agents at various islands who could be applied to in emergencies or for money, and they were told what to buy and sell on the ship's account. Captains had to negotiate the freight with planters, but were given strict limitations on how much they could deviate from the established freight rates. They were warned not to take advantage of shipping scarcities and annoy clients by charging extravagant rates.[13] Captains in the sugar trade, therefore, had a strictly defined role. They were not supercargoes, like captains in other trades, and were not to speculate in the sale of goods, but were to deliver orders and pick up sugar. The limitation of the role helped create a set of standards against which the captains could be judged.

The most significant aspect of the captain's role, aside from getting the ship across the Atlantic, was to act as an agent for metropolitan firms in the West Indies. Hired by the merchants who owned the ships, they became their representatives, engaging with the planters who consigned them sugar and paid for their freight. This meant that there was a good deal of scope for the actions of the captain to harm the reputation of the firm. Goods might be landed in bad order, for example, or there might be suspicions of plunderage, especially if goods were missing, and a captain might find any losses deducted from his wages.[14] Yet how the captain interacted with the planters—their 'civility' with these West India gentlemen—mattered a great deal. The experience of Charles Maies here is instructive. As an agent of the firm, he became embedded within the credit networks that tied the people of Nevis to the merchant firm in Bristol. As Figure 2.2 shows, his interaction with the community embroiled him within John Pinney's Nevis–Bristol business network. The account books (upon which the network diagram is based) detail his use of bills of exchange, his handling of goods, his debt collection activities, and, significantly, his hiring of enslaved people from the plantation to work on the ship. Though it is not stated, their labour probably involved

---

13 As well as numerous letters to captains Charles Maies and John Shilstone in Tobin & Pinney's letterbooks, see their letter to George Webbe Junior, 16 December 1799, UoBSC, MS DM58/Letter Book/40, the records of the *Triton* (BA, 39654/3) and the *Druid* (BA, 39654/4), as well as Lowbridge & Richard Bright to James Henderson, 7 May 1785 and 25 February 1790, Letters 258 and 263, in Morgan, *Bright-Meyler Papers*.
14 See Tobin & Pinney to Ulysses Lynch, 7 March 1791, UoBSC, MS DM58/Letter Book/38.

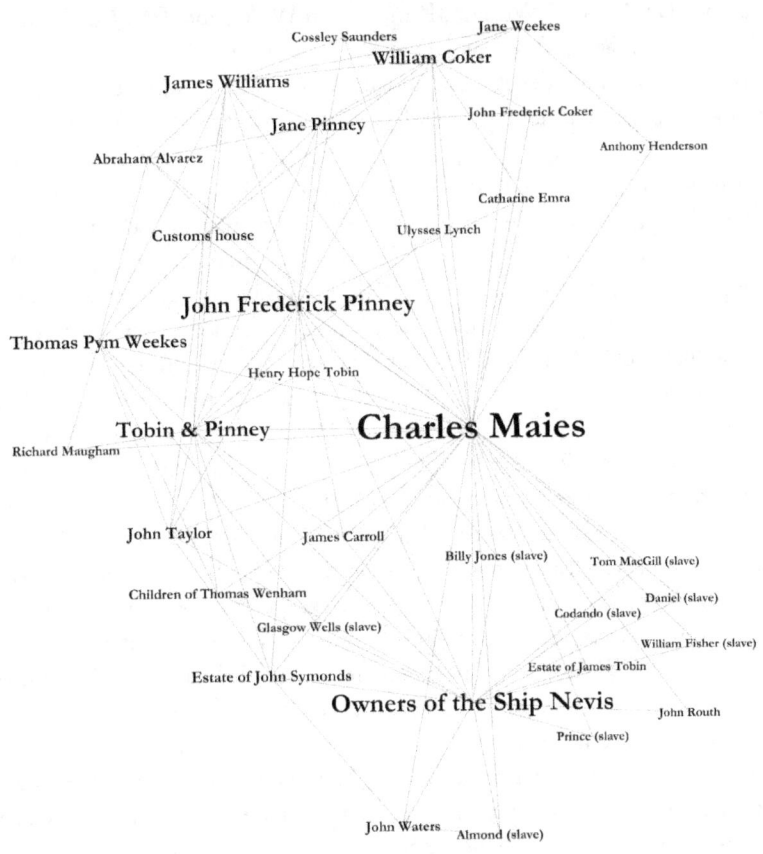

Figure 2.2: Charles Maies' Network within John Pinney's Nevis–Bristol network, 1783–1803

Note: John Pinney has been removed. Rendered in Gephi <https://gephi.org/>.

Source: UoBSC, DM58 Pinney Family Papers, 1538–1948, Account Books 30, 31, 33, 34, 35, 36, 39, 41, 43, 45, 47, 52, 54, 57, and 59.

https://liverpooluniversitypress.manifoldapp.org/projects/crisis-and-resilience/resource/crisis-and-resilience-figure-2-2

carpentry or other manual work, such as loading and unloading the ship. In one instance, Billy Jones is recorded as performing cooperage on some water casks. Other enslaved individuals hired included Glasgow, Codando, Daniel, Tom McGill, Almond, William Fisher, and Prince by Maies, and Glasgow,

Almond, Dr Weekes's William, Prince, John Wilks, and Tom McGill by the ship (and charged to 'The Owners of the Ship Nevis').[15]

Because of how deeply embedded Maies was within the plantation community, his behaviour mattered for the firm's reputation. He appears to have been a fairly competent captain; he was used by the firm for a long period. At times, however, he risked the ire of planters by taking on some sugars and excluding others. The firm explained to the planters whom he risked 'disobliging' that, with a shortage of freight, some clients were bound to be disappointed.[16] When it received complaints of his behaviour after several years of service, the firm promised that it would 'talk very seriously' with Maies about his conduct. Tobin & Pinney felt that this was enough, and told planters that 'we flatter ourselves in future you will have no cause to renew your Complaints of the Conduct of Capt Maies'.[17] Whether Maies was truly at fault, or whether the planters were offended at the ship being full—a matter, in seasons of plenty, that was somewhat beyond the captain's control—is an open question, although it was likely the latter. (Planters were an obstinate bunch. One, who had an argument with a captain bound for London, sent his sugars to Bristol instead.)[18] Tobin & Pinney took particular exception to planters who avoided certain ships because of their captains, pointing out to one planter that 'in not shipping your sugars on any Particular ship from a dislike to the Captain, you are disappointing his owners much more than himself'.[19] Yet eventually the will of the planters would win out. Despite Maies's qualities as a captain, he was eventually let go following some 'dispute between him and the planters in the West Indies', despite the fact that the firm considered him to be an 'excellent seaman' who was 'strictly honest and sober'.[20] Honesty and sobriety did not matter if the planters could not be kept on side. An unpopular captain reflected badly on the firm and induced planters to ship their sugars with someone else.

While ship-ownership therefore involved a great deal of people management, it also meant dealing with a being that more successfully

---

15 See numerous entries across UoBSC, MS DM58/Account Books/30, 34, 35, 36, 41, 45, 47, 52, 54, 57, and 59.
16 Tobin & Pinney to John Hendrickson, 20 August 1793, UoBSC, MS DM58/Letter Book/39.
17 Tobin & Pinney to Edward Huggins, 25 September 1794, UoBSC, MS DM58/Letter Book/39; Tobin, Pinney & Tobin to John Hendrickson, 18 January 1798, UoBSC, MS DM58/Letter Book/40.
18 Tobin & Pinney to Boddingtons & Bettesworth, 3 August 1793, UoBSC, MS DM58/Letter Book/39.
19 Tobin & Pinney to Edward Brazier, 2 December 1793, UoBSC, MS DM58/Letter Book/39.
20 Pares, *West-India Fortune*, p. 221.

resisted human control: the Atlantic Ocean. Vessels would fall victim to the 'perils of the sea', such as hurricanes and winds that drove ships on to land or which resulted in sinking. A ship was lucky to go for more than a few seasons without encountering an environmental hazard that threatened to take the vessel to the depths. It was not just dramatic instances of hurricanes and storms that affected shipping, however. Wet weather impeded and delayed the loading of ships. Contrary winds and tides would prevent a ship leaving port, as would frost in the winter months. A ship damaged in a gale would have to put back into port for repairs, while calms would lengthen a passage.[21] The worst threats of the sea (at least for the owners) could be dealt with through insurance. Though cheaper than at any previous point in history (see below), the purchasing of insurance was not without its drawbacks. Brokers could be inefficient, underwriters could be sluggish or overly demanding, and a significant amount of time was spent collecting evidence, ensuring its accuracy, and waiting for payments.

Insurance was mostly purchased by Tobin & Pinney through the firm's broker. Brokers were used as intermediaries between the merchants and underwriters, and charged 5% on the cost of the premium as a brokerage fee. It was their job to negotiate the premium and collect payments on behalf of merchants in the case of loss. Further, they provided a means of connecting underwriters and merchants, and were in a position to verify the character, reputation, and creditability of the parties involved. A broker with a good reputation was also more likely to get a claim successfully settled with an underwriter than if the underwriter was dealing with someone less well known to them.[22] A poor broker, especially one who could not obtain the same rates as others, would be a drag on a mercantile firm's finances. Moreover, it was easy enough for firms, especially those that had shared ownership of vessels with other partnerships, to find out how much their compatriots and competitors were paying. Tobin and Pinney, who had given their broker, John Warren, the freedom to order insurance 'upon the best terms', found themselves frequently disappointed that other merchants

---

21 See, for example, Pinney & Tobin to Edward Brazier, 12 January 1789, UoBSC, MS DM58/Letter Book/37; Tobin & Pinney to Ulysses Lynch, 1 October 1789, UoBSC, MS DM58/Letter Book/38.

22 See Pearson and Richardson, 'Insuring', pp. 431–34; Adrian B. Leonard, 'From Local to Transatlantic: Insuring Trade in the Caribbean', in *The Caribbean and the Atlantic World Economy: Circuits of Trade, Money and Knowledge, 1650–1914*, ed. by Adrian B. Leonard and D. Pretel (London: Palgrave Macmillan, 2015), pp. 137–60 (p. 138); Christopher Kingston, 'Marine Insurance in Britain and America, 1720–1844: A Comparative Institutional Analysis', *The Journal of Economic History*, 67:2 (2007), 379–409 (pp. 382, 387).

shipping 'on the same vessel' were 'insured on terms so much lower', and so they decided to switch to the services of Noble & Hunt.[23]

While brokers might be unable to obtain the 'best terms' for clients, a more significant drawback to using insurance was the time taken between the incidence of loss occurring and the merchant or shipowner receiving payment from the underwriter. Between the initial claim and payment, documentation had to be gathered which could demonstrate the loss. It could take several months or longer to get everything together. There was a wide array of documents required, and these sometimes had to be gathered from across the Atlantic. In the more routine instances this was not too consequential. To get a rebate for short shipment (i.e., shipping less than originally insured for), for example, the merchant only needed to send a copy of the ship's manifest and the landwaiter's account of goods landed, or if no sugar was sent in the end, a letter confirming this. To get a rebate for sailing with convoy, a certificate was needed as proof (to qualify as having sailed with convoy, the ship needed to receive official instructions from the commodore before departing).[24] Claims for damages required more evidence. Bills of lading were required to demonstrate that goods were actually on board. In one case, for a damaged container of molasses, Tobin & Pinney presented 'a Survey of Captains, Coopers, and Mates, on the state of the Mollasses on board the Nevis who all agreed the damage was intirely owing to the bad Weather, and they have signed a report accordingly, which will intitle those who insured to recover against the Underwriters'.[25] For damaged sugars, the sugar broker would conduct a survey to check that they were stowed properly (underwriters would not be liable for bad casks, only improper stowage or damage incurred at sea).[26] Many of these documents were created in the routine of business or were already to hand, such as when merchants claimed for rebates (which underwriters expected to pay).

Not every claim was so straightforward, however. Some required a mass of paperwork as underwriters attempted to 'verify or disprove events that had

---

23 Tobin & Pinney to John Warren, 22 October 1793, 23 and 27 March 1794, UoBSC, MS DM58/Letter Book/39; Tobin, Pinney & Tobin to Noble & Hunt, 6 May 1799, UoBSC, MS DM58/Letter Book/40.
24 See numerous letters from Tobin & Pinney to John Warren; see also Tobin & Pinney to Charles Chabert, 8 January 1795, UoBSC, MS DM58/Letter Book/39; Tobin, Pinney & Tobin to James Huggins, 18 September 1800, UoBSC, MS DM58/Letter Book/42.
25 Tobin & Pinney to John Scarbrough, 18 June 1792, UoBSC, MS DM58/Letter Book/38.
26 Tobin & Pinney to John Warren, 13 January 1794, UoBSC, MS DM58/Letter Book/39; Tobin, Pinney & Tobin to James Huggins, 6 February 1801, UoBSC, MS DM58/Letter Book/42.

occurred in distant ports or at sea'.[27] When the *Betsey* foundered off Bermuda, some goods were claimed as salvage and sold to 'benefit the underwriters', that is, to make what they could and reduce the underwriters' payment. To prove this was the case, however, various documents had to be sent from Bermuda. These included:

> No.1. A Deposition from Capt. White, and Duncan Campbell his Mate, of the particulars of the accident which happened to the Sloop Betsey – with a Protest under the Seal of Gov.r Hamilton, of Bermuda, countersigned by his Secretary, Henry Tucker – dated 29th March. 1794.
>
> No.2. A Survey and Certificate of the damage which the Sloop sustained, under the hands and Seals of the Master and Wardens of the Port of Crow Lane – (vizt.) Tho.s Dickinson, Master – John Trimingham, & Tho.s Godet Sen.r Wardens – dated the 16th April. 1794.
>
> No.3. Certificate under the hand and seal of Governor Hamilton, of the deposition of the Capt. as to the amount of Costs and Damages incurred at Bermudas, amounting to £380~4~4¾ – countersigned by the Govern.r's Secretary – July 4th 1794.
>
> No.4. Certificate under the hand and Seal of John Hamilton, the British Consul at Norfolk, in Virginia, that the Register of the Sloop Betsey was properly endorsed on the command of her being transferred from Rob.t Roberts to Miles White – dated 20th May. 1794.[28]

Tobin & Pinney found out that the ship had run ashore on Bermuda by July 1794. The above letter with various documents was sent in October 1795—it had taken over a year to get it all together. The account for the underwriter's payment was not received until November 1795, but as it was less than expected, the dispute continued. 'After much trouble', the loss was finally adjusted in January 1796, though it was 'materially less' than the claimant expected.[29] Tobin & Pinney might have been lucky that the process took only this long. As Emma Hart and Cathy Matson observe, disputes might last for years at a time.[30] This incident further shows not just the large amount of paperwork shipping created, but how much was needed to prove a loss.

---

27 Kingston, 'Marine Insurance', p. 382.
28 Tobin & Pinney to John Warren, 2 October 1795, UoBSC, MS DM58/Letter Book/39.
29 Tobin & Pinney to John Warren, 19 July 1794 and 7 November 1795, and Tobin & Pinney to Thomas Pym Weekes, 26 January 1796, UoBSC, MS DM58/Letter Book/39.
30 Hart and Matson, 'Situating Merchants', pp. 672–75.

Problems occurred, and delays were exacerbated, when these documents were improperly completed. The *Mary* went ashore at Tortola, and, like the *Betsey*, goods that were damaged were sold on the spot to reduce the payment due from the underwriters. The remaining sugars that went unscathed were reshipped after the *Mary* was repaired, and she arrived in Bristol in September 1797 after her transatlantic crossing with an account of sugars sold and a manifest of those still on board. Unfortunately, these were not filled out correctly—sugars said to have been sold in Tortola had arrived in Bristol. Thanks to the erroneous accounts and manifest, the sugars were liable to seizure by the Customs officers. Furthermore, the sales and general average had to be recalculated with the underwriters in light of the errors, and so Tobin & Pinney needed to send a further twelve documents. The delay, the need to send various documents as proof, and the calculations of adjustments unnecessarily ate up the firm's time, and this meant that the account did not get settled until February 1798.[31] Hence it was five months after the arrival of the ship before the account was settled, notwithstanding that these underwriters at least appear to have been understanding enough. Underwriters were not always understanding (at least, not in the way that merchants desired). In one case, an underwriter, Mr Van Dam, made frequent requests on one claim for damages to a ship (a claim that co-owners Protheroe & Claxton had already had settled) for tradesmen's bills to be disaggregated into various charges, which Tobin & Pinney maintained was impossible. Tobin & Pinney told Warren to 'settle with Mr Van Dam on the best terms you can – after which, you will inform him that his conduct has been such, that we cannot allow his Name to appear again on any Policy of ours'. The delays meant that the case, which should otherwise have been routinely settled, lasted from September 1796 to June 1797.[32]

Merchant-shipowners therefore faced a variety of risks in the form of moral and natural hazards. Captains, as agents for the firm, could harm the reputations of the firms that they represented, and merchants tried their best to seek reputable captains, pay them well, and keep them adhered as closely as possible to the firm's instructions. When they underperformed or irritated clients, despite their seamanship, they had to be let go. Threats from the sea could be dealt with through the use of insurance, though this engendered its own moral hazards, with incompetent brokers, delays, and, at times, obstinate

---

[31] See numerous letters from Tobin, Pinney & Tobin to Thomas Latham & Son and John Lyons from 4 September to 21 December 1797, and Tobin, Pinney & Tobin to John Warren, 22 February 1798, UoBSC, MS DM58/Letter Book/40.

[32] Tobin, Pinney & Tobin to John Warren, 18 September 1796, 9 and 20 January 1797, and 15 June 1797, UoBSC, MS DM58/Letter Book/40.

and obstructive underwriters. This was enough during peacetime. During war, however, risks were heightened, and further measures were needed to ensure the continuation of trade.

The challenges of warfare

Warfare presented one of the most significant challenges to shipping in this period. Even during periods of peace, the threat of war led to delays. During the Dutch Crisis of 1787, Samuel Span's *Union Island* was delayed by press gangs, which scared sailors out of the city. Similarly, in 1790, during the Nootka Sound Crisis, a hot press over the summer was said to have led to the impressment of 700 men, with some men jumping overboard and drowning while swimming to shore to avoid impressment (see quote at the beginning of this chapter).[33] Tobin & Pinney, hoping to send goods by Evan Baillie's ship, was disappointed by delays. The commercial environment was deeply unsettled: matters were 'in such a critical state of Suspense that nobody seems forward in dispatching their Ships, as they are at a loss to conjecture whether they must be fitted & prepared for Peace or War'. This uncertainty delayed the shipment of provisions and, when tensions had died down, the firm lamented that 'could this have been foreseen much money might have been saved to the Merchants in fitting out, & insuring their ships'.[34] Freight rates had risen in Bristol by 25%, and in London by 50%. Insurance rates had risen from 2% to 3%.[35] The anticipation was enough to bring a halt to shipping as shipowners began preparing for the worst.

The worst was realised three years later when Britain and Revolutionary France declared war. Warfare affected shipping in several ways. First, war led to 'The amazing advance of All Articles of Ship Building &c', increasing the costs of buying and repairing ships. Further, with the increased demands from the government, 'ships of all kinds are … very scarce and dear'. With increased naval shipbuilding, as well as an expanding merchant fleet, planks became scarce—especially oak; on at least one occasion, the *Nevis* had to be

---

33 Edward Shiercliff to William Dickinson, 1 October 1787, SHC, MS DD/DN/4/2/22(2); Rogers, *Manning the Royal Navy*, pp. 131–32.
34 Tobin & Pinney to Ulysses Lynch, 10 June, 4 August, and 8 November 1790, and Tobin & Pinney to B. & T. Boddington & Co., 21 August 1790, UoBSC, MS DM58/Letter Book/38.
35 Tobin & Pinney to Edward Brazier, 19 November 1790, UoBSC, MS DM58/Letter Book/38; Thomas Harris to William Dickinson, 2 October 1790, and 5 January 1791, SHC, MS DD/DN/4/2/33(1), 36(2). See purchases of insurance in UoBSC, MS DM58/Account Books/32 and 40.

repaired with fir instead. Sailcloth was similarly hard to come by.[36] It was not just materials that increased in price, but labour costs, too. Bristol's merchants, operating through the West India Association, attempted to keep these as low as possible. When shipbuilders came to the WIA with requests from their employees to increase their wages, these were denied by the merchants. Furthermore, crews became more expensive to hire. The WIA attempted to keep wages down by establishing rates of pay for crews in 1793. Wages rose during wartime as merchants competed with the Navy and privateers for seamen; some ships were forced to put to sea below complement. This issue was exacerbated by the press gangs.[37] Tobin & Pinney preferred to sail with fewer crew, arguing that new hires were an 'additional, and unnecessary expence' when 'Seamens wages are so high'. Indeed, these costs could add up. Tobin & Pinney paid its captains £6 a month, the first mate £5 10s, the second mate, boatswain, steward and carpenter £4 10s, and seamen between £3 10s and £4 10s a month based on ability.[38] Freight rates had to be raised to cover these costs. From 1793, rates rose quickly (quicker in London, as Tobin & Pinney informed its clients), until they were double the peacetime rate.[39]

These costs were offset by the rising price of sugar, however, as the following chapters show, meaning that the most significant threat to shipping during wartime came from commerce raiding. Privateers threatened shipping lines, while offering belligerent merchants an opportunity for profit. This was such that, as Kenneth Morgan has argued, throughout the eighteenth century Bristol's use of privateers hindered its development by reducing investment elsewhere.[40] By the French Wars, however, the merchants of Bristol engaged less in privateering.[41] Yet the threat from French privateers still persisted. The

---

36 Tobin, Pinney & Tobin to John Hendrickson, 18 July 1797, and Tobin, Pinney & Tobin to George Webbe Junior, 16 December 1799, UoBSC, MS DM58/Letter Book/40; Tobin & Pinney to Martin & William Krause, 25 September 1794, and Tobin & Pinney to George Webbe, 28 March 1796, UoBSC, MS DM58/Letter Book/39.

37 BA, MS SMV/8/3/2/1 WIA; Tobin, Pinney & Tobin to George Webbe Junior, 16 December 1799, UoBSC, MS DM58/Letter Book/40; Clive Emsley, *British Society and the French Wars, 1793–1815* (London: Macmillan, 1979), pp. 34–36, 52–53; Knight, *Britain Against Napoleon*, pp. 76–77.

38 Tobin & Pinney to Charles Maies, 30 December 1793, UoBSC, MS DM58/Letter Book/39; Tobin, Pinney & Tobin to George Webbe Junior, 16 December 1799, UoBSC, MS DM58/Letter Book/40.

39 Tobin & Pinney to Curtis Crippen, 26 October 1795, UoBSC, MS DM58/Letter Book/39.

40 Morgan, *Bristol*, pp. 21, 27.

41 See Henning Hillmann and Christina Gathmann, 'Overseas Trade and the Decline of Privateering', *The Journal of Economic History*, 71:3 (2011), 730–61.

French may have been in a weaker position than in previous wars, but they were still active.[42] Over 1793–1795, Tobin & Pinney fell victim to several attacks. In April 1793, the firm wrote to its attorneys indicating its plans to send goods out on a 'running ship' sailing alone without a convoy. The partners believed that 'The French Privateers have been so destroyed that we have little fear of her arriving safe.' Goods were thus sent out on the *Mercury*, which was outfitted with six nine-pound cannons, plus small arms and a letter of marque. This did her little good, however: she was captured on the outward journey. Tobin and Pinney did not hear of her capture until 'two months after it happened'.[43] Once they heard, they outfitted their own ship, the *Edward*, with replacement goods, along with two carriage guns and eighteen men. She arrived at Nevis, and was sent on to Jamaica. Between Nevis and Jamaica, she was captured and taken to Saint Domingue. Before learning of this development, Tobin & Pinney, still believing the seas to be 'pretty well scoured of French Cruisers', continued to send goods out on running ships, to much the same end.[44] The *Albion* was captured near Guadeloupe. The *Fame*, carrying herrings, was captured by a French privateer, and then recaptured by a Spanish ship and taken into Cadiz, from where the owners failed to negotiate her release. The *Russia Merchant* was sent to Tortola and St Croix as a running ship, and was captured by the French and taken into Brest.[45] The firm's consignments from St Croix and Tortola were harmed by the capture of this and other ships; the partners had expected 100 hogsheads of sugar, but received only 11.[46] Tobin and Pinney's belief that French privateers did not pose a significant threat turned out to be wrong. They learned this the hard way. There was only one real solution: convoys.

---

42 Patrick Crowhurst, *The French War on Trade: Privateering 1793–1815* (Aldershot: Scholar Press, 1989), p. 46.

43 Tobin & Pinney to Edward Brazier & Thomas Pym Weekes, 16 April 1793, and Tobin & Pinney to George Webbe Junior, 18 May 1793, and Tobin & Pinney to Edward Brazier, 5 August 1793, UoBSC, MS DM58/Letter Book/39.

44 Tobin & Pinney to John Warren, 24 August 1793, 20 March and 19 September 1794, Tobin & Pinney to Edward Brazier & Thomas Pym Weekes, 21 September 1793, and Tobin & Pinney to John Hendrickson, 4 May 1794, UoBSC, MS DM58/Letter Book/39.

45 Tobin & Pinney to John Taylor & Edward Brazier, 6 August 1794, Tobin & Pinney to Edward Brazier, 25 September 1794, Tobin & Pinney to Charles Chabert, 5 November 1794 and 18 February 1795, UoBSC, MS DM58/Letter Book/39.

46 Tobin & Pinney to William Colhoun, 26 October 1795, and Tobin & Pinney to Martin & William Krause, 31 October 1795, UoBSC, MS DM58/Letter Book/39.

The convoy system

Despite the fact that the West Indies were a significant source of state revenue, it was the merchants, rather than the government, who led the introduction of the convoy system. As Douglas Bradburn argues of the Virginia tobacco trade during the war in 1690–1715, government-provided convoys were not imposed as a means of controlling merchant populations: 'they were there because they had been demanded by the local oligarchs ... and their partners, kin, and allies in the English merchant community'.[47] As then, in 1793 the convoy system was not simply imposed top-down by a government anxious to protect a vital source of revenue. Merchants were petitioning for convoys well before the government introduced the Compulsory Convoy Act in 1798. This gave commanders greater control over convoys, but only to the degree that it prevented ships abandoning the convoy in order to be the first to market. Licences were still given out until 1812 to any ship that wanted to travel without convoy, so long as it was sufficiently armed.[48] It was the communities of merchants who called on the government to provide them with ships to guard their convoys.

The records of the Bristol West India Association show that convoys were organised on an *ad hoc* basis. Though they were expected to leave at around the same time each year, the dates were rarely certain more than a few weeks before. In 1795, the Association expressed its frustration to the Admiralty, demanding a clear date, and—pointedly—for that date to be adhered to. Applications for a convoy to be appointed for 25 November were typically sent off around October. Attempts to get convoys fixed each year did not occur until the Napoleonic Wars, however, when the Association sent proposals for convoys to sail every five weeks on fixed dates from October to April.[49] Why it took so long to begin fixing dates is not clear. According to Tobin & Pinney, 'with respect to Convoys Government for political reasons seem rather to evade fixing particular days for their sailing or to be very punctual if they are fixed'.[50] The Admiralty might not have wanted to hold

---

47 Douglas Bradburn, 'The Visible Fist: The Chesapeake Tobacco Trade in War and the Purpose of Empire, 1690–1715', *The William and Mary Quarterly*, 68:3 (2011), 361–86 (p. 364).

48 Horsfall, 'West Indian Trade', pp. 188–89; N. A. M. Rodger, *The Command of the Ocean: A Naval History of Britain, 1649–1815* (London: Penguin, 2004), pp. 559–60; Roger Knight, *Convoys: The British Struggle Against Napoleonic Europe and America* (New Haven, CT: Yale University Press, 2022), p. 22.

49 BA, MS SMV/8/3/2/1 WIA.

50 Tobin, Pinney & Tobin to George Webbe Junior, 13 February 1799, UoBSC, MS DM58/Letter Book/40.

itself too closely to any particular date to avoid making promises that it could not keep, given that convoying depended on the availability of naval vessels. Alternatively, it might not have wanted knowledge of dates get into French hands, which could lead to a large convoy of merchant vessels becoming a target for French privateers and naval vessels.[51] Either way, the records of the WIA show that it was the merchants who, in the early stages of the war, lobbied the government for help in protecting their shipping.

Convoys were not infallible. Merchants complained that some convoys were protected by only a small naval vessel—in one case a 12-gun brig—when there were supposed to be at least two ships guarding the fleet. If there were multiple escorts, they would part at Madeira after the initial danger of sailing past France had passed, leaving the ships uncomfortably exposed on the Atlantic crossing.[52] Previous wars had seen the capture of entire convoys. In 1780, 55 merchant ships bound for the East and West Indies were caught near Madeira by a Spanish fleet, a loss valued at around £1.5 million.[53] Something similar occurred during the French Revolutionary Wars when a great number of the Jamaica fleet were lost in 1795.[54] On the whole, however, the protection proved to be effective. Estimates from Lloyds put merchant losses as a result of enemy action at around 2–3% of the total fleet.[55] Indeed, the British merchant fleet was able to expand throughout the wars.[56]

Yet despite their effectiveness in protecting shipping, convoys were not without their downsides. Merchants such as Tobin and Pinney, who experienced the costs of privateers, lobbied for convoys because they had a direct interest in shipping and the safe import of sugar. However, they also knew that there were drawbacks and, where these could not be mitigated, trade-offs had to be made. First, as Richard Pares has previously argued,

---

51 The effect of French raiders could be devastating: in October 1795, a Levant convoy with over sixty merchant ships accompanied by three 74-gun escorts lost thirty-three of their number, along with one of the 74-gun naval vessels, to six French ships of the line. See Knight, *Convoys*, p. 21.
52 Tobin, Pinney & Tobin to John Taylor & Edward Brazier, 20 December 1796, and Tobin, Pinney & Tobin to George Webbe Junior, 15 March 1798, UoBSC, MS DM58/Letter Book/40; Horsfall, 'West Indian Trade', p. 190.
53 Knight, *Convoys*, pp. 18–19.
54 Adrian B. Leonard, 'Underwriting Marine Warfare: Insurance and Conflict in the Eighteenth Century', *International Journal of Maritime History*, 25:2 (2013), 173–85 (pp. 176–77); Pares, *West-India Fortune*, p. 197.
55 Rodger, *Command of the Ocean*, p. 559; Knight, *Convoys*, p. 23.
56 Knight, *Britain Against Napoleon*, p. 180; Michael Duffy, *Soldiers, Sugar, and Seapower: The British Expeditions to the West Indies and the War against Revolutionary France* (Oxford: Clarendon Press, 1987), p. 387.

convoys amplified the seasonal nature of Bristol's West Indies shipping.[57] This meant that merchants had to accept a loss of control over when they sent off their ships. It also increased congestion in the ports. The impact of this on the market was limited, however. Secondly, this concentration of shipping into convoys presented challenges for communications. Yet this was mitigated by the use of packet ships, which had developed substantially since mid-century. Finally, convoys could lead to delays, though delays were not unusual anyway, especially due to weather. If a ship missed the convoy, however, it would have to wait for the next one—or brave the seas as a running vessel. These were not simply costs that were imposed on merchants—the merchants asked for convoys, and where these drawbacks could not be mitigated, they accepted the trade-offs as the costs of safety.

Convoys and the seasonality of shipping

One of the key drawbacks of convoys, frequently complained about by merchants, and thus a complaint that is frequently repeated by historians, was the congestion in the ports that convoys encouraged.[58] Congestion was a symptom of the exacerbation of seasonal patterns of shipping. In peacetime, shipping between Bristol and the West Indies operated with a seasonal rhythm. Ships would load goods for the West Indies in the late summer and autumn, aiming to leave around October or November to arrive in the islands before Christmas. They would stay in the West Indies for the harvest—merchants, knowledgeable about the production process, were anxious that their ships arrived in time—and leave in spring and summer before the hurricane period (beginning officially, as per the conventions of insurance, on 1 August), arriving back in Bristol by the summer and autumn.[59] Other Atlantic trades followed a similar pattern, though in contrast, many ships in the American line would make two voyages a year, aiming to arrive in America in April or May, return in the summer, and leave again to arrive in September or October.[60]

---

57 Pares, *West-India Fortune*, pp. 196–97.
58 Bristol was a port already understood to be congested, a problem for which plans had been repeatedly drawn up—the failure to find a timely solution has attracted a significant amount of attention from historians. See, for example, Morgan, *Bristol*, pp. 28–29; Morgan, 'Economic Development', pp. 51–53; Minchinton, 'The Port of Bristol in the Eighteenth Century', pp. 135–41.
59 See Chapter 1.
60 Herbert Heaton, 'The American Trade', in *The Trade Winds: A Study of British Overseas Trade during the French Wars, 1793–1815*, ed. by C. Northcote Parkinson (London: George Allen and Unwin, 1948), pp. 194–226 (pp. 198–99); Haggerty, *Trading Community*, p. 188.

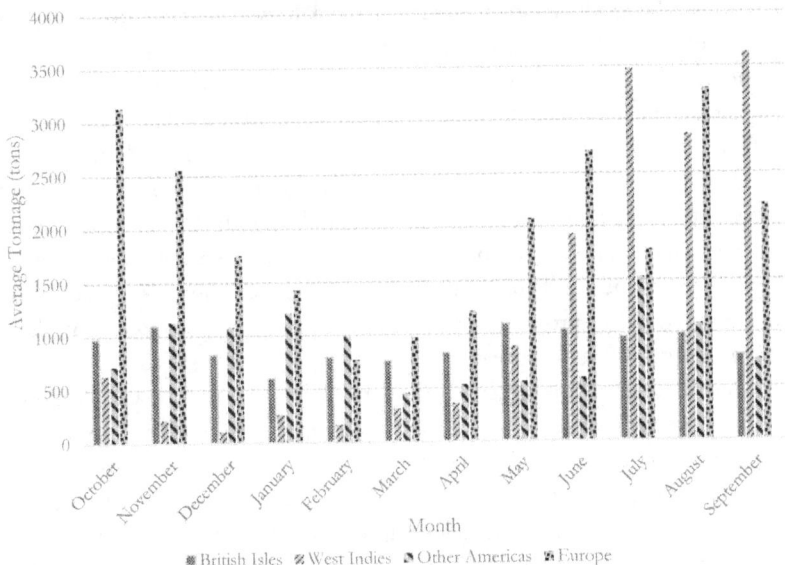

Figure 2.3: Average Monthly Shipping Tonnage Entering Bristol, 1784–1792 (tons)

Source: BA, MS SMV/7/1/1/72-76 Wharfage Books, 1784–1792.

The peacetime pattern for Bristol's major trades is shown in Figure 2.3. The data, collected from Bristol's wharfage books where entries were recorded, shows that arrivals from the West Indies were most pronounced from May to September, while for those from the other Americas (including the United States), peaks occurred from November to January and from July to August. Arrivals from Europe were spread out mostly between May and November. Arrivals from the British Isles were more consistent throughout the year, but each trade experienced a lull from February to April (which was, not coincidentally, the time when merchants began balancing their accounts). In the West India trade, though many ships were engaged in circuitous routes calling at multiple ports, the majority were used in direct trades, with ships that were employed as regulars serving a particular island or region.[61] The *Pilgrim* and *Venus* were regulars to St Kitts, for example; Tobin & Pinney's *Rachel*, as well as the *Nevis*, were the 'regular and Stationed' ships for Nevis.[62] These seasonal rhythms were influenced by oceanic currents and patterns

---

61 Morgan, *Bristol*, pp. 59–74, 80–88; Haggerty, *Trading Community*, pp. 187–88.
62 Tobin, Pinney & Tobin to Cossley Saunders, John C. Mills & James Williams, 6 August 1799, and Tobin, Pinney & Tobin to Patrick Burke, 7 October 1799, UoBSC, MS DM58/Letter Book/40.

of winds—the trade winds—which dictated how (and how quickly) these wind-driven vessels traversed the oceans.

The north-east trade winds took the ships south-west past Madeira and across the Atlantic, to arrive at Barbados. From there they travelled northwards to the Leeward Islands, and then westwards to Jamaica. They would exit the Caribbean to the north-east, north of Bermuda, and then sail eastwards past Newfoundland.[63] As understandings of these patterns improved, merchants were able to make better use of multilateral voyages. The inconsistencies and uncertainties that remained, however, made direct trade a much better prospect for most in the West India trade, as the risk of missing harvests was too great.[64]

Tobin & Pinney attempted to maximise the organisational efficiency of its shipping by sending one ship on two voyages in a year. This was not uncommon, and, as noted, occurred frequently in the trade to mainland America. Though the partners sent their first ship, the *Nevis*, with instructions for planters to load her up quickly so she could make another trip, the realities of the harvest, delays owing to wind and weather, and the threat of war left them disappointed. On one occasion they managed to get the *Nevis* out for a second time in 1792, but she was so late that she had to return after 1 August in the hurricane season. Attempts to get two trips out of the *Edward*, though not always unsuccessful, were equally fraught with difficulties.[65] As Morgan has noted, it could take around a month to collect the hogsheads from multiple plantations at the harbour.[66] The seasonal rhythms were, thus, inherent to the trade, and dictated the departure and arrival of transatlantic shipping.

The convoys had to conform to this pattern. Their imposition, as Pares states, amplified the seasonal nature of trade.[67] Data from the wharfage books can nuance this picture. Figure 2.4, which compares the average share of tonnage per month entering Bristol in wartime and peacetime, confirms that the seasonal nature of trade with the West Indies remained intact, with some important distinctions. Entrances remained just as concentrated around the summer months, though August became more significant. Entrances at other points of the year, especially November to May, were even rarer. The biggest

---

63 Morgan, *Bristol*, p. 55; Horsfall, 'West Indian Trade', pp. 157–58.
64 Nuala Zahedieh, *The Capital and the Colonies: London and the Atlantic Economy, 1660–1700* (Cambridge: Cambridge University Press, 2012), pp. 176–77; Morgan, *Bristol*, pp. 78–80.
65 See Tobin & Pinney to Edward Brazier, 28 April 1792, UoBSC, MS DM58/Letter Book/38; Pares, *West-India Fortune*, pp. 227–28.
66 Morgan, *Bristol*, pp. 199–200.
67 Pares, *West-India Fortune*, pp. 196–97.

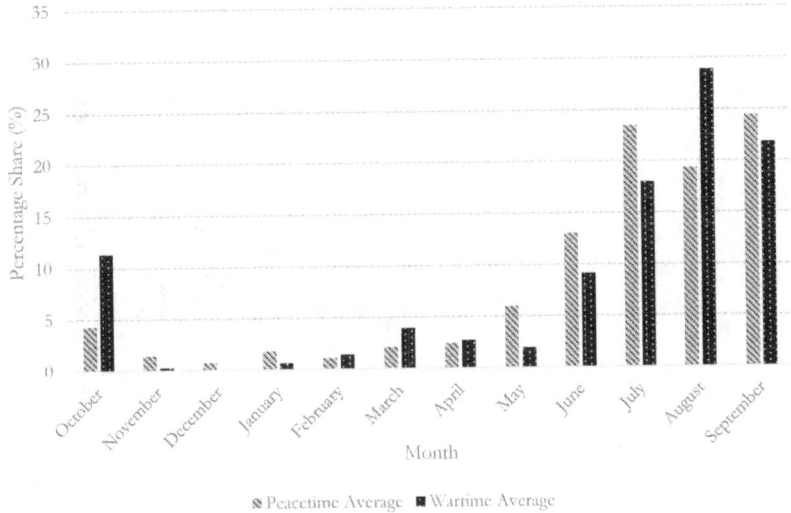

Figure 2.4: Average Share of Shipping Tonnage Entering Bristol from the West Indies by Month, 1784–1801 (%)

Source: BA, MS SMV/7/1/1/72-81 Wharfage Books, 1784–1801.

difference, however, was the shift of the bulk of entrances from between May and September in peacetime to between June and October in wartime. The rise in entrances from October represents arrivals in the last influx of ships leaving the West Indies with the '1st August Convoy'.[68] Rather than sailing when ready, ships would wait for the convoy to form, pushing back the date of sailing. The pattern, on average, therefore remained similar, but shifted by a month in this wartime period. These figures, which represent the averages of every recorded month in peace and war, do not reveal the amplifications that Pares speaks of. When we take a sample year from peacetime and wartime, however, this feature becomes more apparent. Figure 2.5 shows that the 1788/89 period conformed to the peacetime average, while the wartime average masks significant differences between the years: the dramatic spikes in June and especially August in 1797/98 demonstrate the seasonal amplification to which Pares was referring.

That convoys worsened congestion in an already congested port is therefore not hard to see. A more subtle, and perhaps more pernicious, problem, however, and one that was among Tobin & Pinney's greatest complaints, was

---

68 Tobin, Pinney & Tobin to John Lyons, 4 September 1797, UoBSC, MS DM58/Letter Book/40.

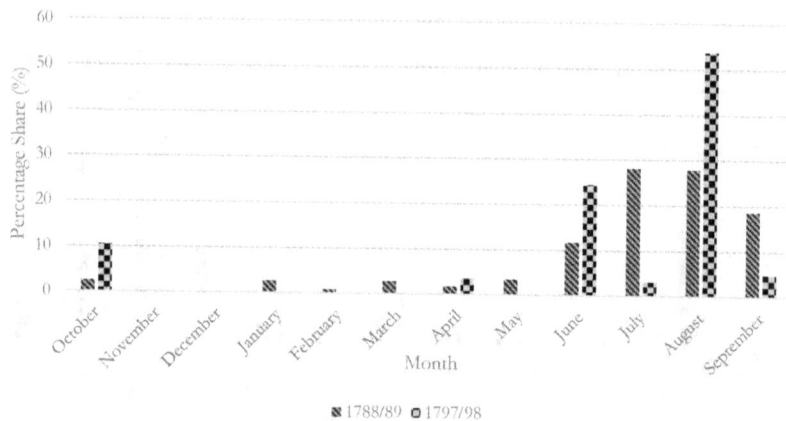

Figure 2.5: Share of Shipping Tonnage Entering Bristol from the West Indies by Month, 1788/89 and 1797/98 (%)

Source: BA, MS SMV/7/1/1/77 and 79 Wharfage Books, 1788–89 and 1797–98.

that convoys led to a loss of control. The decision about when to sail was now down to the collective body of merchants, rather than each firm individually. Instead of shipping goods and collecting sugars on their own terms, shipping was tied to the allocation of convoys; rather than sending the ship as soon as loaded, winter shipments could only be promised with the first convoy. As Tobin & Pinney noted to William Jones, 'Our first convoy is appointed to sail from hence on the 25th of next month [November] … which will be some disappointment to ourselves as well as our friends, but it is not in our power to prevent it'.[69] Tobin & Pinney similarly informed an attorney in Nevis that the firm would 'not be able to dispatch our first regular Ship so soon as usual, being obliged to wait the motions of the Convoy'.[70] With several ships leaving later than usual in November, later convoys might be without a ship for the smaller islands, and the firm, for example, remained 'quite uncertain whether any Vessel for Nevis may go in a second Convoy'.[71] Furthermore, because

---

69 Tobin & Pinney to William Jones, 23 October 1793, UoBSC, MS DM58/Letter Book/39.

70 Tobin & Pinney to John Taylor, 2 December 1793, UoBSC, MS DM58/Letter Book/39.

71 Tobin, Pinney & Tobin to George Webbe Junior, 17 October 1797, and Tobin, Pinney & Tobin to George Webbe Junior, 15 March 1798, UoBSC, MS DM58/Letter Book/40.

ships were sent by the last convoy, travelling in spring, no orders could be sent until the next convoy in autumn.[72] The return fleet was organised by the admiral stationed in the Royal Navy's base on Antigua or Jamaica. These would be appointed throughout the spring and early summer, the latest being the 1st of August fleet, sailing before the onset of the hurricane season.[73]

One trade-off for safety was, therefore, putting up with a more congested port. Furthermore, having to adhere to these predefined sailing times, despite whatever influence each individual merchant might have over the WIA's decisions, meant a loss of control over shipping as each ship now sailed together. Yet these were problems that one could put up with if the system kept one's ships safe from French privateers—the only thing worse than too many ships in port at one time was no ships at all.

Convoys and communications

The shipping that connected Britain to the West Indies was a significant piece of infrastructure, not just for the outbound passage of goods and the return of sugar, but for the passage of information. Letters, accounts, promises of credit, and news (personal and business) were sent by friends, associates, and family—and combinations thereof—across the Atlantic. Importantly, access to timely information was critical for the operation of business. It was important, as we have seen, for merchants and absentee planters to be able to communicate with correspondents in the islands.[74] Merchants such as Tobin and Pinney received orders from clients who demanded that they be completed in a timely manner and arrive as early as possible. As they informed one planter in 1792, 'We seldom receive the bulk of our orders till late in September, when many things are to be manufactured which require time, at a Season when all our tradesmen, and manufacturers are particularly busy.'[75] Early orders remained important with the convoys. As the firm exasperatedly informed a client late in the war, 'We must again repeat (what we have already done so often) that unless our Correspondents furnish us with their orders in time it is impossible for us to get them made properly or early enough to Ship in the first fleet.'[76] Much of this communication was done via merchant vessels, whereby captains picked up and deposited letters at taverns or coffee

---

72 Tobin, Pinney & Tobin to Henry Keyworth, 23 March 1797, UoBSC, MS DM58/Letter Book/40.
73 Horsfall, 'West Indian Trade', pp. 190–91.
74 See Chapter 1.
75 Tobin & Pinney to Edward Brazier, 17 March 1792, UoBSC, MS DM58/Letter Book/38.
76 Tobin, Pinney & Tobin to Edward Brazier, 18 September 1800, UoBSC, MS DM58/Letter Book/42.

houses.[77] This system worked well, though at times letters destined for Bristol might be delayed, arriving instead at somewhere like Liverpool.[78] Further, as Tobin & Pinney explained, when a ship was delayed, this would at least give the firm the 'opportunity of sending a second, a third, or even a fourth Packet by the same Vessel'. Yet given the seasonal nature of shipping, with fewer ships sailing during the spring, merchants' use of merchant vessels in this way was limited. During wartime the situation was worsened with the amplification of these seasonal rhythms and the concentration of shipping times around the departure of convoys.

This problem was mitigated through the use of transatlantic packet ships, which travelled from Falmouth. Used intermittently before 1763 during wartime, after the Seven Years War these became a permanent fixture in transatlantic communications infrastructure. Serious investment was made in improving them. From 1778, the packet ships were copper-bottomed, and from 1788 they were standardised as 170-ton vessels, able to make a round trip to the West Indies in ten weeks. By 1793, the packet ships offered a monthly service, with ten West India packets in use, five for Barbados and the Leeward Islands, and five for Jamaica.[79] This meant that, when Tobin & Pinney was operating, communications between the West Indies and Britain were more sophisticated than ever. Merchants had their pick of packet ships and merchant vessels.

One of the most significant factors influencing their choice was cost. Packet ships, as with convoys, offered a solution that was not without its own drawbacks. Tobin & Pinney sometimes found the packets too costly to use, especially during war. If having timely information was not important, the firm chose to wait and answer letters in one go, or send updates on sales and accounts all at once, rather than sending regular and periodical updates. The partners received complaints from clients for not sending regular information, but they defended their decision on the basis that they were protecting their clients from unnecessary postage costs. Letters could be sent by packet ships if planters did not 'dread the expense'. They could not win, however, for if they sent out regular updates via the packets then they received complaints

---

77 McCusker, *Essays*, p. 122; Howard Robinson, *Carrying British Mail Overseas* (London: George Allen and Unwin, 1964), p. 35; A. C. Wardle, 'The Post Office Packets', in *The Trade Winds: A Study of British Overseas Trade during the French Wars, 1793–1815*, ed. by C. Northcote Parkinson (London: George Allen and Unwin, 1948), pp. 278–90 (pp. 287–88).

78 See Pinney & Tobin to John Scarbrough, and John Tyson, 16 January 1787, UoBSC, MS DM58/Letter Book/37.

79 Robinson, *British Mail*, pp. 32–35, 43, 47–48, 57–67; McCusker, *Essays*, pp. 124–25.

about the cost of postage.[80] The costs of postage therefore factored into their decision making. Merchant vessels were the cheaper option, but the packets were quicker and more regular.

Furthermore, packet ships faced the same natural hazards that merchant vessels did. In 1794, a packet ship was delayed after having to retreat to Antigua 'in distress', seemingly affected by the weather. Another ship later in the year was feared taken, but that, too, had been forced back into Antigua 'owing to some accident'.[81] Packet ships were wood and sail, just like the merchant vessels, so they faced the same risks. Furthermore, though fast, and despite attempts to fend them off—there are several accounts of valiant captains defending the ships and the precious cargo in their charge—packets could still fall prey to privateers. French privateers disrupted not only the transatlantic packets, but also the smaller craft that carried mail between the islands. By 1798, ten of the required 16 packet services were in operation; over 1793–1798, 19 of the Falmouth packets were captured, and over 1793–1802, 46 packet ships overall (including the European packets), along with ten West India mail boats, were taken by privateers.[82]

An example shows what this meant for business operations. Tobin & Pinney found its business disrupted in late 1799 and 1800, when three packet ships in a row were captured. Significantly, the firm was awaiting a report on the state of the crop to know whether or not to send out another vessel, and was forced to make a decision based on reports about the weather that came from Barbados. A fourth packet ship eventually arrived with more correspondence, leaving the partners, in the meantime, without substantial information from the Leeward Islands for about six months.[83] This is a particularly extreme example of disruption, and Tobin and Pinney were able to use their initiative and get information from elsewhere. Between the merchant vessels sailing in convoys and the packet ships, with copies of letters sent by different means, merchants were thus able to maintain communications.

---

80 See Tobin, Pinney & Tobin to Edward Huggins, 4 October 1797, UoBSC, MS DM58/Letter Book/40; Tobin & Pinney to Edward Brazier, 3 August 1795, UoBSC, MS DM58/Letter Book/39.

81 Tobin & Pinney to James Huggins, 4 May 1794, Tobin & Pinney to William Colhoun, 12 September 1794, and Tobin & Pinney to George Webbe, 22 September 1794, UoBSC, MS DM58/Letter Book/39.

82 Robinson, *British Mail*, pp. 69–74; Wardle, 'Packets', pp. 278–90.

83 See Tobin, Pinney & Tobin to Edward Brazier, 6 December 1799, 17 and 25 March 1800, Tobin, Pinney & Tobin to George Webbe Junior, 24 and 31 May 1800, Tobin, Pinney & Tobin to John Colhoun Mills, 4 June 1800, UoBSC, MS DM58/Letter Book/40.

Convoys and delays

Of more material significance were the delays that merchants experienced when their ships were travelling in convoys.[84] Initial delays to shipping early on in the war stemmed from waiting for the first convoys to be organised. Tobin & Pinney's *Nevis* ended up waiting for three months for the first convoy, having been ready to sail 'when the French convention thought proper to declare war'. The late appointment of the convoy by October 1793 meant the *Nevis* would not arrive before Christmas. As Tobin & Pinney stated, 'after all where we are to depend so much on wind and weather, we can never be on a certainty, more especially in time of War when we must also wait upon the Motions of Convoys'.[85] Direct threats to the convoys also caused delays. Reports of a 'strong French Squadron' waiting to prey on the Cork convoy kept the ships in port. Similarly, the 'uncertain destination of the Brest Fleet' delayed the Portsmouth convoy another year.[86] It is difficult to blame the latter on the convoy system itself, for the need to safeguard shipping understandably took priority (given that this was the reason convoys were formed).

Bad weather proved disruptive most often, however. This was a problem in peacetime as well as war. Yet where before individual ships might have been able to set sail while the weather was good, while some sailing later or earlier might have been detained, now entire fleets—sometimes a season's worth of ships—were unable to sail. Once at sea, fleets might be 'terribly scattered' by harsh and heavy gales, making them easy pickings for privateers.[87] At points when groups of ships sailing from Kingroad for the Cork convoy were delayed, the convoy would at least wait for these large numbers of ships to arrive—there were benefits to being delayed together.[88] The West India Association could intervene, sending requests to delay the convoys, or to

---

84 This is a common criticism of convoys in the historiography. See MacInnes, *Gateway*, p. 232; C. Ernest Foyle, 'The Employment of British Shipping', in *The Trade Winds: A Study of British Overseas Trade during the French Wars, 1793–1815*, ed. by C. Northcote Parkinson (London: George Allen and Unwin, 1948), pp. 72–86 (p. 82); Horsfall, 'West Indian Trade', pp. 167–68, 174; Emsley, *British Society*, p. 28.

85 Tobin & Pinney to Frederick Fredrichs, 15 March 1793, Tobin & Pinney to John Scarbrough, 23 October 1793, and Tobin & Pinney to John Hendrickson, 25 November 1794, UoBSC, MS DM58/Letter Book/39.

86 Tobin & Pinney to Simon Pretor, 21 January 1794, UoBSC, MS DM58/Letter Book/39; Tobin, Pinney & Tobin to Edward Brazier, 1 June 1799, UoBSC, MS DM58/Letter Book/40.

87 See, for example, Tobin & Pinney to John Lyons, 4 March 1794, and Tobin & Pinney to George Webbe, 22 September 1794, UoBSC, MS DM58/Letter Book/39.

88 See Tobin, Pinney & Tobin to John Taylor, 6 December 1797, UoBSC, MS DM58/Letter Book/40.

appoint new ones, for groups of ships that were detained by contrary winds, or which had difficulty leaving the Avon.[89] This kind of delay happened frequently anyway, so relatively little changed for ships waiting with a convoy for the weather to turn.

Of more consequence was when individual ships missed the convoy because of the weather, for they would then have to wait for the next one. This situation was not unusual during the war. The *Hebe* and *Duke of Clarence* missed the convoy because they ran aground on a mudbank on the Avon. Another ship was delayed when a vessel sailing ahead of it sank.[90] Such a delay was deeply consequential. Tobin & Pinney's own *Nevis* once missed the Cork convoy by two days, and ended up waiting three months for the next convoy to form. So too did the *King David*, which was 'two days too late' for the Cork convoy 'owing to contrary Winds alone'. Those 'two days we may safely say were fatal ones' for Tobin & Pinney, for 'had she sailed with the Convoy, she would have been back again with the Fleet that lately arrived and fully Loaded with the Sugar of our own Friends'.[91] Missing the convoy would prove especially frustrating, given that the ship would have to wait months for the next one.

It was not just the delay, however, but the cost of missing a convoy that made merchants particularly anxious. Ships still required upkeep and captains and crews still needed to be paid while they were waiting for the convoy.[92] Delays also made shipping livestock much more difficult, as they would have to wait on board for the convoy and would require provisioning for an uncertain length of time.[93] It was not all bad, however: one upside of delay was that it allowed ships to take orders on board that might otherwise have been left out.[94] Yet delays were not ideal for merchant-shipowners or their planter clients. Some shipowners simply chose to send their ships out

---

89 BA, MS SMV/8/3/2/1 WIA; Tobin, Pinney & Tobin to George Webbe, 21 November 1800, UoBSC, MS DM58/Letter Book/42.

90 Tobin & Pinney to John Lyons, 26 December 1793, and Tobin & Pinney to John Warren, 28 December 1793, UoBSC, MS DM58/Letter Book/39; Tobin, Pinney & Tobin to Mitchel & Cockburne, 12 December 1800, UoBSC, MS DM58/Letter Book/42.

91 Tobin, Pinney & Tobin to Edward Huggins, 18 July 1797, and Tobin, Pinney & Tobin to George Webbe Junior, 2 October 1799, UoBSC, MS DM58/Letter Book/40.

92 Tobin, Pinney & Tobin to George Webbe Junior, 16 December 1799, UoBSC, MS DM58/Letter Book/40.

93 Tobin & Pinney to John Budgen, 7 April 1795, UoBSC, MS DM58/Letter Book/39; John Fisher Weare to William Dickinson, 11 and 13 November 1794, SHC, MS DD/DN/4/2/42(2); Thomas Harris to William Dickinson, 2 March 1793, SHC, MS DD/DN/4/2/41(1).

94 See Tobin, Pinney & Tobin to Edward Brazier, 26 January 1797, UoBSC, MS DM58/Letter Book/40.

regardless: the *Guiana Planter*, for example, missed the convoy at Cork, but was sent on to Madeira 'immediately' anyway.[95] Yet this was a risk on the part of the shipowners, and required the purchase of more expensive insurance. Missing the convoy could prove costly, and the wait for the next one would be fraught with uncertainty. This was a small drawback, however, when compared with the protection that convoys offered.

Convoys and insurance

Convoys were not the only protection that merchants had against the risks of warfare. While insurance protected shipowners in peacetime against losses arising from natural hazards, in wartime, insurance worked symbiotically alongside the convoy system. During periods of warfare, insurance costs typically rose, and quite dramatically, as some historians have pointed out. Julian Hoppitt, for example, comments that 'in wartime insurance rates often went so high that many could not afford them'.[96] Scholars interested in the relationship between the slave and slave-related trades and insurance have been drawn to the higher rates that accompanied warfare. Joseph Inikori, for example, finds evidence that rates could rise dramatically from 2% to 14% during wartime. This figure is validated with reference to the accounts of the Jamaican planter Simon Taylor.[97] It has been corroborated by Robin Pearson and David Richardson, who used the records of the slave trader James Rogers to show that premiums during wartime could reach 13.5%.[98] Yet these figures are problematic, and the insistence that dramatic rises in insurance could put merchants out of business is something of an exaggeration, at least for the end of the eighteenth century. While the figures presented by Inikori and Pearson and Richardson are not inaccurate in themselves—ships sailing without convoys were liable to pay these amounts—they do not account for how much cheaper the use of convoys made insurance for merchant-shipowners. Data gathered from Tobin & Pinney's accounts are instructive.

Premiums were calculated based on the ship, the port and destination, and the time of year of sailing. When insuring sugar in the West India trades, however, the actual ship the sugar travelled on mattered little, as many were 'regular' to the route and well known to underwriters. Underwriters took note when the ship was not usual to the trade, for example if it was a prize ship.[99]

---

95 Tobin, Pinney & Tobin to Edward Brazier, 3 July 1801, UoBSC, MS DM58/Letter Book/42.
96 Morgan, *Bristol*, pp. 26–27; Julian Hoppit, *Risk and Failure in English Business, 1700–1800* (Cambridge: Cambridge University Press, 1987), p. 98.
97 Inikori, *Africans*, p. 353.
98 Pearson and Richardson, 'Insuring', pp. 435, 438.
99 Tobin, Pinney & Tobin to George Webbe Junior, 16 December 1799, and Tobin,

Tobin & Pinney, as a merchant firm, shipped provisions for the plantations of its clients and returned the sugar home. As a ship-owning firm, it also sent its ships out. The partners therefore procured insurance for their ships, their outward cargoes, and the return cargoes belonging to the planters. We can, thus, use their account books to assess the cost of insurance at each stage.[100] While insurance was priced in guineas, pounds, or shillings per £100, these figures can be converted into percentages to facilitate comparison.

During peacetime, ships were insured either for single voyages or for a return rate that covered the outward and return legs of the journey. This was cheaper than buying two single voyages: single voyages were priced at 2%, and the rate for there-and-back voyages varied from 3.15% to 3.5%. Single-voyage insurance rates doubled to 4% during the hurricane season from 1 August, so merchants and shipowners were incentivised to avoid shipping during these months. The double rates lasted until January, but only applied to ships returning from the West Indies, not those outbound, which would be leaving Britain from October.[101] During wartime, Tobin & Pinney stopped buying outbound and return rates, either because underwriters preferred to price each voyage singly, or because the firm was unsure of the nature of the ship's return, and so preferred to purchase single voyages. Insurance was cheaper when the convoy, and thus its strength, was known in advance. Convoys were more uncertain for the return journey, as they would be organised in the West Indies. The range for outward and return journeys was, therefore, the same for ships sailing in convoy—4.2–5.25% (or 4–5 guineas per £100)—but the average rate was 4.33% outward and 4.84% return, showing that returns were costlier, with the firm more often paying the 5.25% rate.

The cost of insurance for cargoes behaved similarly. As with ships, the rate during peacetime for the outward voyage was 2%. The rates during wartime were higher. The range of rates was slightly wider for goods, at 3.15–6%. This reflects the variance in the ships used (Tobin & Pinney did not just use its own ships to send goods), the strength of the convoys, and the different nature of the risks posed to the goods than to the ships. The average rate Tobin & Pinney paid on any given day over the war period, based on the surviving data, was 4.94%, while the most common premium it paid was 5.25%, or 5 guineas per £100. The peacetime rates for the return cargo were similarly 2%, with the exception of a rise to 3% in June and July 1790. This was due to the anticipation of war with Spain during the Nootka Sound

---

Pinney & Tobin to Samuel Athill, 7 June 1797, UoBSC, MS DM58/Letter Book/40.
100 See insurance entries in UoBSC, MS DM58/Account Books/32 and 40.
101 UoBSC, MS DM58/Account Books/40, fols. 425–28, 476–79; Pares, *West-India Fortune*, p. 227; Horsfall, 'West Indian Trade', p. 183; Morgan, *Bristol*, p. 202.

Crisis. As with ships, the return voyage for the cargo during wartime was more expensive to insure than the outbound leg of the voyage. The most common rate was again 5.25%, as with the insurance on the ship, but it was used much more frequently, meaning the mean rate was effectively equal. The range of insurance rates was wider, at 3.15–8.4%, reflecting the uncertainty of how the sugar would be coming to England, and the different nature of the risks posed to sugar. There was uncertainty over which ship it would be going on (though this rarely affected the premium, as most ships were regulars known to insurers), whether it was travelling by convoy, and, if so, which port it would be going to. Rebates were built in to cover these variables, but this made the insurance more expensive than if these variables were known when the insurance was purchased. Returning ships could be insured to sail with or without convoy, with returns offered if the ship arrived with convoy. Even with the rebate, this would work out more expensive than if the ship was just insured to sail with convoy.[102] Furthermore, some sugar was sent to London, and, as Tobin & Pinney frequently reminded its clients, 'the risque of the English Channel is at present considered as equal to one Guinea pC^t above that of the Bristol Channel'.[103] That is, Bristol was a guinea cheaper to ship to than London.

There are a number of outliers to this data that reveal more about how these premiums were constructed. First, planters and merchants could still purchase insurance against the 'dangers of the sea only' during wartime, which covered the usual risks faced in peacetime, but not the added risks of warfare. These were charged at the peacetime rate of 2%.[104] Any merchant or planter confident enough in the strength of the convoy could insure against the 'dangers of the sea' and trust the convoy system to protect against capture. Secondly, additional insurance could be procured to insure against specific risks in the West Indies, such as the use of droghers (local watercraft, typically piloted by enslaved men or free Blacks and people of colour) to load the sugar on to the ships. These, in one case, appeared to add 14s 6d per £100, or 0.73%, to the cost of insurance.[105] Thirdly, running ships—those travelling without convoys—were charged much higher premiums than those travelling in convoy. These premiums rose as the war went on. The earlier runners could be insured as low as 7.35% outward. One return premium for sugar cost 8.4%, which included the use of droghers, and offered a 2% rebate if the sugar was

---

102 Tobin, Pinney & Tobin to John Warren, 14 June 1797, UoBSC, MS DM58/Letter Book/40; Pares, *West-India Fortune*, pp. 22–29.
103 Tobin & Pinney to Edward Brazier, 28 June 1793, UoBSC, MS DM58/Letter Book/39.
104 UoBSC, MS DM58/Account Books/40, fols. 560, 568.
105 UoBSC, MS DM58/Account Books/40, fol. 425.

shipped on a running ship with more than ten guns. The cheapness of these rates might have contributed to Tobin & Pinney's misconception of the risks that it faced from privateers. As the war progressed, premiums on runners were rarely less than 10.5%, and reached heights of 15.75%. Shipments for herrings from Glasgow were similarly insured at 10.5–15.75%, suggesting that these ships were being sent as runners.[106] Fourthly, as mentioned above, uncertainty meant that various conditions had to be built into the premiums that offered rebates, but which raised their costs. One particularly complex conditional premium charged 8 guineas to sail without convoy, promised a rebate of £6 if the ship sailed with the '26th July fleet', £4 with any other fleet, but required payment of an additional 2 guineas if the ship sailed after 1 August.[107] These exceptional cases show that the premiums constituted a variety of risks that were priced separately: the usual 'dangers of the sea' were priced at 2%, the threat of capture when in convoy was priced at 2.2–3.25%, and the threat without convoy much higher. In hindsight, this turned out to be a fairly accurate reflection of the risk, if not a better deal for the shippers and shipowners. As N. A. M. Rodger notes, 'careful calculations by the Secretary of Lloyd's suggested that over the whole period 1793 to 1815 British merchant losses ... in deep-sea trades [were] as much as 5 or 6 per cent, half to marine causes and half to enemy action'.[108]

The premiums paid by Tobin & Pinney were not unusual. Rates paid by John Pinney as a planter and by his compatriots on other islands, collated by J. R. Ward, are in line with what Tobin & Pinney was paying for its clients. The premiums Ward cites from the 'other West Indies' (i.e., the Windward, Leeward and Virgin Islands) to London were 3% in peacetime and 8% for 1793–1800.[109] These are higher than those Tobin & Pinney paid on its shipments—2% to insure sugar to London in peacetime (the extra guinea only appears to be factored in during wartime).[110] Even in wartime, 8% is slightly higher than Tobin & Pinney was paying, with 6.3% being more normal. That Bristol was a cheaper option for planters during wartime seemingly does not factor into Ward's assessment of profitability (his aggregate is possibly skewed by the inclusion of planters who shipped only to London). Yet Ward accounts

---

106 See numerous policies, UoBSC, MS DM58/Account Books/32 and 40.
107 UoBSC, MS DM58/Account Books/32, fol. 496.
108 Rodger, *Command of the Ocean*, p. 559. Indeed, the threat of capture when in convoy may well have been overpriced: as Roger Knight argues, 'winter weather and hurricanes were responsible for the loss of far more ships, cargoes and lives than were sustained from enemy action'. See Knight, *Convoys*, p. 24.
109 J. R. Ward, 'The Profitability of Sugar Planting in the British West Indies, 1650–1834', *The Economic History Review*, n.s., 31:2 (1978), 197–213 (p. 200).
110 UoBSC, MS DM58/Account Books/40, fols. 165, 260, 382.

for the commission charges of 0.5%, and the 0.25% cost of making out the policy, which this assessment has not.[111]

This demonstrates the strength of the British insurance market in conjunction with the convoy system, especially compared to that of the French. Silvia Marzagalli quotes French merchants facing 40% premiums on French ships, and 15% on American ships, while British merchants, who benefited from the convoy system and powerful naval protection, were paying as low as 4.2–6.3%.[112]

Conclusion

Shipping infrastructure was vital not just to the passage of goods between Britain and the West Indies, but to the passage of people, knowledge, and information. Wood and sail were central to maintaining the socio-economic networks that were the foundation of early modern business. Merchant-ship-owners, the actors who guided this system, faced significant challenges in both war and peace—challenges that could easily amount to crises on both personal, regional, and national levels. Peacetime risks included failure to fill the ship, ineffective captains (who acted as agents and representatives of the firm), and the perils of the sea. These were dealt with by paying captains well and limiting the scope of their responsibilities, and by using marine insurance (though this introduced similar principal–agent risks and moral hazards, as well as significant costs in terms of time, which had to be dealt with in their own way). Periods of warfare added considerably to these challenges. Press gangs disrupted access to maritime labour (even with the threat of war), while costs of materials and the price of labour increased. Merchants organised to keep these costs down, though they found that the rising price of sugar offset such costs anyway. More central to their concerns was privateering, which Bristol's merchants were less likely to engage in, but the pains of which they were still likely to feel.

The wartime crisis of shipping in the Bristol–West India trade was averted through the organisation of convoys, the use of which was supported by the system of insurance. These were familiar, tried-and-tested systems that merchants had, through their experience of previous wars, and with the knowledge handed down from previous generations, become accustomed to. Adapting their shipping and finances around these systems (and complaining about their drawbacks) was as natural to merchants as managing their

---

111 Ward, 'Profitability', p. 200.
112 Marzagalli, 'Trade Networks', p. 829.

shipping during peacetime. Such drawbacks included increased congestion in the port that followed the exacerbation of the seasonality of shipping, the narrowing of communication via merchant vessels (which was offset by the use of packet ships), and delays felt by ships that missed convoys. These drawbacks could either be put up with or mitigated, however, and convoys provided a substantially safer means of transatlantic travel than allowing ships to go it alone. Significantly, using convoys meant that insurance was much cheaper, reducing rates from 10.5–15.75% to 4.2–6.3%, with structures of premiums that suited the well-prepared. Altogether, these systems enhanced the resilience of the trade.

The shipping that supported the knowledge and networks that contributed to the production of sugar was, therefore, able to continue lubricating the cogs of the plantation machine. It was, in the same way, also able to contribute to the shipment of stable quantities of sugar to Bristol's market. Unsurprisingly, the market itself also faced significant threats to which those working within it and benefiting from it had to respond. To understand these threats, we must first understand the structure of the Bristol sugar market.

3

Merchants, Brokers, and the Structure of the Bristol Sugar Market

> It is commonly said that a sugar planter expects that the rum and molasses should defray the whole expense of this cultivation, and that his sugar should be all clear profit. If this be true, for I pretend not to affirm it, it is as if a corn farmer expected to defray the expense of his cultivation with the chaff and the straw, and that the grain should be all clear profit.
>
> Adam Smith, *The Wealth of Nations*, 1776[1]

BRISTOL REMAINED ONE OF BRITAIN'S major sugar importation centres up to the end of the eighteenth century. Indeed, sugar was Bristol's most valuable product. Despite the fact that Bristol's share of total imports fell towards the end of the century, volumes of imports remained steady, while the value of the sugar imported increased. This stability, even as the value increased, greatly benefited Bristol's West India elites, and especially those few who dominated sugar imports. The market was oligopolistic, with the largest five sugar importers consistently importing over half of the port's sugar, and with only nine to twelve firms each season controlling around 80% of the market, each with market shares of 3% or higher—the 3% mark acting as a clear cutoff between these leading merchants and a trail of smaller importers. Raw sugar (the name inappropriately given to the sugar that left the plantations, which had already undergone an initial refinement process) was bought by sugar refiners in Bristol—as it was, too, in London, Liverpool,

---

1 Smith, *Wealth of Nations*, pp. 244–45.

and elsewhere across Britain—who further processed it. Grocers, who sold the product directly, also bought up the finer sugars that needed little further processing.

Merchants were the most visible party in the act of selling, and have, as such, received the greater part of historians' focus. They did not act alone, however. Responsibility for selling sugar was diffused among brokers, coopers, captains, and clerks, whose hands were present at various stages. The main responsibility of the merchant was to decide when to sell the sugar. Timing was important for overcoming gluts or taking advantage of shortages. Yet they faced something of a face-off with sugar refiners, who bought as much sugar as they could when cheap in order to stockpile, and so during times of dearth or plenty the two sides played chicken, seeing who would break first—would the merchant accept lower prices in times of plenty? Would the refiner pay higher prices in times of dearth? Merchants, given their oligopolistic position, got the better of this deal. The seasonal rhythms of the market, dictated by the shipping and, thus, inherent to the trade, meant that information arrived over the year about the crop, and so the song and dance played between buyers and sellers was a year-long affair, the suspicions of each confirmed or denied only when the fresh batch of imports arrived over the summer. The price each year was determined predominantly not by how much sugar was on hand at any particular point (though this had a minor influence), but by the size of the crop.

We will explore how crisis affected the market and the nature of mercantile resilience in the following chapter. We start here by examining the size and structure of Bristol's sugar market, before exploring how the diffusion of roles and responsibilities allowed buyers to have confidence in the market. We then explore the mechanisms at play that influenced prices and movements within the market.

The size and structure of Bristol's sugar market

The volume and value of sugar imports into Bristol, 1784–1801
Estimating the size of Bristol's sugar market at this time is no easy affair. Imports were recorded by contemporaries, who noted the number of hogsheads and tierces of sugar landed on Bristol's wharves, as well as the smaller number of puncheons, barrels, kegs, and bags that contained sugar. Historians who have attempted to calculate the size of Bristol's market previously—most notably Kenneth Morgan—have stayed true to this system, measuring the size of the market in hogsheads, and converting other container sizes as proportions of a hogshead. The reason for not converting

these calculations into hundredweight—the actual measure of the amount of sugar the hogsheads contained—is not clear, especially when Morgan uses such measures elsewhere (the British Parliament, notably, measured the amount of sugar imported into Britain in hundredweight).[2] Adopting this practice would avoid miscalculations when estimating the total value of sugar imported into Bristol. Morgan estimates a hogshead to have contained 600 lb of sugar; at the long hundredweight (112 lb), this works out at $5\frac{1}{3}$ cwt.[3] However, this was not the case for at least the last twenty years of the eighteenth century: evidence for this period shows that a hogshead contained at least 12 cwt of sugar, meaning that Morgan underestimates the capacity by more than half. Landing at the 12 cwt figures is still unstable, however, not least because the size of a hogshead varied owing to idiosyncrasies in their construction. William Dickinson complained, when he began measuring the output of his estates in hogsheads, that 'competitions of Overseers upon the different estates' were 'carried too far as to make their hh^{ds} little more than Tierces'. They were purposely making their hogsheads smaller to bump up their numbers.[4]

Yet despite these idiosyncrasies, contemporaries still provided their own estimates for how much sugar the average hogshead contained. Hogsheads were commonly thought to contain around 12–15 cwt when they arrived in Bristol. John Pinney thought a good weight for a hogshead to be 13 cwt net as weighed in Bristol at the King's Beam (i.e., after shipping, and when being weighed by Customs). He used this as the average for his own personal calculations.[5] His firm considered 12 cwt net per hogshead to be on the lighter side, the minimum that a hogshead should contain, although this was normal: when providing estimates of Bristol's imports, Tobin & Pinney stated 'By a Hogshead we mean a Cask of at least 15 cwt neat in the Country [i.e., the West Indies], and which generally turn out ... about 12 cwt neat in England' owing to drainage.[6] The net weight of 20 hogsheads sold by Thomas Harris for William Dickinson, as reported to Dickinson by John Maxse, averaged just under 12 cwt.[7] Finally,

---

2 Morgan, *Bristol*, pp. 190–91.
3 Morgan, *Bristol*, p. 190. Morgan acknowledges that the size of the hogshead tripled between 1670 and 1770, so he is possibly using estimates based on a size from an earlier period. See Morgan, *Bristol*, p. 50; McCusker, *Essays*, p. 53.
4 William Dickinson to John White, 4 August 1794, SHC, MS DD/DN/4/2/40(1).
5 Tobin & Pinney to Thomas Pym Weekes, 4 February 1792, UoBSC, MS DM58/Letter Book/38.
6 Tobin & Pinney to James French, 2 December 1793, UoBSC, MS DM58/Letter Book/39; Tobin & Pinney to Monsieur Texier, 28 December 1789, UoBSC, MS DM58/Letter Book/38.
7 John Maxse to William Dickinson, 7 October 1791, SHC, MS DD/DN/4/2/35(3).

Bristol's contemporary authority on the sugar trade, the West India Association, in a draft petition in 1783, used 12 cwt net per hogshead at the King's Beam as its estimate, and in 1789 referred to hogsheads as casks weighing 12–15 cwt.[8] S. D. Smith calculates the mean weights of hogsheads received by the Harewoods in the early nineteenth century to be 13.29 cwt, and references bounds of 10 or 12 cwt to 16 cwt in the first half of the eighteenth century.[9] By the nineteenth century, however, hogsheads had increased further in size.[10] An estimate of 12 cwt per hogshead, then, is taken as a reasonable and conservative conversion for this period.

Where Morgan's estimates are more reliable are in his conversions between container sizes. The estimates provided here follow Morgan by calculating a tierce as three-quarters of a hogshead and a barrel as one-quarter of a hogshead. Kegs and bags, for which Morgan does not provide a ratio, I have assumed to be smaller than barrels: for mathematical simplicity, I have calculated a 'keg' as one-twelfth of a hogshead and a 'bag' as one-twenty-fourth. A hogshead is calculated as three-quarters of a puncheon, in accordance with the English wine measure as it was understood by the nineteenth century.[11] Puncheons, kegs, and bags are rarely entered in the wharfage books as they were rarely used by planters, the hogshead being the most common container, followed by the tierce, so miscalculation of these has little impact on the overall estimates.[12] Moreover, as John McCusker said of his estimates regarding the size of the money supply in France,

> there are several things to notice about the data cited here. The first is that they represent best-informed estimates. Measurement errors are likely, but in our judgment corrections will not significantly change the basic trends ... that are observed and inferred here.[13]

If the precise interrelation between the size of puncheons, kegs, and barrels is inaccurate, it is unlikely to affect the trends in overall estimates for the amount of sugar imported into Bristol.

Table 3.1 shows the total amount of sugar imported into Bristol in hundredweight, according to estimates derived from the wharfage books. Hogsheads, tierces, and other containers are converted into hundredweight, taking hogsheads as 12 cwt, and other containers as proportions of this using

---

8 BA, MS SMV/8/3/2/1 WIA.
9 Smith, *Slavery*, p. 249.
10 Ryden, *West Indian Slavery*, p. 291.
11 See W. Waterston, *A Manual of Commerce* (Edinburgh: Oliver and Boyd, 1865), p. 143.
12 Morgan, *Bristol*, p. xviii.
13 McCusker, *Essays*, p. 192.

Table 3.1: Estimates of Sugar Imports into Bristol, by Primary Source, 1784–1801 (cwt)

Period	Wharfage Books	Period	Parliamentary Papers
Oct 1784-Sept 1785	296,657		
Oct 1785-Sept 1786	227,346		
Oct 1786-Sept 1787			
Oct 1787-Sept 1788	267,663		
Oct 1788-Sept 1789	252,074		
Oct 1789-Sept 1790		1790	248,801
Oct 1790-Sept 1791		1791	229,802
Oct 1791-Sept 1792	247,492	1792	244,358
Oct 1792-Sept 1793	186,074	1793	
Oct 1793-Sept 1794		1794	
Oct 1794-Sept 1795		1795	
Oct 1795-Sept 1796		1796	
Oct 1796-Sept 1797	237,735	1797	
Oct 1797-Sept 1798	208,711	1798	
Oct 1798-Sept 1799		1799	314,039
Oct 1799-Sept 1800	251,184	1800	269,362
Oct 1800-Sept 1801	303,457		

Source: BA, MS SMV/7/1/1/72-83 Wharfage Books, 1784-1803; Kenneth Morgan, *Bristol and the Atlantic Trade in the Eighteenth Century* (Cambridge: Cambridge University Press, 1993), p. 190.

the ratios outlined above. These differ slightly from the estimates Morgan provides from the *British Parliamentary Papers* (from here on *Papers*), which have been placed alongside for comparison.[14] This might be because the periodisation is slightly different: the *Papers* appear to use calendar years, rather than the October–September period used in the wharfage books. They also probably draw on Customs records, which might differ from the wharfage books. The amount the *Papers* provide for 1792 is not far from the

---

14 Morgan, *Bristol*, p. 190. His source is *British Parliamentary Papers*, Commons, 1802–3, VIII, pp. 1099–427 (no. 138).

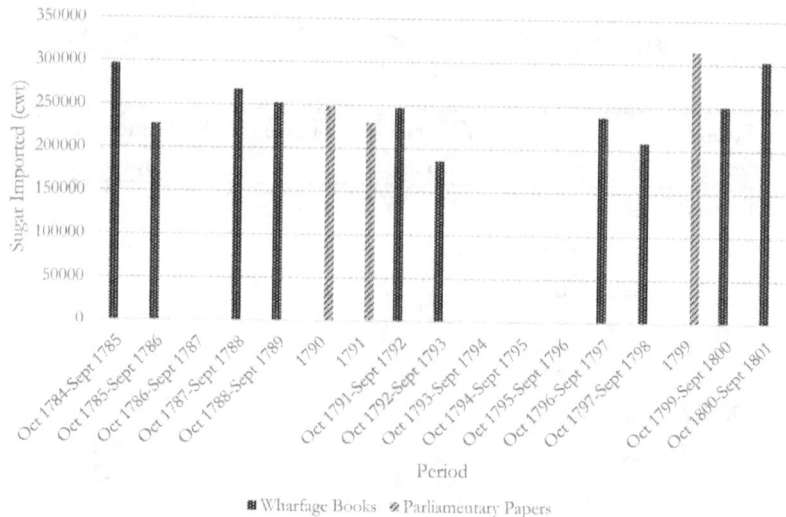

Figure 3.1: Estimates of Sugar Imported into Bristol by Primary Source, by Year and Season, 1784–1801 (cwt)

Source: BA, MS SMV/7/1/1/72-83 Wharfage Books, 1784–1803; Kenneth Morgan, *Bristol and the Atlantic Trade in the Eighteenth Century* (Cambridge: Cambridge University Press, 1993), p. 190.

estimates for October 1791–September 1792 in the wharfage books (244,358 cwt to 247,492 cwt), though the *Papers* estimate a slightly higher import for 1800 than the October 1799–September 1800 estimate (269,362 cwt to 251,184 cwt). If we use the *Papers* to fill in some of the gaps in the wharfage books, though this is slightly crude, we see a relatively consistent series of imports for Bristol in this period (see Figure 3.1).

The figures show that the amount of sugar imported into Bristol in this period remained reasonably consistent, rising and falling dependent both on the amount of the sugar produced in the West Indies and the amount that merchants were able to persuade their clients to ship to Bristol. The consistency is out of step with the overall trends of sugar imports into Britain, however. As we shall explore in the next chapter, the revolution in Saint Domingue led to an increase in sugar imports into Britain. This dramatic rise affected London and Liverpool more, however, with London's imports reaching over 2 million cwt in 1799, Liverpool reaching almost half a million cwt in 1800, while Bristol's peaked at 314,039 cwt in 1799.[15] This disparity is further demonstrated in the statistics compiled by Elizabeth Schumpeter,

---

15 Morgan, *Bristol*, p. 190.

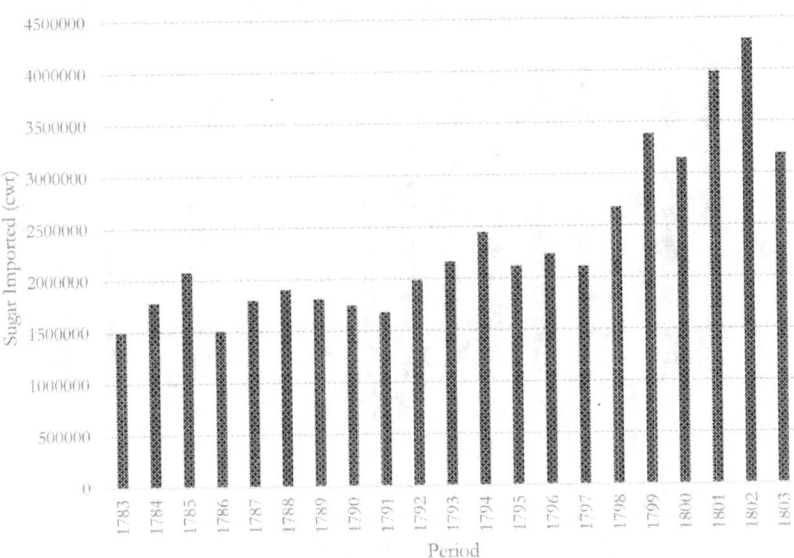

Figure 3.2: Sugar Imports into England/Britain, Estimates by Elizabeth Schumpeter, by Year, 1783–1803 (cwt)

Source: Elizabeth Schumpeter, *English Overseas Trade Statistics, 1697–1808* (Oxford: Clarendon, 1960).

which are recreated in Figure 3.2.[16] Though her figures are for England and Wales before 1791, and for Great Britain from 1792, they still show the tremendous rise that, from 1797, appears to have surpassed Bristol, whose imports in 1799 and 1801 barely surpass its own imports of 1785. Figure 3.3 shows Bristol's share of these totals. Notwithstanding the incorporation of Scotland into Schumpeter's figures from 1792, and the slight misalignment of the periods (I have aligned the year with that in Bristol for which most of the months fall), this shows that Bristol's imports of sugar represented an ever-declining share of total English and British imports, even though they remained stable. This is one example of Bristol's relative decline, which has been the subject of much debate.[17]

The available price data allow us to estimate the total value of sugar imported into Bristol in this period. The estimates below use the prices, in shillings per hundredweight (s/cwt), collated by Morgan.[18] The average price

---

16 Elizabeth Schumpeter, *English Overseas Trade Statistics, 1697–1808* (Oxford: Clarendon Press, 1960).
17 See Introduction.
18 Morgan, *Bristol*, p. 210.

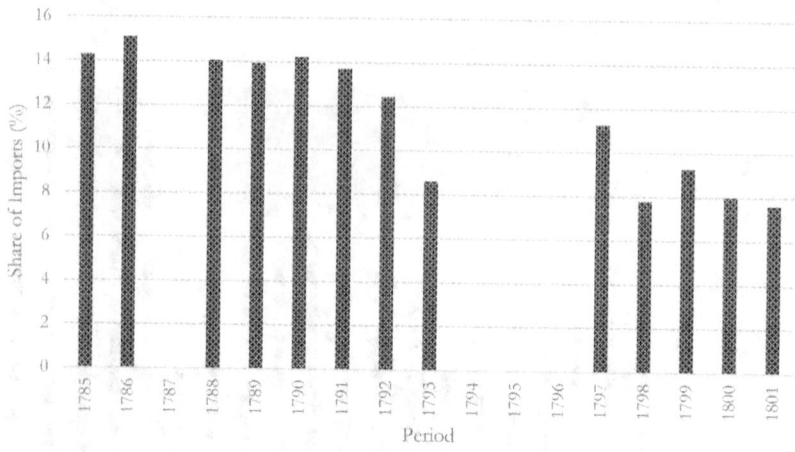

Figure 3.3: Bristol's Share of British Sugar Imports by Year, 1785–1801 (%)

Source: BA, MS SMV/7/1/1/72-83 Wharfage Books, 1784–1803; Elizabeth Schumpeter, *English Overseas Trade Statistics, 1697–1808* (Oxford: Clarendon, 1960).

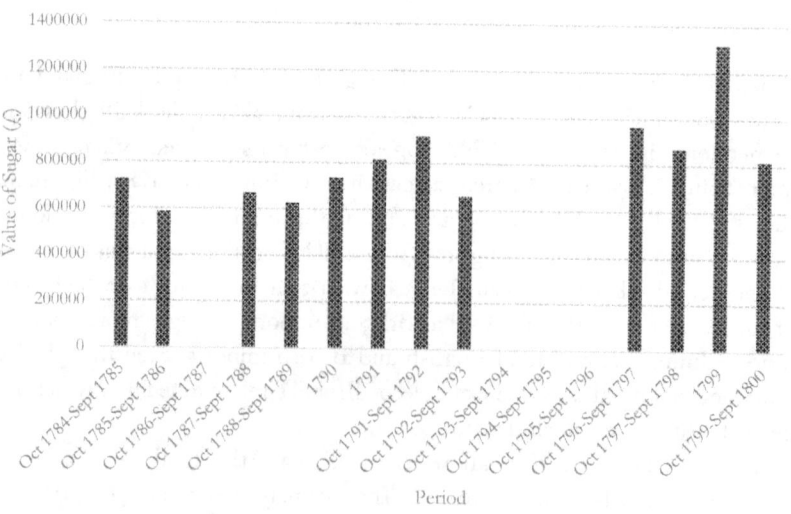

Figure 3.4: Value of Sugar Imports into Bristol by Year, 1784–1800 (£)

Source: BA, MS SMV/7/1/1/72-83 Wharfage Books, 1784–1803; Kenneth Morgan, *Bristol and the Atlantic Trade in the Eighteenth Century* (Cambridge: Cambridge University Press, 1993), p. 210.

over the corresponding twelve-month period is multiplied by the estimates for the volume of sugar imports: October–September for the wharfage books, and the calendar year for the *Papers*. This is made feasible by the conversion of hogsheads into cwt. The result is in Figure 3.4. This shows us that the value of imports increased over the period. There is a spike in 1799 that corresponds both to a peak in the price and a peak in imports.

These data show the general trends in the development of the sugar market over this period. The market was characterised by stable sugar imports and a declining share of Britain's overall imports, but with an increase in the total value of sugar being imported. This is the landscape within which Bristol's sugar importers operated.

Bristol's sugar importers

The sugar imported over these two decades contributed to the immense wealth of Bristol's leading sugar importers, a small number of whom dominated the space. While the number of importers fluctuated from 93 in the 1784/85 season to 50 in the 1792/93 season, reaching 70 in the 1800/01 season, the leading five firms in each season imported, at the least, 50.87% in 1791/92, to over 61% in 1799/1800. Table 3.2 shows the top 20 most prolific importers for the peacetime and wartime periods for the seasons over the last two decades for which we have data. Only six of the firms in the top 20 in peacetime ceased to be in the top 40 for the following period—of these six, two involved the break-up of firms, after which most of the partners continued importing under some other guise. This included Bright, Baillie & Bright, which continued to operate separately as Evan Baillie & Son and Lowbridge & Richard Bright. There are other familiar names in Table 3.2: Protheroe & Claxton, who jointly owned ships with Tobin & Pinney; William Miles, a leading merchant who acted as chairman of the WIA and who was a guarantor for slaving voyages; and Thomas Harris and John Fisher Weare, who both acted as factors for William Dickinson.

Data from the wharfage books confirm that the number of firms importing into Bristol was decreasing, suggesting, as Morgan observes, a concentration of the trade into fewer hands, which seemingly began from the start of the period, but accelerated from at least 1791/92. The figures presented in Table 3.3 nuance Morgan's findings.[19] The number of firms importing more than 3% of the total imports remained relatively stable, with the exception of 1787/88 and 1788/89. In the early peacetime years, the percentage share of those importing more than 3% remained relatively stable, at 77–79%, but this increased to 85% in 1791/92, and remained at around 87–89% until

---

19 See Morgan, *Bristol*, p. 158.

Table 3.2: Top 20 Largest Sugar Importers in Bristol, 1784–1801

1784–1792	1792–1801
William Miles & Son	Protheroe & Claxton
Protheroe & Claxton	Evan Baillie & Son
William & John Gordon	William Miles & Son
Evan Baillie	Thomas Daniel & Son
Thomas Daniel & Son	John Maxse
John Maxse	John Gordon
Samuel Span	John Fisher Weare
Lowbridge & Richard Bright	Munckley, Gibbs & Co.
Munckley, Gibbs & Co.	Tobin, Pinney & Co.
Walter Jacks	Samuel & John Span & Co.
Thomas Harris	Lowbridge & Richard Bright
John Fisher Weare	Walter Jacks
Tobin & Pinney	Ralph Mountague & Son
Jeremiah Meyler	Bright & Daniel
John Gordon Jr	Bruce & Moens
Bright, Baillie & Co.	Charles Payne
Richard Fydell	James Bonbonous
Samuel & John Span	William Gibbons & Co.
James Rogers	Bush, Elton & Co.
John Gordon	Joseph & Thomas Powell

Source: BA, MS SMV/7/1/1/72-83 Wharfage Books, 1784-1803.

1800/01, when it went down to 82.24%, just as the total number of firms importing increased. This suggests that any major changes occurred before the war in 1791/92. The share of the largest importer fluctuated around 12–17%. Outlying years were again 1791/92 and 1799/1800, which were especially low and especially high, respectively. This further indicates that 1791/92 and 1799/1800 were exceptional. Moreover, the largest importer was not always the same firm: in 1784/85, 1796/97, 1799/1800, and 1800/01, it was Protheroe & Claxton; in 1785/86, 1787/88, and 1788/89, it was William Miles; in 1791/92 it was Thomas Daniel & Son, and in 1792/93 and 1797/98 it was Evan Baillie. These merchants were rarely out of the top five. The

Table 3.3: Summary Statistics for Bristol's Sugar Importers, 1784–1801

Period	No. of firms	No. of firms with over 3% of market share	Percentage share of firms importing over 3%	Percentage share of Top 1	Percentage share of Top 5	Herfindahl–Hirschman Index
Oct 1784–Sept 1785	93	11	79.04%	12.12%	56.24%	757
Oct 1785–Sept 1786	90	11	78.86%	16.49%	56.34%	807
Oct 1786–Sept 1787						
Oct 1787–Sept 1788	88	9	79.02%	14.66%	55.08%	821
Oct 1788–Sept 1789	82	9	77.28%	16.35%	58.55%	867
Oct 1789–Sept 1790						
Oct 1790–Sept 1791						
Oct 1791–Sept 1792	55	11	85.25%	10.75%	50.87%	763
Oct 1792–Sept 1793	50	12	89.39%	13.41%	54.42%	813
Oct 1793–Sept 1794						
Oct 1794–Sept 1795						
Oct 1795–Sept 1796						
Oct 1796–Sept 1797	53	11	88.42%	15.96%	58.82%	884
Oct 1797–Sept 1798	55	11	87.80%	14.48%	59.82%	892

Period	No. of firms	No. of firms with over 3% of market share	Percentage share of firms importing over 3%	Percentage share of Top 1	Percentage share of Top 5	Herfindahl–Hirschman Index
Oct 1798–Sept 1799						
Oct 1799–Sept 1800	57	11	87.27%	19.71%	61.94%	982
Oct 1800–Sept 1801	70	11	82.24%	16.53%	56.73%	836

Source: BA, MS SMV/7/1/1/72-83 Wharfage Books, 1784–1803.

final column shows the Herfindahl–Hirschman Index, which is a measure of market concentration.[20] It shows, again with the exception of 1791/92, a trend towards increasing concentration in the market. The measure is not actually that high, indicating considerable room for competition between the leading firms.

Together, however, these statistics show an increasingly oligopolistic market dominated by fewer, larger firms over this short period. The number of firms importing sugar decreased from 93 in 1784/85 to 50 in 1792/93. The trend began, however, before the French Revolutionary Wars. Though these wars might have amplified this trend, the timing suggests that they was not the key driver. The lack of data for 1789–1791 is frustrating, but there appear to be two reasonable alternatives: either there is a linear trend between 1788/89 and 1791/92, or the trend from 1784 to 1789 continued, and 1791/92 represents a sharper change. Given the impact of the Saint Domingue Revolution, the latter is more probable.[21] Indeed, 1791/92 was a pivotal season, as revealed by the data. In 1791/92, fewer firms were entering—55, from 82 in 1788/89—while the market share of the largest firms reached its lowest at just over 50% for the top five, and just over 10% for the largest importer. Conversely, the number of firms with more than 3% of the market share increased to a new high. This suggests a significant degree of competition between the leading firms in this year. After that, and with

---

20 See A Note on Methodology, above.
21 See Chapter 4.

the onset of the war, the largest firms again began to increase their share of imports, with the top five importing over 61% of Bristol's sugar in 1799/1800. The smaller firms managed to retain their share, however, with as many firms importing more than 3% of Bristol's sugar in 1799/1800 as in 1791/92, and their share increasing to over 87%.

The oligopolistic structure of Bristol's market, coupled with, as we shall see, the strategy of withholding sugar until the price was more favourable, might appear to indicate a cartel in the sugar trade. This would not be unusual. Pierre Gervais argues that the Bordeaux sugar market in the 1750s shows evidence of cartelisation (albeit, as Gervais cautions, it did not necessarily constitute a formalised cartel).[22] Yet this was probably not the case here. There is no evidence to suggest cartelisation in Bristol, and such a feat would have been far too difficult given the dependency on production. Indeed, as we shall see, the market was driven predominantly by production, so any cartel would have to begin in the West Indies. This would have required a much larger form of cartelisation across several islands, and a strict management of production that was not feasible given the variations that occurred as a result of the weather.[23] At any rate, contemporaries denied the existence of such a cartel in the West Indies, and this is confirmed by historians, notably David Beck Ryden.[24] Furthermore, information about the size of production was freely available within the community, and came from a wide variety of sources.[25] Finally, the fact that in 1793 merchants sold their sugar quickly under pressure from the credit crisis, without condemnation or penalty from their peers, shows that, where they were able, merchants withheld sugar from the market in their own interests.[26] The market was, therefore, dominated by several key independent merchants and merchant firms that exercised considerable oligopolistic control over the market. Yet they did not act alone—indeed, their role, though the best compensated, was marginal compared to the actions of others.

---

22 Gervais, 'Surviving War', pp. 84–85.
23 See Chapter 1.
24 Ryden, *West Indian Slavery*, pp. 223–24.
25 Morgan, *Bristol*, p. 215; Pares, *West-India Fortune*, pp. 201–03.
26 See Chapter 4.

The separation of roles and confidence in the sugar market

The sugar market was organised, on the face of it, in a way that helped merchants delegate a range of roles to other individuals, freeing up their time for (what they would consider to be) more important tasks. This kind of organisation also had the positive effect of reducing a number of risks. The sugar, even after it arrived in port, was susceptible to a number of moral and natural hazards which—though this was not the language that contemporaries used—was something that they understood well enough. There might be mistakes when collecting sugar from the ships; sugar could be pilfered on its way to the warehouse. After it arrived at the warehouse, it was at risk of fire and flooding. Most of these issues were the concern of the planter, and, because his commission would be affected, the concern of the merchant. The buyers faced risks, too, however. Would the quality of the sugar be as they expected? Would they end up paying more for oversized hogsheads that added to the weight? In order to mitigate these risks and protect both buyers and sellers, a variety of safeguards were put in place. Merchants communicated with each other about the sugars they were bringing in, and they used insurance and diffused responsibilities among captains, crew, and coopers to protect sellers. To attract buyers, they used brokers as intermediaries who independently assessed the quality of the sugar, calculated prices, and oversaw the sampling process. They also tared the hogsheads (that is, deducted their weight from the gross weight), and came up with a complex of regulations for the taring process.

Most sugar entering Bristol was consigned to particular merchants by the planters. The commission system, as it was known, had superseded the older model whereby merchants bought sugar in the West Indies to transport on their own account and risk. Instead, the sugar remained the property of the planter, with the merchant selling it on their behalf for a 2.5% commission.[27] Merchants knew which hogsheads of sugar were meant for them because they arrived with a mark imprinted on their sides that matched that on the bill of lading, the paper document that defined the goods and signified the captain's responsibility for ensuring their safe arrival.[28] The process was prone to human error, with assumptions made about particular hogsheads. Planter

---

27 Morgan, *Bristol*, pp. 193–96. On the development of the commission system, see Richard B. Sheridan, *Sugar and Slavery: An Economic History of the British West Indies, 1623–1775* (Barbados: Caribbean Universities Press, 1974), ch. 13.

28 On bills of lading, see Hannah Farber, 'Sailing on Paper: The Embellished Bill of Lading in the Material Atlantic, 1720–1864', *Early American Studies*, 17:1 (2019), 37–83 (pp. 40–42, 46–47).

George Webbe, for example, consigned some of his sugars to Bright, Baillie & Bright, which Tobin & Pinney picked up and sold by mistake because they were Webbe's usual factors and assumed the sugar was for them.[29] One manager made the mistake of endorsing the bill of lading to his absentee employer, and not Tobin & Pinney, the firm that collected the sugar. For Tobin & Pinney to claim the sugars, it needed a written order from the absentee planter allowing the firm to collect the shipment on his behalf.[30] If in doubt, it was, therefore, best to check who the sugar was intended for. When 30 hogsheads of sugar arrived on John Maxse's ship from William Beckford's estate in Jamaica, Tobin & Pinney wrote to Beckford's agent in London to confirm that it could indeed collect them on Beckford's behalf.[31] The commission system was therefore popular, but there was room for error, and open communication was needed to resolve issues before they escalated into disputes.

Pilferage was a particular risk that sugars faced, and planters, suspicious of the crewmen and others who handled their hogsheads along the commodity chain, were often quick to assume that any difference in weight between the departure and arrival of the sugar was caused by theft. This was not necessarily the case, however. Sugars naturally drained in transit and thus lost weight. Hogsheads that weighed 15 cwt when filled in the West Indies would weigh around 12 cwt on arrival in Britain. This meant that approximately 156 lb of molasses would be drained over the four to eight weeks at sea, though this varied according to the quality of the sugar (or the quality of the cask); and some sugar (or the casks) might be damaged in transit.[32] Merchants had to make this clear to planters, who might seek compensation for perceived slights that were actually a natural occurrence, which the merchant had no obligation to compensate them for. Merchants assured planters that various structures had been carefully put in place to ensure that pilferage would not happen. Captains were carefully selected. Losses attributable to the ship

---

29 Pinney & Tobin to William Hendrickson, 1 August 1785, UoBSC, MS DM58/Letter Book/37.

30 Tobin, Pinney & Tobin to William Colhoun, 26 December 1798, and Tobin, Pinney & Tobin to Coles, Godwin & Coles, 27 August 1799, UoBSC, MS DM58/Letter Book/40.

31 Tobin, Pinney & Tobin to Richard White, 27 September 1797, UoBSC, MS DM58/Letter Book/40.

32 Tobin & Pinney to Monsieur Texier, 28 December 1789, UoBSC, MS DM58/Letter Book/38; Horsfall, 'West Indian Trade', p. 168. With 15 cwt in the West Indies measured at the short hundredweight (100 lb), and the 12 cwt when weighed in England at the long hundredweight (112 lb), the difference works out at 156 lb. See McCusker, *Essays*, p. 53.

would come out of the crew's wages. Brokers conducted surveys of the ships to check that the hogsheads had been properly stowed.[33] The captain and the mates watched the unloading of the sugar, and the firms had their own coopers and clerks who oversaw the process. Only coopers were allowed in the warehouse with the sugars.[34] Some merchants, such as Thomas Harris, employed a constable to prevent pilferage while the sugars were transferred to the warehouse.[35] Further, the West India Association voted in 1783 to pool funds to prosecute anyone caught committing petty theft. In 1805, when plunderage was getting worse, it mandated that mates should keep a record of every article left on the ship, and that the ship's hatches should remain padlocked when in port, with the keys shared between the mate and the Customs officer.[36] The system was hardly perfect; that more measures were needed in 1805 demonstrates this. Yet there was at least some level of surveillance and accountability which gave planters enough confidence to ship their sugars to Bristol.

While the sugar was warehoused, it was at risk of fire and flood damage. In one case in London, Stephen & Rose Fuller observed that 2,000 hogsheads of sugar, worth somewhere between £80,000 and £90,000, were lost to a fire.[37] This risk could be mitigated through insurance. Thomas Harris of Bristol kept sugars consigned to him covered by insurance valued up to £12,000, and Woodbridge, Dyer & Co., a London firm, was instructed by Tobin & Pinney to purchase insurance against warehouse fire for sugars sent to London.[38] In Bristol, on an 'unprecedented' occasion, a warehouse was flooded by a large tide following a storm. Tobin & Pinney consoled some clients, claiming that the few sugars that were 'a little wetted' were—conveniently—'very indifferent' anyway.[39] Just as the sugars were at risk to the perils of the sea during shipping, so too were they at risk from natural hazards when in the warehouse. Freak events could be dramatic, and while they were a serious

---

33 See Tobin & Pinney to George Webbe, 31 December 1792, and Tobin & Pinney to John Warren, 13 January 1794, UoBSC, MS DM58/Letter Book/39.

34 Tobin & Pinney to Edward Brazier, 25 March 1790, UoBSC, MS DM58/Letter Book/38.

35 Thomas Harris to William Dickinson, 19 February 1790, SHC, MS DD/DN/4/2/30(1).

36 BA, MS SMV/8/3/2/1 WIA.

37 Stephen & Rose Fuller to William Dickinson, 3 December 1793, SHC, MS DD/DN/4/2/41(1).

38 Thomas Harris to William Dickinson, 19 February 1790, SHC, MS DD/DN/4/2/30(1); Tobin, Pinney & Tobin to Woodbridge, Dyer & Co., 4 July 1800, UoBSC, MS DM58/Letter Book/40.

39 Tobin & Pinney to Edward Brazier, 12 November 1795, UoBSC, MS DM58/Letter Book/39.

threat to the sugars themselves, through the use of insurance they were not a serious threat to the planters' returns.

Buyers faced particular risks, too. Significantly, they risked not getting the quality of sugar they desired. Sugar, as it arrived from the West Indies, was far from homogeneous.[40] Its quality varied considerably, and contemporaries had a commonly understood framework whereby the spectrum of 'good' and 'bad' sugars were sorted into different grades, with a number of signifiers used to determine what grade the sugar was. Colour was prized most, followed by strength and texture.[41] The lowest end of the spectrum consisted of sugars that were in a treacle-like, 'running state'.[42] Slightly higher were sugars that were very dark or dirty grey, and damp with too much molasses. One particularly bad lot was described as being 'more like Tar than sugar'.[43] Brown sugars were above those that were very dark. These lower grades, determined by their colour, might be redeemed by their strength. Yet some might be too difficult to get out of the cask; one buyer complained to Thomas Harris that 'bird lime' would be easier to get out.[44] At the higher end was the yellower and straw-coloured sugar. The best was white. As Tobin & Pinney informed a client, 'the brighter the color the freer of foot and the better they are cured the greater Price they will fetch the Proprietor & the more credit they will do the Manager'.[45] Quality supposedly varied by island, too. Sugar from Nevis tended to fall lower down the scale than that from Jamaica, while Barbados clayed was considered the best.[46] This mattered to buyers because they had particular preferences for certain qualities. Importantly, the quality determined the price, and the buyer had to be confident that the quality they were getting matched what they were paying.

To mitigate this fear, merchants had brokers independently—or at least with the appearance of independence—assess the quality of the sugar. Sales were privately arranged via brokers, unless the sugars were damaged particularly badly, in which case they were sold through auction.[47] The

---

40 On achieving homogeneity, see David Roth Singerman, 'The Limits of Chemical Control in the Caribbean Sugar Factory', *Radical History Review*, 127 (2017), 39–61.
41 Ryden, *West Indian Slavery*, p. 84.
42 Stephen & Rose Fuller to William Dickinson, 21 August 1794, SHC, MS DD/DN/4/2/42(3).
43 Tobin & Pinney to Edward Brazier, 25 October 1790, UoBSC, MS DM58/Letter Book/38.
44 Thomas Harris to William Dickinson, 7 November 1789, SHC, MS DD/DN/4/2/29.
45 Pinney & Tobin to William Ferrier, 20 September 1786, UoBSC, MS DM58/Letter Book/37.
46 Pares, *West-India Fortune*, p. 189.
47 Tobin & Pinney to Samuel Span, 29 May 1789, UoBSC, MS DM58/Letter Book/38; Morgan, *Bristol*, p. 204.

broker offered a price to the potential buyer, basing this on the quality and market conditions.[48] Each merchant had a particular broker that they used. Thomas Harris had Thomas Booth, a broker in Bristol. He commented on the prices that Harris wanted to receive for his clients, telling him which prices were tenable and which were not. Stephen & Rose Fuller similarly used the services of Mr Tiers in London for this same purpose.[49] The broker's role was as a mediator between buyer and seller. In the case of a dispute over quality, they would arrange a discount: when a hogshead of sugar sold at 90 s/cwt by Tobin & Pinney was not up the buyer's standards, 'the Broker, who is always the person employed on such occasions, judged it right … that the price should be reduced to 87 [s/cwt]'.[50] The role of the broker was, therefore, particularly important in reducing the appearance of opportunism or price gouging. This independence was not always completely clear, however. Some brokers could also act as merchants. James Bonbonous is listed in the 1775 trade directory as a broker at the same time as he was importing sugar.[51] Yet brokers typically retained some independence from the merchant and proprietor. The buyer had to be confident that the interests of the broker were sufficiently separated from the interests of the merchant to allow independent judgement, though they knew that the broker remained the merchant's agent.

Importantly, the buyer had to be confident that the sampling process had been conducted fairly and consistently. Samples were used by buyers and brokers to assess the quality of the sugar. They also allowed merchants to see the quality for themselves. Samples were often sent between markets, so the merchants could judge the sugar going to other ports, or they could be sent back to the planters so they could see how their sugar turned out.[52] Buyers expected there to be a fair and reliable process by which the sample was drawn, which Tobin & Pinney at least believed was the case. As the partners explained, the hogsheads were marked as they lay in the ship by the ship's mate. The mate drew a circle in chalk on the upper bilge of the barrel through which a hole was made, and from which the sample was drawn. About a pound of sugar was removed from the hogshead and given to one broker

---

48 Pares, *West-India Fortune*, p. 187.
49 Thomas Harris to William Dickinson, 10 May 1792, and 6 August 1792, SHC, MS DD/DN/4/2/37(2)–38(1); Rose Fuller to William Dickinson, 9 March 1790, SHC, MS DD/DN/4/2/30(1).
50 Tobin, Pinney & Tobin to Daniel Wane, 12 April 1799, UoBSC, MS DM58/Letter Book/40.
51 James Sketchley, *Sketchley's Bristol Directory, 1775* (Bath: Kingsmead Reprints, 1971 [1775]); Morgan, *Bristol*, p. 195.
52 See numerous examples in UoBSC, MS DM58/Letter Book/37–42. See also Forestier, 'Commercial Organisation', p. 136.

(it was rare for more than one broker to compete to sell the same sugar). Sometimes the prospective buyers might want to draw their own samples, but even if they did, this was overseen by the seller's cooper. When the sugar was ready for sale, the samples were sent to the broker's office to be shown to prospective buyers, and a price was offered. In the broker's office, the samples sat in drawers on 'common brown paper', presumably of a uniform colour that would reveal the whiteness of the sugar.[53] Tobin & Pinney believed that other merchants should be able to inspect the brokers' samples, though not everyone seemed to agree. On one occasion they were prevented from seeing the samples drawn of one of their client's sugars when the sugar was consigned to another merchant. The firm could not arrange a meeting with the broker in his office, suggesting that the sugars were 'kept purposely from our Inspection'. They noted their own desire to keep their sugars 'open to every Bodys Examination, as we wish to do no kind of Business in a hugger-mugger way'.[54] The sampling process was therefore supposed to be reasonably transparent, at least by Tobin & Pinney's standards. There were structures in place that diffused responsibility, with careful monitoring of the people involved. Buyers were assured that the sample had been drawn in a fair way to give them confidence to enter the market.

To make sure that buyers were only paying for the sugar they could use, a system of taring was introduced. The tare was not to account for moisture seeping into the casks from the outside that inflated the weight of the sugar, as S. D. Smith implies, but for the weight of the hogshead itself.[55] This weight was affected by the amount of wood and metal used, and the quality of the cooperage. Dirt and remaining syrup that could not be removed from the cask was referred to as the 'breakage' in Bristol and the 'clough' in London, and this was calculated separately from the weight of the hogshead, and was sometimes differentiated in the account of sales.[56] The taring process was not closely regulated until after 1781. Morgan points out that it was the sugar bakers that pressed for the tare, but it appears to have been the West India Association that outlined the procedure.[57] The WIA passed several

---

53 Pinney & Tobin to Thomas Bettesworth, 2 February 1789, UoBSC, MS DM58/Letter Book/37; See also several letters from Thomas Harris to William Dickinson, SHC, MS DD/DN/4/2/28(1), 35(3), 36(2) and 37(1).
54 Pinney & Tobin to John Arthurton, 12 May 1786, UoBSC, MS DM58/Letter Book/37.
55 Smith, *Slavery*, p. 249.
56 Pinney & Tobin to Thomas Bettesworth, 2 February 1789, UoBSC, MS DM58/Letter Book/37; Thomas Harris to William Dickinson, 29 September 1791, SHC, MS DD/DN/4/2/35(2).
57 Morgan, *Bristol*, p. 216.

resolutions over 1782–1789 outlining how the 'customary tare' should be regulated. In 1786, it declared that the buyer could take the customary tare or have the casks weighed. If an average of several casks was taken, it had to be the same for all the casks. In 1789, it further clarified that the first five casks of up to twenty could be weighed, or the first ten of twenty-one or more, and that these should be the nearest casks, with the sugars weighed within two calendar months of the sale.[58] The casks should be weighed when empty.[59] This process was introduced at the buyers' behest to ensure that they were not paying for the weight of the casks or for the sugar that could not be removed from the inside. The sellers acquiesced in order to give the buyers enough confidence to come to the market.

Contemporary evidence suggests some figures that might be typical for the tare. The customary tare appears to have been a standard value of 1¼ cwt 14 lb, or 154 lb. The breakage would typically come to about 1–3 lb in barrels and would be between 4 and 8 lb in tierces and hogsheads.[60] In a letter to William Dickinson, John Maxse notes that an average of 1¼ cwt 11 lb tare was given on average for 20 hogsheads, alongside 5.85 lb average for breakage.[61] In another sale, 1¼ cwt 13 lb was given as tare, with breakage unspecified.[62] The main point of dispute between the clerks and coopers who oversaw the process and the buyer would be whether or not the hogsheads qualified for the 'super tare'. Super tare was invoked when the hogsheads were particular heavy, whether from the weight of the staves or the thickness of the headings. Allowing this was particularly 'disagreeable' for merchants, and they encouraged the planters to more closely regulate the weight of their hogsheads. Other issues would arise if the hogsheads were inconsistent in size. Larger hogsheads were considered better, as they would comprise a smaller portion of the overall weight than smaller casks, which risked having more than their actual weight taken off the total if the buyers took the customary tare.[63] It is not clear whether super tare was some defined value, or whether

---

58 BA, MS SMV/8/3/2/1 WIA.
59 Thomas Harris to William Dickinson, 19 February 1790, SHC, MS DD/DN/4/2/30(1).
60 Customs officers in Bristol offered 1¼ cwt tare on hogsheads weighing 12–15 cwt, and the King's Tare was 14 lb less that the customary tare. See Pinney & Tobin to John Hendrickson, 6 March 1787, and Pinney & Tobin to Thomas Bettesworth, 2 February 1789, UoBSC, MS DM58/Letter Book/37; BA, MS SMV/8/3/2/1 WIA.
61 John Maxse to William Dickinson, 7 October 1791, SHC, MS DD/DN/4/2/35(3).
62 Account of sales enclosed in John Fisher Weare to William Dickinson, 11 October 1794, SHC, MS DD/DN/4/2/42(3).
63 See Tobin & Pinney to Edward Brazier, 4 June 1789, UoBSC, MS DM58/Letter Book/38; Pinney & Tobin to Richard Crosse, 13 October 1788, UoBSC, MS DM58/Letter Book/37.

it referred to values considered by merchants to be extraordinary. Regardless, that they were willing to offer this to buyers, however 'disagreeable' it might have been, shows that they would comply with buyers' demands if it meant guaranteeing a sale.

Finally, the brokers surveyed the buyers to ensure that they were satisfied. This allowed buyers to raise concerns and initiate disputes that could be mediated through the broker. It was not uncommon for them to be displeased if the sugars 'did not answer Sample'. Thomas Harris, whose integrity in this situation may or may not be representative of the merchant body as a whole, informed William Dickinson that he had sold his sugars at an 'extraordinary price', noting, however, his fear that 'the buyer will expect a considerable reduction when he comes to open them'. As well as the quality not matching the sample, the hogsheads might have a 'very abundant quantity of foot', which was the poor-quality sludge that collected at the bottom of the hogshead as it drained, for which the buyer would be given a rebate.[64] To avoid this, sellers often repacked sugars into fresh hogsheads to get rid of it. This dispute resolution mechanism also allowed buyers to bring to the merchant's attention sugars that had the 'appearance of having been <u>false packed</u>', with the 'much fairer' sugar placed in the middle from which the sample would be drawn, and browner sugars packed on the top and bottom. This particular phenomenon could also be caused (as Tobin & Pinney once claimed) by the addition of hot sugar to a cask that already had cold sugar in it, which impaired its curing; whatever the truth, only the manager would know what really happened.[65] These various processes were introduced to give buyers the confidence to purchase sugar. Throughout, responsibilities were diffused among different agents, whose division facilitated monitoring and accountability.

The merchant, in whose interest it was to fetch the best price possible for their clients' sugars, hired the captains, crews, clerks, and coopers, and carefully selected the broker. Aside from this, they sat apart from the sampling and taring processes, and from direct negotiation with the buyers. Yet they had other responsibilities. First, they communicated information about the quality of the sugar back to the planter. This gave the planters information on how crops from different regions performed (should planters have multiple or extensive estates), which they could use to inform their

---

64 Tobin, Pinney & Tobin to Daniel Wane, 12 April 1799, UoBSC, MS DM58/Letter Book/40; Thomas Harris to William Dickinson, 30 October 1789, SHC, MS DD/DN/4/2/28(2).

65 Tobin & Pinney to John Budgen, 26 January 1793, UoBSC, MS DM58/Letter Book/39.

production processes. It also gave planters some qualitative information to work with when improving their production. Some sugars might show evidence of having been burnt in the boiling process, for example. Merchants might have been guarding against complaints about poor prices by accentuating the poor quality of the sugar, while also limiting the planters' expectations of remittance or credit advances. Either way, Tobin and Pinney did not mince their words. They bluntly told George Lowman that his were 'without exception the worst lot of Sugar which has been consigned to us this Season'. Josiah Webbe Hendrickson's sugars were similarly the 'worst lot of Sugars we have yet received'. William Jones's sugars they described as 'dreadfully bad indeed'.[66] This was, therefore, an important responsibility that influenced the production process through feedback on how the sugar was received. Indeed, it gave the planter something more material to work with than prices, which, on their own, would not indicate to a planter how they could improve their crop in the same way as the merchant's qualitative assessment (however bluntly delivered).

Secondly, the merchant dealt with a lot of the paperwork. He handled the bill of lading, which kept a record of the shipping, indicated the weight on loading, and could be used as proof to claim the sugar on its landing. This was sent to the merchant often independently of the ship that the sugar sailed on, and the entries stated on the bill of lading were transferred into an import book. In the absence of a bill of lading, the ship's manifests would have to be checked to make sure the sugars were on board.[67] The merchants used this form of accounting to log inaccuracies or inconsistencies in the weight of sugar that might indicate faults in the plantation weights, or help identify pilferage.[68] They wrote out the account of sales, which laid out to the proprietor of the sugar the gross revenue from the sales, minus the duties, freight, landwaiters charges, costs of weighing, brokerage, any abatements, and commission on the sale.[69] Tobin & Pinney chastised Coles, Godwin & Coles, its agents in London, for omitting from the accounts of sale the date that the duties were paid and the time given to purchasers before they had

---

66 Tobin & Pinney to George Lowman, 23 October 1793, Tobin & Pinney to William Jones, 15 October 1794, UoBSC, MS DM58/Letter Book/39; Tobin & Pinney to Josiah Webbe Hendrickson, 29 August 1791, UoBSC, MS DM58/Letter Book/38.

67 Tobin, Pinney & Tobin to Coles, Godwin & Coles, 25 September 1799, and 21 May 1800, UoBSC, MS DM58/Letter Book/40; Farber, 'Sailing on Paper', p. 42.

68 Pinney & Tobin to Richard Crosse, 30 August 1788, UoBSC, MS DM58/Letter Book/37.

69 See account of sales enclosed in John Fisher Weare to William Dickinson, 11 October 1794, SHC, MS DD/DN/4/2/42(3).

to pay, which Tobin & Pinney included.[70] This accounting of imports and sales was a significant responsibility, and formed part of the broader activity of tracking credit and debts.

Finally, and most importantly, the merchant was responsible for deciding when to sell the sugar. Once the broker had assessed the quality and value of the sugar and compared this to the market conditions, the merchant would have the final say on whether or not to take the sugar to market. Merchants could hold on to the sugars in their care until the price was right, and they would order them to be sold when the market picked up.[71] Morgan has observed how 'a glut of sugar after the arrival of the West India fleet at Bristol usually led to poor sale prices'.[72] While this might be the case, it did not mean that merchants necessarily had to sell. They could choose to hold their sugars back from the market and wait for conditions to change. Given the oligopolistic structure of the sugar market, they exercised considerable power and were certainly in a good position to do this. They were happy to abide by any instructions their clients had, for example if they wanted their sugars to be 'brought to an earlier market'.[73] Yet Tobin & Pinney only held on to sugars, so it claimed, 'to promote the Interest of the proprietor: as it must ever be for his own advantage [i.e., the merchant's] to sell as soon as possible'.[74] Indeed, as the firm informed another client, 'it is every way against the Merchants Interest' to keep sugars.[75] This is a bit of an overstatement—they also did not want any interference from planters who wanted an immediate sale. While the merchants might have preferred a quicker turnover of stock, they still received a larger commission with a higher-priced sale. If the sugar was sent as debt repayment, which it commonly was, keeping sugars until the price had risen was certainly in their interests, too. Regardless of who benefited most, this was the merchants' most important role in the marketing process. It required the ability to read market patterns and take in the mood of the market in order to make predictions about the expected direction of

---

70 Tobin, Pinney & Tobin to Coles, Godwin & Coles, 26 December 1798, UoBSC, MS DM58/Letter Book/40.
71 Pares, *West-India Fortune*, p. 187.
72 Morgan, *Bristol*, pp. 212–14; Pares, *West-India Fortune*, pp. 200–01.
73 Pinney & Tobin to William Colhoun, 17 November 1786, UoBSC, MS DM58/Letter Book/37; Tobin & Pinney to John Lyons, 21 October 1794, UoBSC, MS DM58/Letter Book/39.
74 Tobin, Pinney & Tobin to Nicholas Williams, 6 August 1799, UoBSC, MS DM58/Letter Book/40.
75 Tobin & Pinney to John Scarbrough, 18 June 1792, UoBSC, MS DM58/Letter Book/38.

the price. If they were right, they boosted their reputation by getting a higher price for their client and earned themselves a healthier commission.

There were still things that they had to consider other than market conditions. The risk of further natural drainage had to be weighed up against the expectation of a price rise. The only condition under which they would sell immediately was if the sugars were of such poor quality that they were rapidly draining weight. In one instance, so much molasses had drained out of the sugar casks that it had almost flooded the warehouse floor. Tobin and Pinney

> had at the <u>particular desire of the Cooper</u> visited the warehouse where [Edward Brazier's] Sugars by the *Nevis* were deposited in order to be witness to the uncommon quantity of Mollasses which run from those sugars, which was actually so much as to be nearly over their shoes[76]

Sugars that arrived in this state could not be feasibly kept, so were sold as soon as possible.

Furthermore, they did not have complete control over this process. Some planters wanted a bigger say in when their produce was sold.[77] This was the case with William Dickinson, who would accept the opinion of Rose and Stephen Fuller or his Bristol factors on the matter of withholding, but wanted the final decision to be his. When the price was too high to justify speculation, the Fullers had no qualms about selling immediately if they thought this best, but they usually offered their opinion and deferred their decision.[78] Given that Dickinson, an absentee planter, spent his time in London or Kingweston, he was at most only a few days away from the sugar markets. Planters residing in the West Indies had no choice but to allow the merchant to make this decision. Yet this did not stop them complaining. John Pinney himself chastised his factor when he was a resident planter in the West Indies in 1777 for selling too early.[79] Merchants who sold against the planters' wishes could be vindicated by a fall in the market. Robert Lovell sold Dickinson's rum before knowing that he wanted it kept, but sold it high before a fall.[80] The merchants' role was, therefore, to decide when to sell, and at the very least to advise their clients on when they should authorise a sale. To better understand the decision-making process, and how these merchants

---

76 Tobin & Pinney to Edward Brazier, 4 June 1789, UoBSC, MS DM58/Letter Book/38.
77 Pares, *West-India Fortune*, pp. 187–88.
78 See numerous letters from Stephen & Rose Fuller, James Sutton and John Fisher Weare to William Dickinson in SHC, MS DD/DN/4/2/1(2)-42(5).
79 Morgan, *Bristol*, p. 214.
80 Robert Lovell to William Dickinson, 9 November 1782, SHC, MS DD/DN/4/2/16(3).

used withholding as a tool to weather poor market conditions, we have to understand the market itself.

The mechanisms of the sugar market

As important to the price of sugar as its quality (and the judgement of brokers) were the forces of supply and demand. As has been previously noted, prices across different grades would remain fixed in relation to one another (browns would not exceed lighter sugars in price), but the range between the best and worst would widen and shrink.[81] The other important component, or measure, of the market was the briskness at which the sugar would sell. Briskness was a function of demand especially as it related to price and the expectations or realities of supply. A change in briskness was occasioned by the anticipation of a fall or rise in the price, and, because prices tended to be sticky as both buyers and sellers attempted to maintain prices that suited them, this meant that the pace of sales could be quite volatile. Expectations about the size of the crop were the key driver of this mechanism throughout the year. If there were rumours of a bumper production, for example, buyers would wait until the whole of the import had arrived and merchants were forced to lower their prices in response. Rather than accept lower prices, sellers preferred to wait until buyers' stocks ran low and they were forced to come to the market—rumours of a poor crop helped.

Demand

There were two main groups of purchasers in the Bristol sugar market: grocers and refiners. They would exercise their influence on the market in different ways. Grocers were interested in the best-quality fine sugars that needed little further alteration before retail.[82] They had no interest in the browner or wetter sugars, but their demand was year round as they bought small amounts more frequently.[83] Their influence was thus steady, and they maintained a 'brisk demand' for finer sugars, even if demand for browns was 'very heavy'.[84] Even when the refiners were standing back, the grocers might still 'buy a little briskly'.[85] Because their needs were relatively consistent, and

---

81 Morgan, *Bristol*, pp. 206–07.
82 Thomas Harris to William Dickinson, 6 August 1792, SHC, MS DD/DN/4/2/38(1).
83 Pares, *West-India Fortune*, p. 190.
84 Tobin & Pinney to John Warren, 5 September 1792, and Tobin & Pinney to William Jones, 10 September 1792, UoBSC, MS DM58/Letter Book/38.
85 Pinney & Tobin to B. & T. Boddington & Co., 24 August 1788, UoBSC, MS DM58/Letter Book/37.

because storage space was restricted, they could not exert their influence over the market by standing back. Instead, they attempted to exert influence over prices through lobbying. On one occasion, for example, there was a meeting of grocers and consumers, who sought an investigation into the scarcity of sugars to determine its accuracy. Tobin & Pinney hoped this would be productive, 'by bringing forward <u>enquiries</u> which will plainly prove the present scarcity of Sugars to be <u>real</u>'.[86] The demand of grocers was therefore year-round, but was predominantly for the highest-grade sugars. This gave them little influence over the market through their purchasing power, though they kept the price of fine sugars high.

Refiners, conversely, exercised more influence. They bought the darker, stronger muscovado sugars that were not suited for immediate retail.[87] Strength was especially valuable, for sugars needed to withstand the refining process. John Fisher Weare commented that some of Dickinson's lighter sugars were too weak for refiners (though they also had too much foot to appeal to grocers).[88] Refiners mixed the muscovado sugar with lime water in copper pans, which would be boiled, skimmed, strained, and boiled again. Eggs might be beaten up with the shells and thrown into the mixture as it was boiled to further remove impurities that would be skimmed from the surface. The mixture would then be poured into moulds and left to drain and set in a similar fashion to the clayed sugars that came from Barbados and the French islands. This process was repeated multiple times until just the pure white sugar was left. The result was a loaf of sugar that could be sold at retail.[89] A number of refineries were established around Bristol's rivers, the Frome and the Avon, which had good access to the hard lime water that was needed in this process. There were at least twenty refineries in Bristol in 1801, as there had been since mid-century.[90] In the 1780s, 200–250,000 cwt of sugar was imported into Bristol annually, which the refiners, alongside the grocers, were able to consume. They represented the final stage of the production process and formed a significant component of Bristol's market.

Their power to influence the market came from their ability to stockpile. They came forward when the price was low, but if they felt the price was too high, they would initiate a standoff with the merchants. At times like these, Tobin & Pinney acknowledged that 'the Buyers seem frightened out of the Market by the prices we ask' and were coming forward 'very cautiously'. They

---

86 Tobin & Pinney to Boddingtons & Bettesworth, 8 December 1791, UoBSC, MS DM58/Letter Book/38.
87 Pares, *West-India Fortune*, p. 190.
88 John Fisher Weare to William Dickinson, 17 July 1794, SHC, MS DD/DN/4/2/42(3).
89 Anon., *The Art of Making Sugar* (London: Willock, 1752).
90 Harvey and Press, 'Industrial Change', p. 5; Morgan, *Bristol*, pp. 185, 216–17.

would be 'not very eager to buy large quantities in hopes of more considerable arrivals'; Tobin & Pinney complained of 'the backwardness of the Bakers to buy at the present prices'. The sellers waited too, however, believing that 'it cannot be long before the Bakers must purchase again'. Indeed, the market might be flat 'not for want of purchasers, but rather because the Sellers do not chuse to give way'.[91] For Tobin & Pinney, if 'the Buyers come forward very sparingly in hopes of compelling the Merchants to reduce their prices', their strategy was to 'stand aloof'. It might have been frustrating for some planters when the refiners were holding back from the market and when the merchants did the same, especially when the quality of their sugars was 'more fit for them than the Grocers'.[92] This standoff was the key mechanism by which prices remained sticky; as Tobin & Pinney explained, the 'Sugar market still continues very dull, but we presume it cannot be long before the Bakers must purchase again, and we have not yet lowered our prices'.[93] The refiners, therefore, kept stocks on hand so they could wait out periods of high prices, and merchants similarly waited out periods of low prices. There was a time constraint facing both: refiners' stocks would eventually run low, while merchants with a lot of sugar on hand would soon receive a new import (a pressure that compounded with the perishability of sugar). Both would wait out the other, seeing who broke first.

This mechanism had broader impacts on the rest of the market. High prices led, at times, to a fall in 'demand for refined Sugars'. Several high-profile failures of sugar refiners in London after years of 'little profits' gave the merchants pause, as their own demand was being eaten away by their unwillingness to lower prices.[94] Yet this does not appear to have been an immediate concern for the merchants and planters, who were more interested in maximising profits than lowering production costs and broadening demand. The refiners, too, sought to minimise their costs. Their ability to stand back from the market when prices were too high (a luxury that grocers did not

---

[91] Pinney & Tobin to John Budgen, 22 June 1786, Pinney & Tobin to B. & T. Boddington & Co., 20 September 1786 and 24 August 1788, Pinney & Tobin to William Colhoun, 8 November 1786, UoBSC, MS DM58/Letter Book/37; Tobin & Pinney to Boddingtons & Bettesworth, 22 November 1791, UoBSC, MS DM58/Letter Book/38; Tobin & Pinney to Alexander Douglas, 12 February 1795, Tobin & Pinney to Edward Brazier, 3 February 1796, UoBSC, MS DM58/Letter Book/39.

[92] Tobin & Pinney to Edward Brazier, 7 February 1792, and Tobin & Pinney to William Colhoun, 23 June 1791, UoBSC, MS DM58/Letter Book/38.

[93] Pinney & Tobin to William Colhoun, 8 November 1786, UoBSC, MS DM58/Letter Book/37.

[94] Pinney & Tobin to Edward Brazier, 25 April 1787 and 23 July 1788, and Pinney & Tobin to Rowland Burton, 2 August 1788, UoBSC, MS DM58/Letter Book/37.

have) made them a powerful group of buyers whose behaviours contributed to the ebb and flow of demand. This influenced the pace of sales, if not always the price. Both merchants and refiners were motivated to wait, and both were pressured to come forward by the limited stock they had on hand.

Supply

The total sugar supply had the greatest impact on the market. With an increase in supply expected to lower prices, or a scarcity expected to raise prices, uncertainty over the size of the season's crop influenced the behaviour of buyers and sellers. Rumours abounded over the size of the crop, and both merchants and refiners tried to anticipate how this would affect the market. In this way, the market functioned similarly to the early nineteenth-century Liverpool cotton market, where 'the construction of price ... includes present supply and demand, but also considerations of future supply and demand'.[95] Supply fluctuated on two levels: throughout the season, as the supply of sugar fluctuated over the year, and yearly, as the import varied year on year.

Fluctuations in the market were driven predominantly by the overall size of the crop, and especially the size of the crop in Jamaica, Britain's largest sugar colony. As Bristol's merchants observed when the first ships arrived in 1787, though the market 'broke better than it did at the begining of last', Tobin & Pinney commented that 'much will depend on the Quantity imported from Jamaica'.[96] Thomas Harris calculated that the total import that year had reached 21,700 hogsheads, surpassing the average of the previous nine years by 3,490 hogsheads, a bumper supply that was the result of the large Jamaica crop and which affected sales.[97] Tobin & Pinney likewise stated in the summer of 1788 that the market was 'very dull, and indeed drooping' owing, in part, to 'a large crop from Jamaica'.[98] The fortunes of planters from smaller islands were therefore heavily influenced by production in Jamaica. The Nevis crop suffered several times over these years at the hands of the borer worm and successive dry periods.[99] Bad luck on the islands was then compounded by arrival to a market that had been depressed by the Jamaica crop. Similarly, in 1785, the large crop from Jamaica coincided with a fall in

---

[95] Sheryllynne Haggerty, 'What's in a Price? The American Raw Cotton Market in Liverpool and the Anglo-American War', *Business History*, 61:6 (2019), 942–70 (p. 945).

[96] Pinney & Tobin to Edward Brazier, 6 May 1787, and Pinney & Tobin to James Tyson, 18 May 1787, UoBSC, MS DM58/Letter Book/37.

[97] Thomas Harris to William Dickinson, 22 November 1787, SHC, MS DD/DN/4/2/25.

[98] Pinney & Tobin to Edward Brazier, 23 July 1788, UoBSC, MS DM58/Letter Book/37.

[99] See Chapter 1.

output in Antigua and Montserrat. The following year, the Leeward Islands benefited from a short crop in Jamaica. When the short Jamaica crop was realised by September, Tobin & Pinney sold some of its clients' sugar at a higher-than-expected price.[100] Refiners would wait to see how the Jamaica crop turned out before coming to the market, especially if they expected it to be large, which would cause a fall in prices as merchants struggled to get rid of stock. The merchants could attempt to wait out the glut. Conversely, if the import was expected to be small, merchants held off until the scarcity had become realised and prices increased, while refiners relied on what stocks they had on hand to see them through.

It was not just the size of the crop that affected the market, as it became apparent *ex post*, but also news arriving from the islands throughout the year that shaped the expectation *ex ante*. In 1786, the market was lifted by 1s 6d–2s in June 'as the accounts from Jamaica are rather unfavourable as to the Crop there'.[101] In 1787, conversely, the market fell by 5s–6s before the arrival of any ships 'owing to the repeated acco.^{ts} of large Crops in most of the Islands', which 'give us but faint hopes of its getting up again'. The situation stayed this way for much of April.[102] The prospect for the next year did not look much better. In December 1787, the reports from Jamaica were already 'very flattering', giving the market 'little prospect' of rising. The market in May 1788 opened 'rather heavily owing to the idea that the Crop in Jamaica is very great', though the 'truth of this will soon be ascertained' with the arrival of that season's sugars.[103] Further, a short importation in one year would lead to the expectation of scarcity in the next as the market suffered a dearth of sugars in the lead-up to the new importation. In cases like these, Tobin & Pinney congratulated their clients on their sugars coming to a 'most excellent market'.[104] It was, therefore, expectation as much as reality that caused fluctuations in the price of sugar and the briskness of the market throughout the year.

The arrival of ships over the summer caused minor fluctuations as the truth of the full extent of production emerged. Further, an influx of sugars over the

---

100 Pinney & Tobin to John Richardson Herbert, 1 August 1785, and Pinney & Tobin to John Scarbrough, 21 September 1786, UoBSC, MS DM58/Letter Book/37.
101 Pinney & Tobin to John Richardson Herbert, 28 June 1786, UoBSC, MS DM58/Letter Book/37.
102 Pinney & Tobin to James Tyson, Thomas Maynard 2 April 1787, and Pinney & Tobin to Edward Brazier, 25 April 1787, UoBSC, MS DM58/Letter Book/37.
103 Pinney & Tobin to Edward Brazier, 8 December 1787, and Pinney & Tobin to Rowland Burton, 26 May 1788, UoBSC, MS DM58/Letter Book/37.
104 See Tobin & Pinney to Francis Canham, 1 November 1790, UoBSC, MS DM58/Letter Book/38.

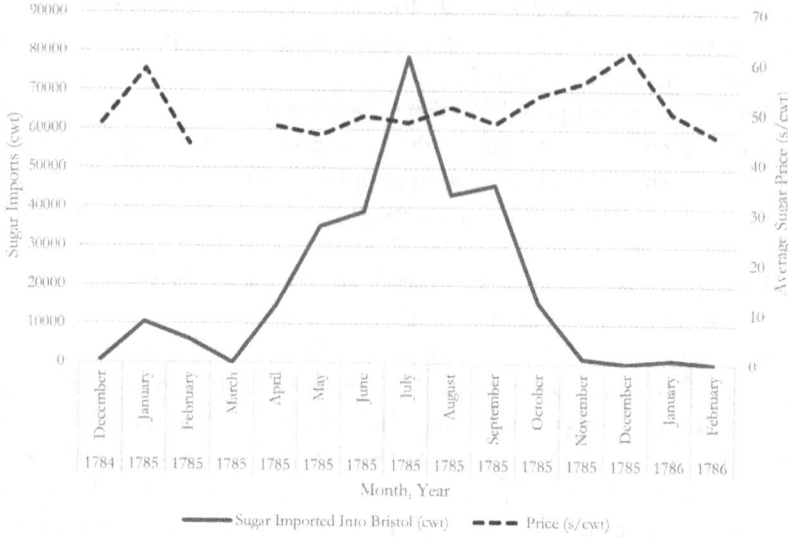

Figure 3.5: Sugar Imports and Average Prices in Bristol by Month, December 1784–February 1786 (cwt and s/cwt)

Source: Price data: Kenneth Morgan, *Bristol and the Atlantic Trade in the Eighteenth Century* (Cambridge: Cambridge University Press, 1993), p. 210; Import data: BA, MS SMV/7/1/1/72-73, Wharfage Books 1784–1786.

summer would 'dampen' the market as the sugars arrived in sequence or at once.[105] The seasonal rhythm, with a dip as the crop was expected, followed by minor fluctuations and a larger price movement as the last ships came in, is illustrated in Figure 3.5, which shows the imports and prices for the period from December 1784 to February 1786. Tobin & Pinney observed a drop in prices over the summer, which it attributed to a large crop from Jamaica that exceeded that of the previous year. As Tobin & Pinney knew well, it was 'the Jamaica Crop which chiefly affects the market and that (taken generally) is likely to be a pretty good one'. The price fluctuated around 50 s/cwt as new imports arrived. The market dipped from a high in January with expectations of the new ships, and became flat with the 'great number of arrivals' which had, over July, lowered the markets 'both here and in London about 2[s] or 3[s]'.[106] Merchants such as Tobin and Pinney sought to wait out these gluts, not bringing their sugar to market until stocks had begun to fall, and prices

---

105 Morgan, *Bristol*, pp. 204–12; Pares, *West-India Fortune*, pp. 194–95.
106 Pinney & Tobin to John Richardson Herbert, and John Scarbrough, 1 August 1785, UoBSC, MS DM58/Letter Book/37.

started picking up again. Indeed, a large crop like this would prompt merchants to hold off from entering the market until winter. Tobin and Pinney believed that withholding their sugar like this could net them an extra 2 s/cwt.[107] This is shown in Figure 3.5, with the price not climbing again until October, reaching a peak in December. In January and February, the price sank back to the levels seen before the summer as news began coming in regarding the next crop. The biggest changes in price came with rumours of the crop, and then later when the full extent of the import was realised.

The seasonal nature of arrivals therefore gave the market a seasonal movement, though there were exceptions. New arrivals did not always affect the price. As Tobin & Pinney informed a client in September 1787, 'Our Sugar market is at present both here and in London, very flat owing to the numerous arrivals lately but the prices are but little fallen as yet'.[108] Later importations would extend the period of flatness.[109] Yet on the whole, prices tended to dip with new arrivals, though it was the expectation of the overall size of the import that materially drove prices up or down. Buyers held back from buying over the summer if they expected a bumper crop that would precipitate a greater fall, even as the price fell in anticipation. As they entered the market, prices began to rise. If the crop was large, merchants might choose to ride out the glut until the late winter. On the other hand, a short import meant that they could take advantage of the scarcity as early as autumn. Buyers depended upon their stocks to wait out periods of high prices, though would be pressed to come to market should their stocks run low. Merchants counted on these stocks running out before they received a new import of sugars as the next season began.

Bristol's relationship with other markets

It was not just supply and demand within Bristol that affected Bristol's market. It was influenced by supply and demand elsewhere, too, significantly in London. Bristol tended to follow the price in London and, for that reason, merchants in Bristol sought frequent updates on how the London market was performing. Yet there were also often price differences between the two markets that merchants and refiners could exploit. Further, planters split their consignments between Bristol and London, while merchants in both cities built up links with the other port to benefit from the sale of their

---

[107] Pinney & Tobin to Rowland Burton, 3 March 1789, UoBSC, MS DM58/Letter Book/37.
[108] Pinney & Tobin to Archbald & Williamson, 3 September 1787, UoBSC, MS DM58/Letter Book/37.
[109] Tobin & Pinney to John Warren, 27 September 1790, UoBSC, MS DM58/Letter Book/38.

clients' sugars wherever it arrived. The ports were, therefore, in a dual state of competition and cooperation, with merchants seeking to exploit the benefits of both and limit the drawbacks. Markets beyond London had comparatively less impact on Bristol.

Sugar prices in Bristol and London often rose and fell together, though London would rise or fall first. Kenneth Morgan argues that 'sugar prices at Bristol "broke" only after the opening of the London sugar market'.[110] This is confirmed by Tobin & Pinney, who told the Boddingtons in London that 'our market is still quite dull, waiting to be set a going by yours'. The buyers would know this, too: Bristol's sugar market would also be dull as 'the Buyers seem to expect a fall in London'.[111] The London market was much bigger than Bristol's, importing around five times as much sugar.[112] For this reason, merchants in Bristol sought frequent updates on the performance of London's market. As Tobin & Pinney observed, 'all markets are subject to temporary fluctuations … we can only say that we spare no pains to get the best information as to any expected rises and falls both of the markets here and elsewhere'.[113] They had various sources. From John Warren, their insurance broker, and merchants B. & T. Boddington and Thomas Bettesworth, they requested 'the best intelligence in your power'.[114] These enquiries were common from Bristol's merchants.[115] Price data were also published, which made it relatively easy to confirm the accuracy of their reports.[116] Such information helped merchants in Bristol predict the price movements in their own market, considering that it often followed movements in London.

Yet there were also differences between the two markets that merchants could exploit. Even if the movement of prices was similar, the prices were not always equal. Figure 3.6 shows that the average price in Bristol tended to be higher than London until at least 1791. Indeed, Bristol had, by the 1780s, gained a reputation for having higher prices than London.[117] Tobin

---

110 Morgan, *Bristol*, pp. 209–11.
111 Pinney & Tobin to B. & T. Boddington & Co., 8 November 1787, UoBSC, MS DM58/Letter Book/37; Tobin & Pinney to Thomas Bettesworth, 25 September 1789, UoBSC, MS DM58/Letter Book/38.
112 Morgan, *Bristol*, p. 190.
113 Pinney & Tobin to B. & T. Boddington & Co., 27 June 1788, UoBSC, MS DM58/Letter Book/37; Tobin & Pinney to Edward Huggins, 31 August 1789, UoBSC, MS DM58/Letter Book/38.
114 See Pinney & Tobin to John Warren, 19 September 1784, and numerous other letters to these individuals in UoBSC, MS DM58/Letter Book/37–42.
115 Morgan, *Bristol*, p. 211.
116 McCusker, *Essays*, pp. 99–121.
117 David Duncombe to Lowbridge Bright, 19 June 1790, Letter 264, in Morgan, *Bright-Meyler Papers*.

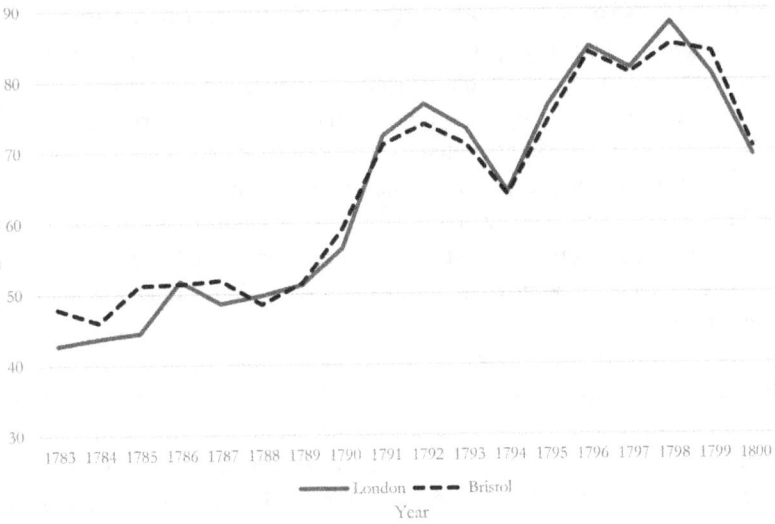

Figure 3.6: Average Annual Price of Muscovado Sugar in Bristol and London, Inclusive of Duties, 1783–1800 (s/cwt)

Source: London prices: Thomas Tooke, *A History of Prices and of the State of Circulation from 1793 to 1837*, Vol. II (London: Longman and others, 1838), p. 414; Bristol prices: Kenneth Morgan, *Bristol and the Atlantic Trade in the Eighteenth Century* (Cambridge: Cambridge University Press, 1993), p. 210.

& Pinney enjoyed pointing this out to clients. Furthermore, the firm argued that, because the costs of shipping to Bristol were lower, the net proceeds would be higher, even if the price was the same. When Edward Brazier, a client of Tobin & Pinney's, made the 'mistake' of shipping his produce to London, the firm pointed out how, in retrospect, he was too 'much in a hurry to send so many of your best Sugars to an <u>early</u> London Market: for had they arrived here [Bristol] and later in the season, it would have turned out much to your advantage'.[118] John Fisher Weare similarly pointed out to Dickinson when Bristol was above London.[119] Some London merchants even sent their sugar to Bristol to take advantage of the higher prices.[120] Speculators would take advantage of the price difference, too, buying in one market to sell in the

---

118 Tobin & Pinney to Edward Brazier, 30 March 1795, UoBSC, MS DM58/Letter Book/39.
119 John Fisher Weare to William Dickinson, 11 November 1794, SHC, MS DD/DN/4/2/42(2).
120 Pinney & Tobin to Wildman & Smith, 17 and 29 July 1786, UoBSC, MS DM58/Letter Book/37.

other, though these adventures were not always successful: Tobin & Pinney noted one occasion when '500 to 800 Hhds' were 'sent round this year on Speculation', though the speculators 'made but very trifling profits on their adventures, and some we believe have lost money'.[121] The major drawback was that higher prices might result in a dull market, as refiners migrated from Bristol to London to take advantage of lower prices there. The transport costs, at 3 s/cwt, were not prohibitive if the gap was wide enough.[122] Merchants could use Bristol's typically higher prices as an advertising point to gain clients, and speculators could take advantage of the price difference—but so could refiners, a point that Tobin & Pinney often failed to mention to planters.

Significantly, however, prices in London could also exceed those in Bristol. Though this might have helped sales in Bristol, Tobin and Pinney were more worried that it might encourage planters to ship their sugars to the higher London market. Such differences could be nuanced, with price variations occurring across grades, for example with browns selling higher in London, even if finer sugars were the same. This was a result of the different preferences of the two major buying groups. Refiners, with brown sugars higher in London, would be induced to come to Bristol for their stocks. Conversely, when sales of brown sugars in Bristol were slow, even Tobin and Pinney, who were cheerleaders for Bristol's market, sent their sugars to an agent in London via waggon.[123] Speculation was experienced the other way around, too. Tobin & Pinney noted some 400 hogsheads being transferred to London on one occasion, for example.[124] When prices in London exceeded Bristol, refiners would come to Bristol's market, and speculators similarly sought to take advantage of the gap. Merchants such as Tobin and Pinney, however, worried that planters would send their sugar shipments to London instead.

The fears that planters would come to exclude Bristol if prices fell below those in London were overstated. The planters' view of the market was

---

121 Tobin & Pinney to Edward Brazier, 25 March 1790, UoBSC, MS DM58/Letter Book/38; Tobin & Pinney to Monsieur Desalle, 16 November 1794, UoBSC, MS DM58/Letter Book/39.

122 Tobin & Pinney to Boddingtons & Bettesworth, 6 October 1794, UoBSC, MS DM58/Letter Book/39; John Fisher Weare to William Dickinson, 1 December 1794, SHC, MS DD/DN/4/2/42(5); Morgan, *Bristol*, pp. 211–12.

123 Tobin, Pinney & Tobin to Woodbridge, Dyer & Co., 5, 9 and 21 March, and 2 May 1799, and Tobin, Pinney & Tobin to Daniel Wane, 18 March 1799, UoBSC, MS DM58/Letter Book/40.

124 Tobin & Pinney to B. & T. Boddington & Co., 19 August 1789, UoBSC, MS DM58/Letter Book/38.

significantly lagged, with their information on prices often out of date. Their best strategy, therefore, was to split their consignments between the two markets.[125] Some still had a preference. William Dickinson, in 1793, ordered 40 hogsheads to be sent to Bristol and 100 hogsheads to London. His division, weighted in favour of London, was driven by the idea that 'London is certainly the best market for Rum & I think at present it is & has been for 2 or 3 years also rather the best for Sugar'.[126] Frequently, however, planters depended on the availability of shipping (especially in the smaller islands), and would send sugars to whichever port was most convenient at the time.[127] This demonstrates the importance for merchants of having control over the shipping infrastructure. Price variations between the two markets therefore had a significant impact over buying behaviour. Yet it had a more subtle effect on supply, which was influenced to a greater degree by the information lag and availability of shipping.

Price differences and concerns over attracting clients meant that the two ports were in direct competition. However, merchants in both ports, wary of losing out from the effects of planters sending sugars elsewhere, made arrangements to act as agents for one another. These arrangements would be made clear on the bill of lading. If sugars intended for Tobin & Pinney were sent to London, it was noted that another firm, say B. & T. Boddington, would pick them up and sell them on Tobin & Pinney's behalf. Usually, the two firms would split the commission (though Tobin & Pinney waved its share for the Boddingtons). Tobin & Pinney would reciprocate, selling sugars on behalf of London merchants, then remitting the net proceeds.[128] This arrangement was driven by the interlinked credit needs of merchants in both ports. Planters made remittances of sugar to pay down debts, which their merchant creditors required, regardless of the port they were sent to. This process was not without its problems, however. A careless agent might forget to claim some sugars and leave them on the ship, for example.[129] With planters splitting consignments, merchants therefore made mutually beneficial arrangements with their counterparts in the other port that allowed them to take advantage of both markets. This created an environment where

---

125 Morgan, *Bristol*, p. 199.
126 Barnard and William Dickinson to Thomas Salmon, 25 January 1793, and to John White, 24 December 1793, SHC, MS DD/DN/4/2/40(1).
127 See Pinney & Tobin to Edward Brazier, 28 September 1787, UoBSC, MS DM58/Letter Book/37.
128 See Pinney & Tobin to B. & T. Boddington & Co., 20 September 1787, UoBSC, MS DM58/Letter Book/37.
129 See Tobin & Pinney to Boddingtons & Bettesworth, 24 November 1794, UoBSC, MS DM58/Letter Book/39.

merchants in the two ports were both competing and cooperating with one another.

Markets other than London had less influence over Bristol. Liverpool held little sway over Bristol until the end of the century (as we shall see in the following chapter). Only rarely did Tobin & Pinney's clients send their sugars there. Glasgow was a more popular destination, if only because Tobin & Pinney sent orders of herrings to planters that might have been paid for with sugar. Tobin & Pinney's clients on occasion sent sugars there, as did Tobin himself.[130] The Irish markets held more sway than these two. Ireland was a significant trading partner for Bristol, and strong consumer base for sugar. When the markets in London and Bristol were full, Ireland was used as a vent-for-surplus.[131] Yet there were differences in practice that acted as a barrier to further integration. The breakage was taken off when consumed, rather than when sold to the refiners, for example.[132] Bristol's merchants also complained of troublesome Customs officials when exporting rum, given that the weight drained during re-export, making the Customs bonds appear to be false.[133] Ireland was limited as a vent-for-surplus for Bristol's sugar, however, by its exposure to the Liverpool market, which at times fully supplied the Irish market. When this happened, even when Thomas Harris managed to sell some sugar to Ireland, it was through a Liverpool-based merchant.[134] Yet none of these markets had the level of influence over Bristol's market that London had.

Markets in the West Indies held comparatively more sway than Liverpool, Glasgow, and Ireland. Though most sugar was sent by commission, some was still bought in the islands. The presence of this market allowed planters to threaten to sell their sugar on the islands rather than consign it, especially if they were unhappy about the prices they received in Britain. The trouble caused by obtaining remittances from these sales in Britain probably worried merchants, as much as it worried absentees who might otherwise have

---

130 See Tobin & Pinney to Alexander Houstoun & Co., 25 May, 16 August, and 8 September 1792, UoBSC, MS DM58/Letter Book/38; Tobin & Pinney to Archibald Washington, 23 October 1793, UoBSC, MS DM58/Letter Book/39.

131 Tobin & Pinney to John Warren, 3 December 1791, UoBSC, MS DM58/Letter Book/38; Tobin, Pinney & Tobin to John Mair, 21 September 1799, UoBSC, MS DM58/Letter Book/40; Morgan, *Bright-Meyler Papers*, p. 94.

132 Thomas Harris to William Dickinson, 29 September 1791, SHC, MS DD/DN/4/2/35(2).

133 Minchinton, *Politics*, pp. 169–70.

134 Thomas Harris to William Dickinson, 8 October 1791 and 15 November 1791, SHC, MS DD/DN/4/2/35(2)-35(3).

preferred their managers to sell sugars in the islands.[135] Given that selling the sugar in Britain gave the planters (or at least their creditors) a 40% mark-up in price, it is unlikely that many planters preferred the West India markets.[136] It was most likely that sugar that was too poor to ship was sold in the islands. However, rum often sold better in the West Indies than in Britain, where it had to compete with other spirits, notably brandy. It was sold in the islands, typically for export to America, to help planters 'defray the contingencies of the Estate'.[137] On occasion, when the market for rum in Bristol was very low, some was sent to Quebec on speculation, which at times had spikes of demand.[138] The market for sugar in the West Indies was therefore limited, though planters could use it to threaten merchants. The market for rum was better.

Finally, Bristol had some connection to the European market. This was typically indirect. Bristol was predominantly a consumption centre for sugar, rather than a centre for re-exports.[139] At times the re-export market could be 'pretty considerable'; however, the European market had a greater impact when London experienced a strong re-export that raised prices there, leading to higher prices in Bristol.[140] Yet for British merchants generally, the European market was, for much of the eighteenth century, less important. The expansion of Saint Domingue, and its ability to supply the continent with cheaper sugar, led to the effective exclusion of British sugars from the European market. Sugar was re-exported from French ports with strong colonial links, predominantly Bordeaux and Nantes, to Amsterdam, Hamburg, and St Petersburg, which served as continental entrepots.[141] Though British planters were, thanks an Act of Parliament in 1739, allowed to export sugars in British ships to any port south of Cape Finisterre without

---

135 Caleb Dickinson to William Dickinson, 5 May 1790, SHC, MS DD/DN/4/2/32.
136 Klas Rönnbäck, 'Sweet Business: Quantifying the Value Added in the British Colonial Sugar Trade in the 18th Century', *Journal of Iberian and Latin American Economic History*, 32:2 (2014), 223–45 (p. 228).
137 Tobin & Pinney to Thomas Pym Weekes, 4 July 1792, UoBSC, MS DM58/Letter Book/38; Barnard Dickinson to William Dickinson, 27 October 1792, SHC, MS DD/DN/4/2/38(1).
138 See Pinney & Tobin to John Tobin Crosse, 12 August 1786, UoBSC, MS DM58/Letter Book/37.
139 Morgan, *Slavery, Atlantic Trade*, pp. 90–91.
140 Tobin & Pinney to B. & T. Boddington & Co., 27 November 1789, UoBSC, MS DM58/Letter Book/38; Thomas Harris to William Dickinson, 4 September 1789, SHC, MS DD/DN/4/2/28(1).
141 Marzagalli, 'Trade Networks'; Francois Crouzet, 'Wars, Blockade, and Economic Change in Europe, 1792–1815', *Journal of Economic History*, 24:4 (1964), 567–88.

calling at a British port first, there was often little point.[142] The protected British market was better for British planters.

Conclusion

Imports into Bristol's market remained reasonably steady over the period, despite some fluctuations caused by warfare, and despite a decline in the port's share of Britain's imports. The market was dominated by a few leading firms, with several others lower down the strata (including, for the most part, Tobin & Pinney), and a string of casual importers. The structure appears to have been fairly oligopolistic. While merchants might have dominated, however, they did not act alone, for they were supported by a range of other individuals who worked to limit hazards and reduce risks. Captains and crew cared for the sugar while it was in the ship's hold and, along with merchants' clerks, when it was being unloaded. Brokers checked how the sugar was stowed and judged the quality and price, and also surveyed the buyers to check that they were satisfied. Coopers cared for the sugar in the warehouse and orchestrated the taring process. Merchants, for their part, dealt with the paperwork and financial sides, not least purchasing insurance. Importantly, it was they who decided upon that most crucial of questions—when to sell the sugar.

Sugar in Bristol was purchased predominantly by grocers and refiners. Refiners, who were able to stockpile sugar, withdrew themselves from the market when prices were too high. Merchants, meanwhile, used their ability to withhold their sugars from the market to wait out periods of low prices. The resulting standoff would end either when refiners ran out of stocks or when merchants were pressured to sell by new arrivals. This behaviour was driven by the expectation of a large or small crop, predominantly from Jamaica. The seasonal nature of arrivals created a predictable pattern of gluts and scarcities that merchants and refiners used, alongside information about the current crop, to predict the movement of prices. The ebb and flow of supply and demand created periods of briskness and flatness in the market, which was just as significant for buyers and sellers as high or low prices. The market was influenced further by London. Refiners took advantage of price differences between the two markets, as did speculators. Merchants advertised their port when prices were higher in the hopes of gaining more consignments. All the while, planters, whose view of the market was insufficient for them to wholly prize one over the

---

142 Ryden, *West India Slavery*, pp. 1–6; Ragatz, *Planter Class*, pp. 106–07, 126–27.

other, split their consignments between Bristol and London. In response, merchants split their commissions. Other markets had less influence. It was this understanding of the market that guided merchants when they decided to withhold or sell the sugar in their care.

Such roles, responsibilities, and relationships defined the ebb and flow of trade in Bristol's sugar market. But, as with production and shipping, the market was not independent of its wider circumstances. As well as keeping a weather eye on market conditions, merchants also had to keep an eye on events and crises that could cause disruption, and had to use their ability to withhold sugar to overcome the resultant uncertainty. And so it was that in the sugar market merchants would face one of the most significant tests of their resilience.

4

Crisis, Disruption, and Uncertainty in Bristol's Sugar Market

> The sugar market does not get up, we sadly want the report of a War, a Hurricane, or something to give it a lift
>
> Pinney & Tobin, writing to a client, 1788[1]

As noted in the Introduction, several historians see warfare as one of the most problematic crises for eighteenth-century markets. In the words of Pierre Gervais, 'for an eighteenth-century merchant, the ultimate crisis was war'.[2] Similarly, Kenneth Morgan argues that 'the greatest uncertainty about sugar prices was caused by war'.[3] Was this always the case? Not, it seems, for this period. Rather, it was the transition from one condition to another, lasting over several months or as long as a year, that was the greatest cause of price uncertainty. This meant that the transition from war to peace could be just as disruptive as the transition from peace to war. Furthermore, even the expectation of a transition could affect prices and reduce sales. This is shown both in peacetime when war was threatened and during war when peace became a possibility. A similar phenomenon is observed by Sheryllynne Haggerty with regard to cotton prices.[4]

---

1 Pinney & Tobin to Rowland Burton 8 September 1788, UoBSC, MS DM58/Letter Book/37.
2 Gervais, 'Surviving War', p. 79.
3 Morgan, *Bristol*, p. 213.
4 Haggerty, 'What's in a Price?', pp. 951–53.

In this chapter, I show how war itself could be a source of price certainty, as merchants expected (and received) high prices, while other elements of the market remained as they were in peace. The seasonal fluctuations were much the same: convoys might have accentuated gluts, but ultimately they had little influence over the merchants' and refiners' approach to the market. Indeed, given the ability of merchants and refiners to withhold themselves from selling and buying, the impact of convoys on the market has been overstated. Other wartime issues proved more problematic, though even these were mitigated by various forces. Here, as before, merchants used their ability to withhold sugar from the market and their understanding of price movements to their advantage. Refiners similarly continued to rely on their ability to stockpile.

Building on the work of historians such as David Beck Ryden, I argue instead that the biggest crisis and source of disruption to the sugar market came not from the war with France, but with the collapse of Saint Domingue and the European sugar economy. The Saint Domingue Revolution presented an opportunity to British planters and merchants as the immediate scarcity in the European markets increased the price of sugar in Britain. This was sustained until 1799. The realisation that the opportunities presented by the Revolution were also taken by other, newer sugar colonies then led to the collapse of sugar prices.[5] The Hamburg Crisis, as this has become known, revealed to Britain the flaws in its new-found dependence upon the European market, revealed to Bristol the influence that Liverpool could have over its market, and revealed to merchants the limits of their withholding strategy, dependent as it was upon the ability to use past experience to predict future price movements.

Amid all this, the true source of uncertainty came from the transition from one condition to another. Meanwhile, the greatest effect on the sugar market came not from war, but from the revolution in Saint Domingue, which engendered a sudden underproduction of sugar, followed not even a decade later by a crisis of overproduction as other islands sought to fill the void. With crisis thus came opportunity, but the resilience that taking these opportunities built had its limits.

---

5 Cf. Ryden, *West Indian Slavery*. Ryden shows how overproduction and oversupply following the Saint Domingue Revolution contributed to abolitionist narratives regarding the inefficiencies and excesses of a slave-based system, becoming a significant factor in the timing of the abolition of the slave trade.

The return to peace and the threat of war

From 1782 to 1791, the transition from war to peace following the American Revolution and the threat of war in both 1787 and 1790 were the greatest causes of price uncertainty in Bristol's market. The transition out of war with America, as with the Seven Years War before, brought significant changes to the political and economic landscape. The West Indies planters faced new trading restrictions with the former colony, while the merchants of Britain had new opportunities to ship supplies and provisions. In Britain, however, they faced a revised tax regime, with the rate on sugar raised to 12s $3^2/\!_5$d per cwt in 1782. The West India Association feared that, with a fall in prices guaranteed to occur with the resumption of peace, the planters' profits would be eaten away.[6] Yet with peace expected, prices fell even before the war had ended. The market was dull early in 1782 as the season's fleets were awaited. Their arrival was anticipated to keep the price from advancing, but the spectre of coming peace kept the market dull. Only when peace was confirmed did the market begin moving again, as peace prices were certain to continue.[7] When William Miles, one of Bristol's leading sugar importers, commented in May 1783 that 'now peace has taken place things will go on better and with more certainty', he was acknowledging not the uncertainties of war, but the uncertainties of the transition into peace.[8] Indeed, the high prices that Morgan has observed during the war were not a product of uncertainty, for they were to be expected.[9] It was understood as a rule that war prices were higher.[10] The uncertainty was derived from the transition between conditions, with buyers and sellers awaiting confirmation of peace before resuming activity.

The experience during the 1787 Dutch Crisis was similar. In 1787, the Royal Navy was mobilised in response to the Dutch anti-Orangist Patriot Party seizing power from the Stadtholder in the Netherlands and appealing to the French for help.[11] It was unclear whether or not Britain would launch

---

6 BA, MS SMV/8/3/2/1 WIA; Ragatz, *Planter Class*, pp. 189–90.
7 Robert Lovell to William Dickinson, 17 January and 19 February 1782, Caleb Dickinson to William Dickinson, 21 December 1782, SHC, MS DD/DN/4/2/16(1)–16(3).
8 Kenneth Morgan, ed., 'Calendar of Correspondence from William Miles to John Tharp, 1770–1789', in *A Bristol Miscellany*, ed. by Patrick McGrath (Bristol: Bristol Records Society, 1985), pp. 79–122 (pp. 102–03); Morgan, *Bristol*, pp. 212–13.
9 Morgan, *Bristol*, pp. 207–10.
10 Pinney & Tobin to Rowland Burton 8 September 1788, UoBSC, MS DM58/Letter Book/37. See also Gervais, 'Surviving War', p. 83.
11 Rodger, *Command of the Ocean*, p. 364; Knight, *Britain Against Napoleon*, p. 10.

a military intervention, and this had a dampening effect on the sugar market in Bristol. In September, Tobin & Pinney reported to several clients that 'At present every thing seems in a state of uncertainty one day it is all war & the next all peace – it is however certain that Ministry are preparing for the worst.' The firm observed that the 'sugar market both here & in London' was 'but flat lately' with no sales being made, 'nor do we expect any alteration 'till it is determined whether we are to have war or peace – Just now everything bears the face of war'; indeed, they found that 'everything is in a state of great uncertainty'. By 20 October, the market remained flat and sugars remained unsold, with matters 'Still in as much suspense as ever with respect to peace or war'.[12]

When the French proved unable to come to the aid of the anti-Orangists, the Prussians intervened to reinstate the House of Orange.[13] By the end of October there was, therefore, a more 'peaceable appearance'; to Stephen & Rose Fuller in London, war by then seemed 'doubtful'.[14] In November, Tobin & Pinney reported that 'though the political hemisphere is a little cleared up at present, we cannot consider the storm as entirely blown over'. The price soon fell with the confirmation that there was to be no war.[15] The sugars that Tobin & Pinney had kept 'under the idea of a considerable rise in case of a war' looked to sell lower than hoped owing to 'the peaceable turn which matters have taken'. In December, they commented that 'the Market in London as well as here [Bristol] has fallen considerably since the peaceable Settlement of public affairs'. Yet the confirmation, one way or the other, injected some much-needed certainty into the market. There was a period of briskness late in December, which was only cut short when news arrived of a bumper crop from Jamaica for the 1788 market.[16] This shows that episodes of uncertainty could bring a halt to the market, even in peace, as sellers expected a transition into war (and, with it, higher wartime prices). Prices were raised

---

12 Pinney & Tobin to Rowland Burton, Francis Canham, and Thomas Maynard, 27 September 1787, and Pinney & Tobin to John Richardson, 20 October 1787, UoBSC, MS DM58/Letter Book/37.
13 Rodger, *Command of the Ocean*, p. 364; Knight, *Britain Against Napoleon*, p. 10.
14 Pinney & Tobin to Nathaniel Martin, 28 October 1787, UoBSC, MS DM58/Letter Book/37; Stephen & Rose Fuller to William Dickinson, 23 October 1787, SHC, MS DD/DN/4/2/22(1).
15 Pinney & Tobin to Henry Dench, 3 November 1787, UoBSC, MS DM58/Letter Book/37; Ezekiel Dickinson to William Dickinson, 2 and 26 November 1787, SHC, MS DD/DN/4/2/22(1)–25.
16 Pinney & Tobin to William Colhoun, 17 November and 11 December 1787, and Pinney & Tobin to B. & T. Boddington & Co., 9 January 1788, UoBSC, MS DM58/Letter Book/37.

even before war was declared, though buyers withheld their money, awaiting confirmation one way or the other.

This same phenomenon occurred again in 1790 with the Nootka Sound Crisis. Late in 1789, the British government received reports that a fur-trading post at Nootka Sound, near what is now Vancouver Island, had been dismantled by the Spanish. In a bid to claim the whole of the Pacific Ocean as their own, the Spanish had captured two British ships. When news reached Britain, it caused uproar. Pitt began mobilising the Navy in response, and by the spring of 1790, at the height of the crisis, a considerable fleet was formed.[17] This seriously disrupted shipping as sailors were impressed. In July 1790 the *English Chronicle* reported that a 'hot press' had resulted in the impressment of '700 sailors', stripping 'all the outward-bound vessels in Kingroad of their hands'.[18] With the threat of war in this case much more potent, the impact on the market was more pronounced. The 'alarming State of affairs' brought a halt to the market, resulting in a 'dreadful check to all mercantile undertakings'. The price of sugar rose, and Tobin & Pinney excitedly informed a client that sugar promised 'to fetch exceeding good prices, as they have risen several shillings since the Rumour of a War'. Despite being 'in as much suspense as ever as to War or Peace, Under the idea of War however Sugars bear a great price at present'. The market broke high with some sugars selling at around 57s–67s as a result of the expectation of war, which compounded with the expectation of a low crop from Jamaica.[19]

Yet the uncertainty over whether war was going to be declared or not meant that sales were few. Tobin & Pinney reported that the sugar market was 'very dull', with 'both Sellers and buyers ... very shy', as the market remained 'in such a state of uncertainty'. Over the summer, markets were in suspense, with 'War or Peace still as uncertain as ever'. Owing to the 'very critical state of the Sugar Market', the firm asked John Warren, its insurance broker in London, to 'give us a line twice a Week ... to let us know how the prices begin on Tuesday' and how they 'finish on Friday and the days between'.[20] The few sales that were made were reportedly due to 'the dealings of Speculators', who were buying up sugar in the hope of a declaration of

---

17 Rodger, *Command of the Ocean*, pp. 364–65; Knight, *Britain Against Napoleon*, pp. 13–15.
18 Rogers, ed., *Manning the Royal Navy*, p. 131.
19 Tobin & Pinney to George Lowman, 10 June 1790, Tobin & Pinney to Ulysses Lynch, 4 August 1790, Tobin & Pinney to Edward Brazier, 14 June 1790, and Tobin & Pinney to John Arthurton Senior, 24 June 1790, UoBSC, MS DM58/Letter Book/38.
20 Note that a coach from Bristol and London could, thanks to John Palmer's innovation in 1784, take as little as 16 hours to reach its destination. See 'Mail Coaches', *The*

war and, thus, further price rises. By November, the market was still 'a little flat, but we are in hopes of a brisk sale again soon, if things continue to bear the same warlike appearance'.[21] James Sutton similarly expected sales soon, thinking that the refiners must be running low on stocks.[22] These hopes were not realised. By October 1790, the Spanish, waiting for French support that never materialised, realised that they could not match Britain's naval supremacy and backed down. Pitt received word of the capitulation in November and demobilised the fleet in response.[23] The revelation that peace was certain led 'to a fall of about 2[s] or 3[s] to the Sugar-market'.[24] The situation was the same in London: when the talk was all war, little business was done. Though the sellers did not immediately lower the price after news of the peace convention arrived, eventually the price fell by around 2s 6d–3s.[25] Again, the uncertainty saw a rise in prices as sellers hoped for war, while buyers waited, hoping that the result would be peace. The uncertainty brought about a high, but—crucially—dull market for several months. The confirmation of peace brought some certainty back to the market, and, though prices were lower, buyers were again buying.

These events show how the expectation of a transition could affect the market. The expectation of the oncoming peace following the American Revolution led to a fall in prices. Merchants waited until the peace was confirmed before authorising the sale of their sugar. Similarly, in 1787 and 1790, anticipation of war caused price rises, but refiners held back from the market, waiting for confirmation one way or the other. This uncertainty is important. Historians have noted how the threat of war could raise prices, as Richard Pares has for 1787 and 1790.[26] Yet Pares does not acknowledge that high prices did not matter if no sales were made. Until war was confirmed—and high prices were, thus, set to continue—buyers held back.

Post Museum, <https://www.postalmuseum.org/collections/mail-coaches/> [accessed 29 January 2023].

21 Tobin & Pinney to B. & T. Boddington & Co., 13 and 23 July 1790, Tobin & Pinney to Edward Brazier, 4 August 1790, Tobin & Pinney to John Warren, 14 October 1790, and Tobin & Pinney to Ulysses Lynch, and George Webbe Junior, 1 November 1790, UoBSC, MS DM58/Letter Book/38.

22 James Sutton to William Dickinson, 11 November 1790, SHC, MS DD/DN/4/2/33(2).

23 Rodger, *Command of the Ocean*, pp. 364–65; Knight, *Britain Against Napoleon*, pp. 15–17.

24 Tobin & Pinney to Edward Brazier, 19 November 1790, UoBSC, MS DM58/Letter Book/38.

25 Stephen & Rose Fuller to William Dickinson, 21 October 1790 and 11 November 1790, and Rose Fuller to William Dickinson, 6 November 1790, SHC, MS DD/DN/4/2/33(1)–33(2).

26 Pares, *West-India Fortune*, pp. 195–96.

Bristol and the collapse of the European sugar economy

The disruption felt in the preceding decade paled in comparison to that felt from 1791. Before then, the British sugar market was the only real market for British West India sugar. The British islands barely had a foothold in Europe owing to the dominance of Saint Domingue, which accounted for two-thirds of all French sugar production. Production in Saint Domingue surpassed production in Jamaica, if not the entire British West Indies, as early as the 1740s.[27] Yet the revolutions in France and Saint Domingue completely changed this. Production in Saint Domingue collapsed, and Europe was left without its major supplier. A period of uncertainty followed as the world sugar economy transitioned into a new phase. What was a crisis for French merchants and planters turned out to be a golden opportunity for their British counterparts. It led to an elevation of sugar prices, which was followed by a sharp increase in production. More sugar was being imported into Britain than ever before, and more was being re-exported. Yet the transition to this state was a source of uncertainty. It took time for buyers and sellers to adjust to the new normal, especially as the government intervened to control prices. Other sugar producers, significantly those in the East Indies, also sought to take advantage of the high prices in Britain's sugar markets, though this was not realised on any substantial scale. By 1793, it was the West India merchants and planters who seemed set to benefit from this crisis.

With the Saint Domingue Revolution came a sharp reduction in Europe's sugar supply. Bordeaux, which had been the largest re-exporter of sugar to the rest of Europe, was suddenly disconnected. Hamburg and other continental entrepots turned to suppliers from Britain.[28] Britain suddenly became very interested in European consumption; re-exporters became a significant source of demand in Bristol's market. The price incentive was powerful and led to increased production in the sugar colonies. Production in Jamaica increased dramatically—by some estimates doubling—from 1792 to 1805. This was more a result of the increase in the number of plantations rather than an increase in output per plantation, though there were important improvements, including the adoption of the Otaheite cane, which also contributed to the increase in the quantity of sugar produced.[29] Yet the old

---

27 Ragatz, *Planter Class*, pp. 123–26; Burnard and Garrigus, *Plantation Machine*, pp. 34–36.
28 Marzagalli, 'Trade Networks', p. 812; Crouzet, 'Wars', p. 569; Sydney G. Checkland, 'Finance for the West Indies, 1780–1815', *The Economic History Review*, 10:3 (1958), 461–69 (pp. 461–62).
29 Burnard and Garrigus, *Plantation Machine*, pp. 23–24; Tomich, 'Commodity Frontiers', p. 190; Ryden, *West Indian Slavery*, pp. 221–24. See Chapter 1.

colonies were not the only ones to increase production. Expansion occurred elsewhere in the Caribbean basin, significantly in Cuba, and in the Dutch colonies of Essequibo, Demerara, and Berbice.[30] This also led to a substantial disruption of Bristol's market in that year. Fewer firms were importing, but there was more competition between those who were: the share of the largest importers decreased, while the share of those importing at least 3% of the sugar increased. These 11 firms together had a larger share of imports—over 85%—while the share of the largest importers declined. The largest importer that season, Thomas Daniel & Son, imported only 10% of the total sugar, while the top five largest importers had their share reduced to 50%, both of which were the lowest shares for the largest importers recorded in this period.[31] The Revolution therefore led to an increase in prices (which, apart from a pullback in 1794, was sustained throughout the 1790s), an increase in production across the American tropics, and a new reliance on the European market in Britain.

On the eve of the Revolution in the colonies, the market in Bristol was still recovering from the Nootka Sound Crisis. In January 1791, however, the market was looking up. Prices ranged from 61s for brown to 78s for good sugars. In February, Tobin & Pinney reflected on the 'late amazing start' in the sugar market that had added '8[s] or 10[s] [per cwt] to their price'. The causes were as yet unclear. In March, news arrived of 'confusion in the French Sugar Colonies, which last has occasion'd a general and unprecedented scarcity all over the Continent'. Yet this was met by the usual flatness and decline over the summer. Prices continued at around 60s–70s in June. Then news arrived in October of the slave uprising that had taken place in August. The market remained flat after that summer's importation, but it was hoped that 'some recent accounts of a very alarming & ruinous insurrection of the Slaves in St Domingo will ... prove a cause ... of their getting brisk again'.[32] At the same time, there were understandable fears that what happened in Saint Domingue

---

30 Francois Crouzet, 'America and the Crisis of the British Imperial Economy, 1803–1807', in *The Early Modern Atlantic Economy*, ed. by John J. McCusker and Kenneth Morgan (Cambridge: Cambridge University Press, 2000), pp. 278–318 (pp. 278–81); Ryden, *West Indian Slavery*, p. 250; Tomich, 'Commodity Frontiers', pp. 199–208.

31 See Table 3.3 in Chapter 3. Tobin & Pinney imported approximately 6,864 cwt of sugar in that period, 2.8% of the total. Database built from BA, MS SMV/7/1/1/72-83 WB.

32 Tobin & Pinney to Charles Chabert, 29 January 1791, Tobin & Pinney to John Budgen, 21 February 1791, Tobin & Pinney to Edward Brazier, 7 March 1791, Tobin & Pinney to Joseph Chabert, 14 June 1791, and Tobin & Pinney to Charles Maies, 24 October 1791, UoBSC, MS DM58/Letter Book/38.

would happen elsewhere in the British West Indies, especially in Jamaica.[33] Tobin & Pinney requested information from John Warren, writing

> As we conceive the late melancholy and alarming acct from St Domingo must considerably affect the Sugar Market we shall be obliged to you to give us a line or two on the subject once a week or on any Sudden turn. We presume the holders will <u>keep back</u> at least till it is known how this news is likely to affect the foreign Markets[34]

Tobin & Pinney thus anticipated that the sellers would withhold their sugar until the full impact of the event was digested, and that the news, alarming as it was in itself, would be good for prices.

It took some time for buyers to come around to the realisation that the economy had significantly changed. The Fullers reported to William Dickinson in October that the London market remained flat owing to a lack of foreign demand. They hoped that the news from the West Indies would lead to some start in the market.[35] Coffee, along with cotton (both commodities for which Saint Domingue had dominated production), had already taken a 'surprising start'. Tobin & Pinney was able to unload some of its clients' cotton bales.[36] Yet while the sugar market was not yet brisk, prices had certainly responded to the news. Merchants, anticipating the scarcity, were asking for 72s for brown and up to 84s for fine sugar. By November, with sugar prices 'higher than ever', the buyers had started to give in. There were hopes, expressed by Tobin & Pinney, that 'England bids fair to be the great market for sugars for some years to come'.[37] Buyers had waited until the full extent of the situation was known, and until the uncertainty of what this new sugar economy would look like had passed. The scarcity turned out to be real, and, now competing with refiners in Europe, they faced a higher market.

The transition was not yet complete, however, and the uncertainty had not yet passed. In the wake of high prices, refiners and grocers lobbied for government intervention and held back from the market in anticipation of the government's response. This intervention was not looked upon kindly

---

33 Caleb Dickinson to William Dickinson, 22 January and 6 March 1792, SHC, MS DD/DN/4/2/37(1); Petley, *White Fury*, pp. 165–67.
34 Tobin & Pinney to John Warren, 1 November 1791, UoBSC, MS DM58/Letter Book/38.
35 Rose Fuller to William Dickinson, 22 October 1791, and Stephen & Rose Fuller to William Dickinson, 27 October 1791, SHC, MS DD/DN/4/2/35(3).
36 Tobin & Pinney to Joseph Chabert, 24 October 1791, and Tobin & Pinney to Archibald Washington, 25 October 1791, UoBSC, MS DM58/Letter Book/38.
37 Tobin & Pinney to Monsieur Texier, 17 November 1791, and Tobin & Pinney to Jens Freidenreich Hage, 25 November 1791, UoBSC, MS DM58/Letter Book/38.

by the merchants. Tobin & Pinney commented with disdain that the government would 'be forced, for the sake of preserving their popularity, to attend to the cries of the Mob'.[38] The government had already raised the duty on sugar in 1791 to 15 s/cwt (it had previously been raised to 12s 3²/₅d in 1782 and then to 12s 4d in 1787). The drawback, which was essentially a rebate for goods exported, was kept equal to the duty. The drawback on refined sugars was maintained at 26s.[39] The government reassessed these levels in light of the sudden price rise, and buyers held back as they did so. In the spring, the markets were 'at a Stand, owing to the uncertainty of what may be done by the Ministry towards lowering the prices, in consequence of the popular murmurs and discontents'. The uncertainty continued until June 1792, when an Act to regulate the drawbacks was passed. The price at that point remained high, but whether it would rise or fall was unclear. Consumption had decreased.[40] Just as buyers and sellers waited for the confirmation of peace in 1783 and the confirmation of war or peace in 1787 and 1790, they awaited news on how the government planned to regulate prices.

The new Act created a threshold past which the domestic price of sugar had to pass before the drawback would be suspended. The relevant price of sugar was determined by the calculation of an average over a six-week period, which merchants watched closely.[41] It was integrated in a staggered manner: for the first period, the threshold was 60s (pre-duty), for the second it was 55s, and for the rest it was to be 50s. Direct export from the West Indies to Europe under the 1739 Act was suspended.[42] Many of those connected to the West Indies were sceptical of government intervention; the London West India Society opposed it.[43] Tobin & Pinney expected the price of sugar to 'sink considerably at once' if it surpassed the threshold.[44] Yet the Act was not as harmful as they expected. Tobin & Pinney informed a client that

---

38 Tobin & Pinney to William Jones, 17 March 1792, UoBSC, MS DM58/Letter Book/38.
39 Tobin & Pinney to Edward Brazier, 7 March 1791, and Tobin & Pinney to Nicholas Richards, 14 March 1791, UoBSC, MS DM58/Letter Book/38; Ragatz, *Planter Class*, pp. 189–90.
40 Tobin & Pinney to Edward Brazier, 17 March 1792, and Tobin & Pinney to Ulysses Lynch, 14 June 1792, UoBSC, MS DM58/Letter Book/38.
41 Rose Fuller to William Dickinson, 23 August 1792, and 6 November 1792, SHC, MS DD/DN/4/2/38(1)–39.
42 Ragatz, *Planter Class*, pp. 206–07.
43 David Beck Ryden, 'Sugar, Spirits, and Fodder: The London West India Interest and the Glut of 1807–15', *Atlantic Studies*, 9:1 (2012), 41–64 (p. 52).
44 Tobin & Pinney to Edward Brazier, 4 July 1792, UoBSC, MS DM58/Letter Book/38.

Mr Pitt's regulating Bill which was so much dreaded in the West Indies has we really believe hitherto done us more good than harm by a temporary check to the price of Sugars which has encouraged and renewed the <u>Consumption</u> again which had abated before in a very serious and alarming degree[45]

Prices continued at 60s–84s. The Act had checked the rise in prices but kept them high.[46] Significantly, the very passage of the bill had injected certainty into the market—certainty that the price, though high, could go no higher. Buyers came forward because they did not expect the price to change. Briskness—that crucial element—was restored.

The West India communities were not the only ones interested in the fall of Saint Domingue and the new-found demand from the Continent. Sugars were entering Britain from the East for the first time. The first trial shipments arrived in 1789, and 1791 saw the first major shipment. Refiners and consumers welcomed these imports, hoping that they would keep prices in check.[47] Tobin and Pinney noted the first importations, and, like other West India men, connected it to the abolitionist movement, which was increasing in strength.[48] They kept a watchful eye on the impact of East India shipments, which, as they noted with trepidation, 'begins … to be very sensibly felt'. In December 1793, this import increased 'more than was expected'.[49] The fears that East India sugar would somehow supplant the West were not realised, however. Imports from the East, by David Ryden's estimate, only comprised 3.6% of all imports into Britain in 1794–1795. Further, the West India merchants responded quickly to the danger. They demanded protection, which they received in the form of a duty structure that heavily favoured West Indian produce. The East Indian sugars were first entered under the same rate as East India manufactures, which stood at £37 16s 3d per £100 ad valorem, and then were held there. With prices as high as they were, the tax structure thus favoured West Indian imports. The West India merchants, at least until the prices took a downward turn, had the upper hand on the British market.[50] East India

---

45 Tobin & Pinney to John Taylor, 10 September 1792, UoBSC, MS DM58/Letter Book/38.
46 Tobin & Pinney to Nicholas Richards, 18 September 1792, UoBSC, MS DM58/Letter Book/38.
47 Ragatz, *Planter Class*, pp. 209–10; Ryden, *West Indian Slavery*, p. 121.
48 Tobin & Pinney to Nicholas Richards, 14 March 1791, UoBSC, MS DM58/Letter Book/38.
49 Tobin & Pinney to William Jones, 10 September 1793, and Tobin & Pinney to Edward Brazier, 2 December 1793, UoBSC, MS DM58/Letter Book/39.
50 Ryden, *West Indian Slavery*, pp. 120–23; Ragatz, *Planter Class*, pp. 209–12, 289.

sugars, therefore, had little impact on overall supply and did not depress the high price of sugar.⁵¹

The Saint Domingue Revolution upended the global sugar economy. Black freedom from enslavement was catastrophic for white French merchants and planters, but was a considerable boon for their British West India counterparts, who found themselves as near enough Europe's sole sugar suppliers. Prices rose significantly in British markets, including Bristol's. The transition was not smooth and was fraught with uncertainty. The source of uncertainty came first as the impact of the scarcity was realised, and then as the government intervened to prevent prices from rising higher. Buyers returned to the market once it was clear that the scarcity was real, and once the government had administered its intervention. With high prices destined to continue, buyers came forward, and West India planters and merchants could enjoy their new-found prosperity. But for how long could this last?

War in Europe and the West Indies

With Britain and France at war not long after the Saint Domingue Revolution, one might have expected the prosperity of Britain's West India merchants to soon evaporate. The outlook was, indeed, negative; merchants expected the worst, and this affected lending decisions, as we shall see in the next chapter. Yet war was not a source of price uncertainty—rather, war brought with it the certainty of sustained high prices. Uncertainty came from the transition into war (just as it came from the transition out of war) and with the occasional expectation of a return to peace. The seasonal flow of the market was still the same, with the exception that ships were now arriving in convoys, which amplified the seasonal rhythms of arrivals.⁵² As Julian Hoppit has observed, 'the convoy system, which offered reassurance and protection, led to highly distorted markets because of the way the system encouraged gluts'.⁵³ Yet this distortion has been overstated. Merchants were able to ride out these larger gluts in much the same way as they rode out gluts that occurred in peacetime. Price fluctuations were still more dependent on

---

51 East India sugars would take on a greater role in the debates over abolition and emancipation that occurred from the 1800s to the 1820s, especially with the East India Company's insistence that its sugar was created using 'free labour'. See Scanlan, *Slave Empire*, p. 245; Bronwen Everill, *Not Made by Slaves: Ethical Capitalism in the Age of Abolition* (Cambridge, MA: Harvard University Press, 2020), pp. 160–67.
52 See Chapter 2.
53 Hoppit, *Risk and Failure*, p. 128.

the overall size of the crop and the expectation of what this might be, rather than on seasonal fluctuations in supply.

Issues with convoys were outweighed by the other problems caused by warfare. Some of this was unique to the post-1791 world. First, the new dependence on the European market made the markets in Britain more liable to disruption from conflict on the Continent. Yet, as we shall see, it was the rising price in Britain, which triggered the government's price threshold, that had a bigger impact on British exports. Secondly, with French forces present in the West Indies, the source of British sugar was under threat. This was mitigated again, however, with the strengthening of British forces, which turned out to be a greater threat to the French islands. Indeed, the capture of French islands was seen as a potential source of opportunity. Finally, the scarcity of grains that came about with warfare was problematic for the sugar colonies. Again, however, this was mitigated by the government regulation of distilleries, which brought renewed demand for sugar and rum, alongside the reopening of trade with the United States, which helped to alleviate shortages of provisions in the islands. In the end, merchants were, for the most part, able to use their previous experience of trading in wartime and their knowledge of the market to anticipate price patterns and withhold sugar from the market. The rising price of sugar brought about by the collapse of Saint Domingue far surpassed the increasing costs of warfare. This meant that plantations, in some cases, were more profitable during the war than they had been before. War, rather than a source of uncertainty, was a period of manageable disruption.

The declaration of war alleviated the uncertainty that had grown in the build-up to the conflict. Once war was declared, Tobin & Pinney reported a rise in the price of sugar and a start in the market. This coincided with the late winter scarcity. The firm informed its London correspondents that 'Sugars are up with us 6[s] or 7[s] within this fortnight and still on the rise, tho' we have very few left, not more than 500 or 600 hhds'. It sold 17 hogsheads of William Colhoun's sugars 'owing to a sudden start in the Market from the apparent certainty of a War'.[54] As the markets became adjusted to the new normal, buyers expected prices to persist at their current high level, if not to rise further, and so came forward. The new source of uncertainty was the expectation of peace. Tobin & Pinney commented in December 1795, for example, that 'public affairs seem to wear a more promising aspect, and the hopes of peace seem better founded'. This led to a low in the market, which, in January, 'continued to droop'. In March, with sugars 'getting scarce' and

---

54 Tobin & Pinney to Boddingtons & Bettesworth, 10 February 1793, and Tobin & Pinney to William Colhoun, 12 February 1793, UoBSC, MS DM58/Letter Book/39.

'no talk of peace at present', the 'late flatness in the market' was ebbing away, and sugars were 'gradually rising again' as peace seemed less likely.[55] The market in wartime was, thus, in this respect a mirror image of its state in peacetime. During peace the expectation of war raised prices and brought a stillness to the market; during war the expectation of peace lowered prices and brought a stillness.

The market in Bristol continued to be affected by London, just as it was during the peace. There was a flatness in the market in Bristol in December 1794 that was attributed by John Fisher Weare to a fall of 2s in the London market the month before.[56] Similarly, in December 1796, Tobin & Pinney attributed the 'extremely dull' market in Bristol to 'the great fall in the London Market'.[57] Merchants in Bristol continued to seek information about London, albeit with greater appetite. Tobin & Pinney began receiving frequent samples of sugar alongside the price information so it could assess not just how different grades were selling, but how the quality was being interpreted.[58] Buyers would still exploit differences between the markets. When London was lower for fine sugars, for example, grocers went there instead.[59] Similarly, Tobin & Pinney began sending its brown sugars to London to be sold by its brokers in 1800 (it had agents there who could warehouse and sell them). London still led Bristol in price movements, and Tobin & Pinney's strategy for managing this was, in essence, much the same, while buyers and sellers continued to exploit the differences between the two markets.

Markets remained much the same in terms of their seasonal rhythms. Ships now arrived in convoys, but still came during the summer months. As several historians have argued, the arrival of convoys would glut the market and depress prices.[60] This is often stated as if it were a general rule, but the price data show that this was not always the case. As Figure 4.1 shows,

---

55 Tobin & Pinney to Joseph Chabert, 15 December 1795, Tobin & Pinney to John Lyons, 23 January 1796, and Tobin & Pinney to John Taylor & Edward Brazier 14 March 1796, UoBSC, MS DM58/Letter Book/39.

56 John Fisher Weare to William Dickinson, 11 November, 1 and 13 December 1794, SHC, MS DD/DN/4/2/42(2)–42(5).

57 Tobin, Pinney & Tobin to George Webbe Junior, 15 December 1796, UoBSC, MS DM58/Letter Book/40.

58 See numerous letters to John Warren and others, including Thomas Latham & Sons, Richard White, and Coles, Godwin & Coles, UoBSC, MS DM58/Letter Book/39–40.

59 Tobin & Pinney to John Hendrickson, 20 August 1793, and Tobin & Pinney to Edward Brazier, 4 May 1794, UoBSC, MS DM58/Letter Book/39.

60 Pares, *West-India Fortune*, pp. 196–97; Morgan, *Bristol*, p. 203; Hoppit, *Risk and Failure*, p. 128.

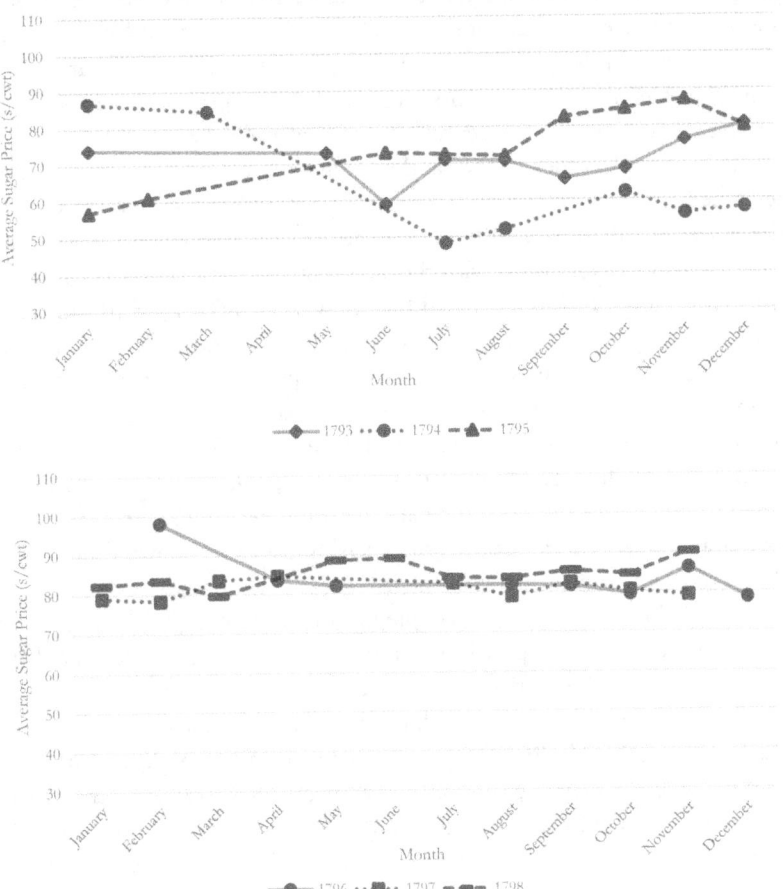

Figure 4.1: Average Monthly Price of Sugar by Year, 1793–1798 (s/cwt)

Source: Kenneth Morgan, *Bristol and the Atlantic Trade in the Eighteenth Century* (Cambridge: Cambridge University Press, 1993), p. 210.

during the French Revolutionary Wars, convoys only had an impact for the first few years, with significant dips occurring during the summer in 1793 and 1794. For the other years, the price remained stable. Prices even increased over 1795. Where the convoys did have an impact, merchants were able to use their ability to withhold sugar from the market to ride out the gluts and short-term depressive effects.

The decreasing impact of the convoys is confirmed by Tobin & Pinney's experience. In 1793, 'the Sugar market was never known so dull', as both buyers and sellers awaited the first convoys. Tobin & Pinney was unsure as to 'what may be the case when large Convoys arrive all at once' from Jamaica and from the Leeward Islands, but it feared a glut so great 'that the prices must fall considerably'.[61] Information on its size and time of arrival was eagerly awaited.[62] When the first sugars arrived, those 'which happened to be <u>first</u> landed out of the Leeward Island fleet, sold the best' before the rest of the fleet could unload. The market soon experienced a 'natural fall', and remained in 'an unsettled state' as more fleets were expected. By October, the price had fallen by 8s–10s from its height.[63] The situation was similar in London as prices fell 3s–4s with the arrival of the Leeward Island fleet.[64] At this point, Tobin & Pinney hoped that 'now the whole import is ascertained it may look up again'. The situation in 1793 was unique, owing to a run of failures and a strain on credit that meant 'some importers' had 'want … for ready money'. They were forced into a sale 'contrary to their inclination', pressurised by the 'unprecedented check given to Credit' and the 'numerous failures' that followed. Many were therefore unable to step back from the market. Tobin & Pinney, whose financial position was more secure, held back its sugars until the full extent of the fleets' impact was known. The firm 'let those <u>force</u> a Sale who may feel themselves under the disagreeable <u>necessity</u> to do so'.[65] John Fisher Weare adopted a similar strategy.[66] Though the glut was large, with more ships arriving at once, merchants that could hold their sugars back from the market did so, just as they did in peacetime.

The imports of 1794 and 1795 show the weakening impact of convoys. The market was dull in April 1794, though prices remained high, with the main fleet not due for several months. It remained dull over the summer. Tobin & Pinney remarked in August that 'buyers … of Sugar seem for some time past to have confined themselves to such supplies only as they absolutely

---

61 Tobin & Pinney to John Warren, 27 March 1793, Tobin & Pinney to Edward Brazier, 14 May 1793, and Tobin & Pinney to William Colhoun, 17 July, UoBSC, MS DM58/Letter Book/39.

62 James Sutton to William Dickinson, 31 August 1793, SHC, MS DD/DN/4/2/41(2).

63 Tobin & Pinney to James Huggins, 20 August 1793, Tobin & Pinney to Walter Maynard and John Smith, 11 September 1793, Tobin & Pinney to George Lowman, 13 October 1793, UoBSC, MS DM58/Letter Book/39.

64 Stephen & Rose Fuller to William Dickinson, 14 August 1793, SHC, MS DD/DN/4/2/41(2).

65 Tobin & Pinney to Edward Brazier, 23 October 1793, Tobin & Pinney to William Jones, 10 September 1793, Tobin & Pinney to Walter Maynard, 11 September 1793, and Tobin & Pinney to George Webbe, 2 October 1793, UoBSC, MS DM58/Letter Book/39.

66 John Fisher Weare to William Dickinson, 3 September 1793, SHC, MS DD/DN/4/2/41(2).

could not do without' as they anticipated a fall in prices.⁶⁷ As Figure 4.1 shows, the market, by July, had dipped substantially. This changed as the full importation became clear, however: the islands had produced a 'short import', which meant that prices 'got up a little' by October. The rise continued into April 1795, while expectations of a fall over the summer that year were not realised. The price was bolstered by the capture of several ships from the Jamaica fleet and slave uprisings in St Vincent and Grenada.⁶⁸ Figure 4.1 shows the price continuing to rise throughout 1795 from its low in 1794. Though the convoys had a short-term depressive effect on the market, by 1795 this was weakening. It was, in the end, the overall size of the crop and the state of demand that had a greater effect, as merchants continued to wait out lows. The import of 1795 shows that other wartime issues, which I will come on to later, outweighed the short-term gluts of convoys.

In 1796, the market continued to withstand the short-term effects of convoys. It was dull in May, with the fleets expected in mid-July. The price was anticipated to be favourable, though the arrival of both 'the Jamaica and Leeward Island Fleets, nearly about the same time' was expected to dent the market. This did not materialise. As it happened, the market was 'not much reduced in price', with highs of 74s–90s by September.⁶⁹ There was no depressive effect, but rather a renewed briskness. Sugars were selling at 80s–90s, despite some flatness when London fell below Bristol in price. There was a minor decline in October, which the firm attributed to 'the arrival of so much Sugar nearly at the same time'; but while this led to a dullness as buyers expected a fall, prices remained at 78s–88s into November. The dullness extended into December as buyers held back. This was a familiar standoff that both merchants and refiners were used to, and prices began advancing in January as merchants refused to give way.⁷⁰ The arrival of the first fleet had no depressive effect, while the later arrivals caused a damp as

---

67 Tobin & Pinney to William Innes, 11 April 1794, and Tobin & Pinney to Joseph Chabert, 6 August 1794, UoBSC, MS DM58/Letter Book/39. See also Ragatz, *Planter Class*, p. 208.

68 Tobin & Pinney to John Lyons, 21 October 1794, Tobin & Pinney to John Budgen, 7 April 1795, Tobin & Pinney to Jeffery Shaw, 18 July 1795, and Tobin & Pinney to George Webbe, 15 October 1795, UoBSC, MS DM58/Letter Book/39.

69 Tobin, Pinney & Tobin to Jeffery M. Shaw, 27 May 1796, Tobin, Pinney & Tobin to William Woodley, 25 July 1796, Tobin, Pinney & Tobin to Samuel Athill, 5 September 1796, and Tobin, Pinney & Tobin to Joseph Lyons Walrond, 7 September 1796, UoBSC, MS DM58/Letter Book/40.

70 Tobin, Pinney & Tobin to John Warren, 25 September 1796 and 13 December 1796, Tobin, Pinney & Tobin to John Hendrickson, 5 October 1796, and Tobin, Pinney & Tobin to John Taylor & Edward Brazier, 2 November 1796, Tobin, Pinney & Tobin to John Budgen, 27 January 1797, UoBSC, MS DM58/Letter Book/40.

buyers expected a fall. The fall did not materialise in the way that they had hoped. Merchants who had withheld their sugars to wait out this glut found themselves rewarded for their patience.

Convoys continued to lose their potency in the following years, too. In 1797, the market was dull in June in anticipation of the new fleets, and little was being done in July after the first arrivals. Prices were maintained at 76s–94s, though the expectation of the Jamaica fleet kept buyers back from the market even after the Leeward Islands fleet arrived. Though the eventual arrival of the Jamaica fleet 'caused a damp in the Market, we [Tobin & Pinney] do not think the prices much reduced', with sugars still selling at 73s–93s. Prices were maintained, with many 'of the first Quality' sugars sent to Ireland.[71] By Christmas, the market had become flat, though Tobin & Pinney thought 'it will be more brisk, as we have no reason to think Sugars will fall'. In January 1798, the flatness continued, though 'prices are looking up'. Eventually, the refiners' stocks of sugars were run down, and by May, sugars were scarce, with the market continuing 'very high' at 80s–96s.[72] The market continued to reach new heights by 1799, so much so that export controls had to be implemented, with the price of sugar exceeding the threshold. The high prices were sustained thanks to the increase in demand from Europe, and the convoys did little to depress this. When buyers held back from the market, the merchants could wait them out until their stocks ran low, and they were compelled to meet the merchants' prices.

The wartime market therefore remained similar to that in peacetime in many respects. The main source of uncertainty was still periods of transition—this time the shift into war, and the expectation of peace. The market was still led by London, and merchants still sought information on how the London market was performing. Finally, the market retained its seasonal rhythm. Convoys might have caused gluts, especially in the first few years, but these were easily waited out by merchants whose financial position had not been compromised by the financial crisis of 1793. The overall size of the crop still mattered more for the price, especially with production in Saint Domingue at a standstill. As the war progressed, and prices continued to rise, merchants found withholding sugars from the market to be all the more

---

71 Tobin, Pinney & Tobin to George Webbe Junior, 14 June and 14 August 1797, Tobin, Pinney & Tobin to John Warren, 22 July 1797, Tobin, Pinney & Tobin to John Taylor, 31 July 1797, Tobin, Pinney & Tobin to John Lyons, 4 September 1797, and Tobin, Pinney & Tobin to Rowland Burton, 20 September 1797, UoBSC, MS DM58/Letter Book/40.

72 Tobin, Pinney & Tobin to Thomas Latham & Son, 21 December 1797, Tobin, Pinney & Tobin to William Colhoun, 17 January 1798, and Tobin, Pinney & Tobin to John Taylor, 2 May 1798, UoBSC, MS DM58/Letter Book/40.

effective. Indeed, Tobin & Pinney's approach to withholding changed little. They conversed more with planters about their intentions, ascertaining their credit needs, and offered advice. Yet they still made the executive decision of when to sell, weighing up the benefits of withholding against the costs of warehousing and wastage.[73] The standoffs that ensued, familiar to both merchants and refiners before the war, now increasingly went the way of the merchants. High demand from Europe meant that prices were little affected by gluts, and all the merchants had to do was wait until refiners' stocks ran low enough to force them to market.

Other disruptive wartime effects had a greater impact than convoys, though even these were mitigated. Britain's new-found connection to (and dependence upon) the Continental market following the Saint Domingue Revolution was liable to disturbance by the conquests of the French Revolutionary Army, especially early on. Holland, for example, was of ever more importance for British West India merchants.[74] There were early fears that 'the unsettled state of Europe will prevent the Call abroad for Raw Sugars, and be a means of keeping down the Market'.[75] News of developments in Europe had a more pronounced impact, especially at the start of the war.[76] Early French successes in Flanders led to a fall in prices, as it was feared that exports would be prevented. This was a short-term phenomenon: when these fears proved less well founded, the price picked up again.[77] Later invasion fears in 1796 and 1797 led to a flatness in the market, but this too was ephemeral.[78] Tobin & Pinney's direct exposure to the European market was limited. It had one client on St Croix who sent his sugar to Amsterdam, with the proceeds to be remitted to Tobin & Pinney.[79] It had sold sugars 'wanted for exportation' before, but this was infrequent.[80] Events on the Continent

---

73 See Tobin & Pinney to George Webbe, 15 October 1795, UoBSC, MS DM58/Letter Book/39; Tobin, Pinney & Tobin to Charles Payne, 3 September 1796, UoBSC, MS DM58/Letter Book/40.
74 Stephen & Rose Fuller to William Dickinson, 16 August 1794, SHC, MS DD/DN/4/2/42(3).
75 Barnard and William Dickinson to Thomas Salmon, 1 December 1792, SHC, MS DD/DN/4/2/40(1).
76 Pares, *West-India Fortune*, p. 198.
77 Tobin & Pinney to John Taylor & Edward Brazier, 6 and 20 August 1794, UoBSC, MS DM58/Letter Book/39.
78 Tobin, Pinney & Tobin to Henry Berkeley, 5 September 1796, and 26 January 1797, UoBSC, MS DM58/Letter Book/40.
79 Tobin & Pinney to Joseph Chabert, 25 May, 6 August and 24 November 1794, and Tobin & Pinney to Hope & Co., 23 July 1794, UoBSC, MS DM58/Letter Book/39.
80 Pinney & Tobin to John Symonds, 8 December 1787, UoBSC, MS DM58/Letter Book/37.

therefore threatened to impact the market, but, in the end, the effect on Britain's exports to Europe was limited. Markets moved with the rumours, but reverted again when fears were not realised.

Conversely, the movement of prices in Britain had a greater effect on sugar exports to Europe. The price controls that the government had enacted after the Saint Domingue Revolution were triggered in 1798. Prices had continued high into that year after the highs of 1797, with prices standing at 70s–93s in December, rising further even as refiners held back. With the stocks of sugar slowly emptying, a late scarcity raised prices to 80s–96s in May. The summer import had little depressive effect, with prices steady at 78s–94s.[81] The export restrictions had long been triggered, having surpassed their pre-duty threshold, but the price was maintained even as exports were prohibited. The market remained flat as prices reached heights of 78s–98s, and then 80s–100s, before the arrival of the next fleet. Tobin & Pinney commented, however, that 'the Sugar Market is under a temporary depression as the Ports are shut against the exportation of that Article', with buyers waiting for the price to fall.[82] It was, therefore, the continued demand from Europe and within Britain that triggered export controls and thus had the greatest impact on exports, rather than France's continental conquests.

Threats to production in the West Indies further affected the market. Significantly, in 1795, prices were sustained by the slave uprisings in St Vincent and Grenada. The 'unfortunate situation' in these islands, which saw their crops destroyed, coupled with a 'short Crop in the other Islands … contributed to keep up the present high price of Sugars'. Initial reports of the uprising speculated that the French had been involved in helping the 'Rebellious Negroes', which was later confirmed, and some newspapers suspected that St Lucia, Antigua, Nevis, and Montserrat had also been affected. Tobin & Pinney hoped that the accounts would turn out to be exaggerated, but believed that 'something very disagreeable must have happened to give rise to them'.[83] There were similar scenes in Jamaica, with a maroon uprising at the same time.[84] Government intervention again alleviated much of the distress. The British organised 'the biggest expedition ever dispatched from British

---

81 Tobin, Pinney & Tobin to John Taylor, 6 December 1797, and 2 May and 25 August 1798, UoBSC, MS DM58/Letter Book/40.
82 Tobin, Pinney & Tobin to Edward Huggins, 13 November 1798, and Tobin, Pinney & Tobin to Rowland Burton, 9 April 1799, UoBSC, MS DM58/Letter Book/40.
83 Tobin & Pinney to George Webbe, 15 October 1795, and Tobin & Pinney to William Jones, and George Lowman 2 May 1795, UoBSC, MS DM58/Letter Book/39; Duffy, *Soldiers*, p. 370.
84 Petley, *White Fury*, pp. 179–80.

shores' in response.⁸⁵ The uprisings in St Vincent and Grenada were violently put down, and the rebels involved were hanged or deported. Many Caribs, native to St Vincent, and with whom the British settlers had (uneasily) shared the island, were also deported, and their lands were confiscated by the Crown. Furthermore, the government made £1.5m in exchequer bills available to those affected, and offered loans at rates of 5%.⁸⁶ The events were particularly shocking, but their impact on the market served, if anything, only to raise prices—a boon for those unconnected with these particular islands. It had more of an effect on investment in the islands, as we shall see. In the end, it was government intervention that safeguarded the West Indies and contributed to their resilience.

Of further concern to the merchants in Britain was the presence of French forces in the West Indies. In previous wars, the West Indies had become a significant theatre of conflict.⁸⁷ In 1794, there were rumours that St Martin had been plundered by French privateers. Tobin & Pinney wrote to a client on that island expressing concern, hoping that 'there is no truth in this rumour'.⁸⁸ Owing to fears of invasion, John Pinney told his manager to hide business papers and stores of rum and to brick up the cellar so invaders could not loot it.⁸⁹ Yet these fears were assuaged by the presence of British forces, which turned out to be a far greater threat to the French islands. The defence of the islands was a key priority for the British government, which relied on the wealth of the plantation economy as a source of revenue, and which, at the same time, sought to deprive the French of income. Tobago, which was British between 1763 and 1776, and which became French during the American Revolution, was retaken by the British in 1793. Martinique, Guadeloupe, and St Lucia were captured in 1794.⁹⁰ News of the capture of these French islands in 1794 led to a fall in the price of sugar and reduced the briskness of sales as merchants were unsure whether they would be ceded or returned. These islands were recaptured in 1795, and this threw 'a <u>fresh</u> gloom' over the West Indies, showing that the French had reinforced their strength.⁹¹ It motivated a substantial response from the British forces, however. The West Indies were reinforced, and when the Dutch and Spanish were forced to enter

---

85 Duffy, *Soldiers*, p. 370.
86 Ragatz, *Planter Class*, pp. 22–25, 221.
87 Colley, *The Gun*, pp. 26–27.
88 Tobin & Pinney to Joseph Chabert, 15 December 1794, UoBSC, MS DM58/Letter Book/39.
89 MacInnes, *Gateway*, p. 322.
90 On these campaigns, see Duffy, *Soldiers*.
91 Tobin & Pinney to Joseph Chabert, 25 May 1794, and Tobin & Pinney to George Lowman, 17 February 1795, UoBSC, MS DM58/Letter Book/39.

the war on the French side in 1796 and 1797, their colonies became targets: Essequibo, Demerara, and Trinidad were captured.[92] As Patrick Crowhurst summarises, 'in the period 1794–1815, French and Dutch colonies fell one by one into British hands'.[93] The threat of French expansion in the West Indies was, therefore, mitigated by the British offensives in the islands.

This expansion of the British West Indies presented opportunities for British merchants. Tobin & Pinney contacted a French planter in Martinique, to whom it extolled the virtues of Bristol's market over London. This contact was made in speculation, given that it was deeply uncertain whether the islands would be retained (Tobin & Pinney had 'connections with Gentlemen of considerable rank', all of whom were 'unable to form any satisfactory opinion on the subject').[94] As Martinique was recaptured, little appears to have come from this new correspondence. The newly captured territories, especially the former Dutch colonies in South America, experienced an influx of new investment that led to an expansion of production. This was a source of anxiety for some, especially the West India Society of London, which lobbied against the free admission of sugars from these territories (though it failed).[95] Yet these concerns did not reflect the reality: with British markets now heavily dependent on Europe, increased production would have affected all the markets equally, regardless of where the sugars ended up.[96] The capture of territories in the West Indies therefore turned out to be a source of opportunity for British merchants.

The final source of concern attributable to the war with France was the scarcity of grain, which was exacerbated by the increased demand from the army and navy. With the West Indies increasingly dependent on Britain for its food supplies since 1783, this was potentially catastrophic. Poor harvests had exacerbated shortages, with the price of flour rising from 44s a sack in 1794 to 83s in 1795. The government organised the importation of grain from America and Canada, while private merchants also took advantage of high prices.[97] Tobin & Pinney noted this scarcity in its letters to planters. In March 1794, the firm was forbidden from shipping flour or oats by a vessel sailing without convoy owing to government restrictions. Exports were regulated by

---

92 Duffy, *Soldiers*, p. 370; Ragatz, *Planter Class*, pp. 227–29.
93 Crowhurst, *The French War on Trade*, p. 30.
94 Tobin & Pinney to Monsieur Dessalle, 16 November 1794, UoBSC, MS DM58/Letter Book/39.
95 Checkland, 'Finance', pp. 462–63; Ryden, 'Sugar', pp. 52–55; Ragatz, *Planter Class*, p. 229.
96 This observation was made by contemporary Joseph Marryatt. See Ryden, 'Sugar', pp. 53–54.
97 Emsley, *British Society*, p. 7; Knight, *Britain Against Napoleon*, pp. 157–58.

quotas, but there were exemptions for exports to the colonies. It was rarely clear in advance whether these exemptions would be enacted, however. Each Customs district set its quotas each quarter, and these might not be sufficient: in January 1796, Tobin & Pinney commented that 'the quantity of Flour in [George Webbe's] last order was engrossed in a day or two'. The situation in the West Indies was becoming untenable. By 1795, Tobin & Pinney noted the 'great scarcity, and high price of everything in the West Indies'.[98] The scarcity of grain was, therefore, one of the most significant threats facing the West Indies, perhaps more so than French forces.

The scarcity was alleviated by the reopening of trade with the United States. When Britain and the United States failed to agree on trading terms involving the West Indies in the 1794 Jay Treaty, trade remained on 1788 terms, with their emergency clauses. These exemptions to the regulations, used frequently before the war, were used almost constantly from 1793 as Canada proved unable to supply adequate provisions and as supplies from Britain and Ireland became increasingly costly. The United States could provide grain and timber more cheaply than Canada, and, unlike the British and British colonial shipping, its vessels were not at risk from French privateers. Fish from Newfoundland was sent to the West Indies via New England to take advantage of American neutrality (the Americans shipped it more cheaply, too).[99] Tobin & Pinney found it 'some comfort ... that the Ports are opened in all the Islands to American and other Neutral Vessels'.[100] William and Barnard Dickinson wrote to their manager that 'we hope you will not be in want of provisions, had you given the least hint we would have sent Flour or Pease from hence', though adding 'probably you will be better supplied from North America'.[101] This was of great consequence for the islands, which, under threat from significant scarcity, finally obtained the trading relationship with the United States that they had sought since 1783.

In Britain, the government began regulating the distilleries to control their use of grain. The distillation of grain was prohibited in 1795 owing to

---

98 Tobin & Pinney to John Taylor, 22 March 1794, Tobin & Pinney to George Webbe Junior, 1 January 1796, and Tobin & Pinney to John Budgen, 3 October 1795, UoBSC, MS DM58/Letter Book/39.
99 Alice B. Keith, 'Relaxations in the British Restrictions on the American Trade with the British West Indies, 1783–1802', *The Journal of Modern History*, 20:1 (1948), 1–18; Ryden, *West Indian Slavery*, pp. 110–14; Crouzet, 'Crisis', pp. 290–97; Basdeo and Robertson, 'Commercial Experiment', pp. 32–40.
100 Tobin & Pinney to John Lyons, 4 March 1794, UoBSC, MS DM58/Letter Book/39.
101 Barnard and William Dickinson to Thomas Salmon, 4 November 1793, SHC, MS DD/DN/4/2/40(1).

a poor harvest.[102] In this instance, sugar was not permitted to be used in its place, which meant that the market was 'flat and fallen 2[s] or 3[s] which is owing chiefly to the talk in Parliament of a Stop being put to the distilling of Molasses'.[103] Just as it had following the Saint Domingue Revolution, the expectation of government intervention brought a pause to the market. While sugar and molasses did not stand to benefit from this intervention, in the end it was rum that took off. The price soared to 6s 6d–7s 6d per gallon, and it was being sold 'before the Mast'.[104] The high eventually gave way as Spanish brandy, a more pleasant and palatable spirit, expanded its share of the market.[105] Conversely, in 1799, sugar was allowed to be used in distillation when the use of grain was banned. This led to sales of very dark sugars at the bottom of the market that even refiners had very little interest in.[106] Government intervention in markets, by allowing the West Indies to use their emergency clauses and trade with the United States, and by preventing the use of grain in distillation, alleviated much of the distress facing the West India community.

Planters still faced high prices, especially as the war increased costs for plantation necessities. Butter and beef were scarce owing to demand from the army and navy. The price of shoes was raised in 1793 as the journeymen combined for higher wartime wages. The price of coal was increased, too.[107] Tobin & Pinney was also asked to find a blacksmith to send out to Nevis, but the firm found itself competing with the army, which was offering bounties that were comparatively more generous. The cost of shipping was also passed on to planters. Freight rates increased progressively to 125% and 150% of the peacetime rate in 1793, and then to double the peacetime rate in 1795.[108] The shippers needed to increase their freight rates to keep up with the inflating

---

102 Tobin & Pinney to John Taylor & Edward Brazier, 15 December 1795, UoBSC, MS DM58/Letter Book/39; Ryden, *West Indian Slavery*, p. 249; Ragatz, *Planter Class*, p. 290; Emsley, *British Society*, p. 43.
103 Tobin & Pinney to John Lyons, 28 November 1795, UoBSC, MS DM58/Letter Book/39.
104 Tobin & Pinney to John Taylor & Edward Brazier, 15 December 1795, UoBSC, MS DM58/Letter Book/39.
105 Tobin, Pinney & Tobin to Archbald & Williamson, 30 July 1796, UoBSC, MS DM58/Letter Book/40.
106 Tobin, Pinney & Tobin to Nicholas Williams, 17 and 23 December 1799, UoBSC, MS DM58/Letter Book/40.
107 Tobin & Pinney to John Scarbrough, 11 September 1793, Tobin & Pinney to Edward Brazier, 12 November 1795, Tobin & Pinney to Joseph Chabert, 18 March 1793, and Tobin & Pinney to George Webbe, 7 November 1793, UoBSC, MS DM58/Letter Book/39.
108 Tobin & Pinney to John Scarbrough, 25 September 1794 and 25 November 1794, and

cost of hiring seamen. Merchant shippers, facing stiff competition from the Royal Navy, raised wages from 30s to 40s a month, increasing the cost per voyage by an additional £40–50.[109] Some of this was not unique to periods of war. Freight rates increased in 1790 with simply the threat of war, and mobilisation raised the cost of provisions. In 1792, Bristol experienced a delay in ships leaving the port owing to 'no less than a <u>rising</u> of all the Seamen in this Port for an advance of wages'.[110] Yet the increased costs for provisions, freight, and labour sustained during wartime were higher and longer lasting.

However, these costs were outweighed by the increasing price of sugar that was sustained for much of the French Revolutionary Wars. Cursory calculations based on the known prices for freight, insurance, duties, and commission show that the rising costs of war were offset by the rise in the price of sugar, with planters rarely seeing net returns below 30 s/cwt after 1784, and after 1789 never below an average of 35s.[111] While plantations faced other costs, including those for plantation stores, and minor fees, such as brokerage, landwaiters' fees, warehousing fees, and other sundry fixed fees, the returns following the initial deductions left considerable headroom. This initial impression is corroborated by the more extensive estimations of other historians. Ryden has shown that, for this period, gross returns on slave labour remained above 15%, and kept rising up to 1795, and did not fall again below the average gross return for 1752–1807 until 1800.[112] Ward, similarly, estimates that the average rate of profits for 1783–1791 in the Leeward Islands was 12.1%, and 6.4% in Jamaica. After the Saint Domingue Revolution, it went up to 13.9% in Jamaica, and remained at 12% in the Leeward Islands. From 1799, the rate sat at 9.1% in the Leeward Islands and 9.6% in Jamaica.[113] Data from both of these sources are combined by Klas Rönnbäck, who shows that planter income net of the cost of subsistence for the enslaved labourers

---

Tobin & Pinney to Curtis Crippen, 26 October 1795, UoBSC, MS DM58/Letter Book/39; BA, MS SMV/8/3/2/1 WIA.

109 Tobin & Pinney to George Webbe, 8 January 1793, UoBSC, MS DM58/Letter Book/39.

110 Tobin & Pinney to Edward Brazier, 1 and 19 November 1790, and Tobin & Pinney to John Taylor, 3 November 1792, UoBSC, MS DM58/Letter Book/38; Thomas Harris to William Dickinson, 5 January 1791, SHC, MS DD/DN/4/2/36(2).

111 This is based on my own calculations of prices after deducting a 'cost of war' index based on these factors. Data are drawn from the following. Prices: Morgan, *Bristol*, p. 210; duties: Thomas Tooke, *A History of Prices and of the State of Circulation from 1793 to 1837*, Vol. II (London: Longman and others, 1838), p. 414; Ragatz, *Planter Class*, pp. 16, 189–90, 210, 380; Ryden, *West Indian Slavery*, p. 128; freight: Ward, 'Profitability', p. 199; insurance: UoBSC, MS DM58/Account Books/32 and 40.

112 Ryden, *West Indian Slavery*, pp. 234–36.

113 Ward, 'Profitability', p. 204.

increased from 40% of these costs in the 1750s to around 100% in the 1790s.[114] The costs of war, therefore, did not offset the gains that merchants and planters experienced after the Saint Domingue Revolution.

For much of the wartime period, then, things were looking up for the planters and merchants connected to the British West Indies. Merchants in Bristol retained much the same relationship with London. They were able to wait out gluts caused by convoys. The fears that the new dependence on Europe would lead to problems as the French army expanded were not realised, nor were fears of French gains in the West Indies. Issues with scarcities in the islands were relieved by the further reopening of trade between the islands and the United States. This situation did not persist, yet it was not war that brought an end to their prosperity. Rather, it was the same mechanism that had led to this prosperity in the first place: changes in production.

The crisis of overproduction in the West Indies

Just as underproduction after the collapse of Saint Domingue brought about renewed prosperity for British planters and merchants connected to the West Indies, the increase in production as a response turned out to be an overcorrection. The increase in production in the 'old' West Indies was met with increased production in the newly settled, underdeveloped territories. Increasing production in Cuba, Berbice, Demerara, Essequibo, and Brazil led to a world-wide overproduction of sugar that failed to be absorbed by the British and European markets at the same high prices.[115] Brazil and Cuba, especially, benefited from having large tracts of fresh land and rich soil that could be cultivated at lower cost, along with access to American shipping that operated more cheaply than the British shippers. The price crash that followed was a result of overtrading and speculation in the Hamburg market in light of this new import. Thanks to Britain's new-found dependence on the European market, this had repercussions in London, Bristol, Liverpool, and elsewhere. Re-exports declined, even as imports into Britain reached unprecedented heights: 3.5 million cwt in 1799, according to one estimate, compared to 2.2 million in 1797 and 2.7 million in 1798.[116] The price fell in 1799, rebounded in 1800, but continued on a downward trend from thereon.

---

114 Rönnbäck, 'Sweet Business', p. 231.
115 Ryden, *West Indian Slavery*, pp. 15–18, 221–25; Williams, *Capitalism & Slavery*, pp. 148–50; Petley, *White Fury*, pp. 184–85.
116 Ragatz, *Planter Class*, pp. 286–88, 337; Crouzet, 'Crisis', pp. 284–85; Ryden, *West Indian Slavery*, pp. 17–18, 237–39.

This crisis brought about major changes for the merchants of Bristol. First, it signalled that Liverpool was now a market with considerable influence over prices in Bristol. Secondly, it marked the first stage in the decline of planter prosperity that continued until the mid-nineteenth century. Finally, it revealed a flaw in the trading strategy of merchant firms such as Tobin & Pinney. Whereas before they were able to wait out gluts in anticipation of a relatively predictable rise in prices, the crisis, having disrupted the normal pattern of price movements, made withholding difficult and led to a paralysis of indecision.

It was business as usual in early 1799, and merchants were still enjoying the high prices of 1798 that had led to export restrictions. Prices in the late winter were expected to continue high, and the market was expected to remain brisk. The market indeed remained high, though, given that prices were up at 80s–100s, with some very fine sugars selling above 100s, buyers were not as forthcoming as merchants might have liked.[117] The buyers were right to wait. They were vindicated by the arrival of the first fleet, which had an immediate and severe depressive effect on the market. Tobin & Pinney indicated its intention to wait out this glut, as the firm would have before, in anticipation of fresh orders from the Continent. Yet these orders never materialised. Reports came instead that foreign markets were 'amply supplied'. The market became more and more unsettled with new arrivals. Refiners were waiting; brown sugars were hardly selling. Liverpool, whose imports had surpassed Bristol's for the first time, was the first to lower its prices, even as Bristol's merchants attempted to maintain theirs.[118] No new sales were expected in Bristol until Liverpool's market was drained or until they matched Liverpool's prices. Eventually it became clear that Hamburg, and other European markets such as St Petersburg, were 'for the present overstocked'. Refiners were waiting for the fall, coming to the market and buying only what they had immediate need for. Only fine sugars would sell, while the low-quality brown sugars were not selling at all. Markets were sought out in Ireland, to little avail.[119] Browns had fallen to 50s, while fines

---

117 Tobin, Pinney & Tobin to Samuel Boddington, 6 February 1799, Tobin, Pinney & Tobin to Rowland Burton, 9 April 1799, and Tobin, Pinney & Tobin to John Colhoun Mills, 20 April 1799, UoBSC, MS DM58/Letter Book/40.
118 Tobin, Pinney & Tobin to Nicholas Williams, 19 July and 2 August 1799, and Tobin, Pinney & Tobin to John Hendrickson, 20 July 1799, Tobin, Pinney & Tobin to Edward Huggins, 20 July 1799, UoBSC, MS DM58/Letter Book/40; Morgan, *Bristol*, p. 190.
119 Tobin, Pinney & Tobin to John Taylor, 15 August 1799, Tobin, Pinney & Tobin to Nicholas Williams, 17 September 1799, and Tobin, Pinney & Tobin to John Mair, 21 September 1799, UoBSC, MS DM58/Letter Book/40.

were selling no higher than 85s. The fall was so bad that 'Merchants in London have resolved to offer no more Sugar for Sale until there appears to be a real demand for the Article'.[120] They indicated their intention to wait out the glut. This time, with markets in Europe fully supplied from elsewhere, it was the buyers whose patience would be rewarded. It seemed that merchants in Bristol and London would have to follow Liverpool, with its new-found influence, and lower their prices.

The other alternative was to lobby for government intervention. In response to the fall, the London West India Society began lobbying for protectionist measures, while the merchants in Liverpool combined to form their own West India Society.[121] Tobin & Pinney joined in the call for an increase in the bounty for exports and a ban on the distillation of grain. Tobin & Pinney saw little prospect of a rise, especially with such a large import still on hand.[122] While the war on the Continent probably did not help, it was the overstocking of the European markets by American shippers that were importing from the new sugar colonies that had the greatest impact. British planters had rushed to fill the place of Saint Domingue and supply both Britain and Europe. Now, with European demand satiated from elsewhere, in particular Cuba, British planters were left with just the British market to soak up their sugar.[123] The market thus witnessed an unsettling reversal to something approximating its pre-1791 state. With the market flat and prices low, Tobin & Pinney was at a loss as to how to act. The firm sold nothing for several months.[124] It had no idea how the market would develop: the patterns upon which it had become dependent to anticipate future prices no longer held true.

Eventually, the fall in prices was met with a revival of demand. With prices as low as 42s–76s, buyers were now entering the market. Distillers, banned from using grain due to a poor harvest, were buying up the lowest grades of sugar. In the late winter, the market saw a brief resurgence as stocks were low before the arrival of the next fleet. Prices in Bristol had risen to 60s–80s in

---

120 Tobin, Pinney & Tobin to Edward Huggins, 1 October 1799, and Tobin, Pinney & Tobin to John Colhoun Mills, 2 October 1799, UoBSC, MS DM58/Letter Book/40.
121 Ryden, *West Indian Slavery*, pp. 239–42; Sydney G. Checkland, 'American versus West Indian Traders in Liverpool, 1793–1815', *The Journal of Economic History*, 18:2 (1958), 141–60 (p. 145).
122 Tobin, Pinney & Tobin to George Webbe Junior, 2 October 1799, and Tobin, Pinney & Tobin to John Colhoun Mills, 29 October 1799, UoBSC, MS DM58/Letter Book/40.
123 Ryden, *West Indian Slavery*, pp. 251–53.
124 Tobin, Pinney & Tobin to William Colhoun, 13 January [1800], UoBSC, MS DM58/Letter Book/40.

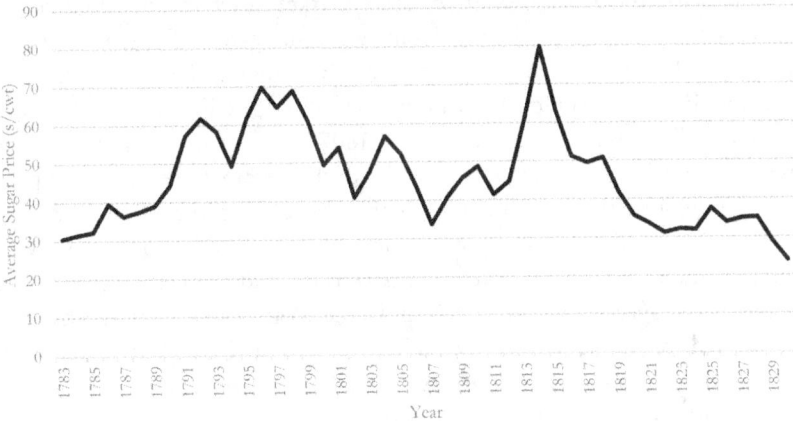

Figure 4.2: Average Annual Price of Muscovado Sugar in London, Before Duties, 1783–1830 (s/cwt)

Source: Thomas Tooke, *A History of Prices and of the State of Circulation from 1793 to 1837*, Vol. II (London: Longman, and others, 1838), p. 414.

early 1800.[125] Yet this resurgence proved fleeting. Liverpool's prices stayed low, and refiners in Bristol, in what was a worrying new development, began buying from the Liverpool market. Though Bristol fell slightly to 58s–75s, the market stayed flat. There was no prospect of an export, and distillers were now allowed to use grain once more. The market picked up over the summer, leading to a renewed optimism. With a new import on the way, however, and little indication that conditions in Europe had changed, the transition was set to continue.[126] The worst fears of overdependence on Europe had thus been realised, not by war, but by overproduction.

Merchants in Bristol were faced with two new realities. First, Liverpool now held significant influence over the market in Bristol. It had, for the first time, surpassed Bristol's market in terms of sugar imports.[127] This realisation left Bristol's merchants contending, in the long term, with their own relative decline, and in the short term, as Tobin & Pinney's experience

---

125 Tobin, Pinney & Tobin to John Warren, 3 December 1799, Tobin, Pinney & Tobin to Nicholas Williams, 17 December 1799, and Tobin, Pinney & Tobin to George Webbe Junior, 24 January 1800, UoBSC, MS DM58/Letter Book/40.

126 Tobin, Pinney & Tobin to John Budgen, 31 January 1800, Tobin, Pinney & Tobin to George Webbe Junior, 29 March 1800, Tobin, Pinney & Tobin to John Colhoun Mills, 4 June 1800, and Tobin, Pinney & Tobin to Joseph Clarke 9 July 1800, UoBSC, MS DM58/Letter Book/40.

127 Morgan, *Bristol*, pp. 188–90.

shows, with the realisation that their market could be manipulated by Liverpool as refiners in Bristol went north in search of sugar. Secondly, the West Indies entered a period of decline from which they would not recover. Prices continued on a downward trend, as Figure 4.2 shows for London. They reached a new low in 1807, even as imports into Britain reached new heights. Furthermore, the decline from 1799 was an impetus for the abolitionist movement, which argued that the slave trade had contributed to the excess of production and that, in order to save the West India planters from themselves, the slave trade had to be abolished.[128] Bar a period of speculation as the Napoleonic Wars came to end, the price continued to tumble as the new additions to the British Empire and Cuba began to out-produce and under-sell Jamaica and the Leeward Islands, and the emancipation movement gained traction.[129]

There was one further effect. The crisis and the unpredictability of prices left merchants such as Tobin and Pinney unsure of how to act. They were no longer capable of making the decision when to sell, so they thrust this responsibility, where they could, back on to their clients. Though there are several examples of this, Tobin & Pinney's response is illustrated best by its sugar sales for William Beckford. Early on in its correspondence with his agents, the firm made it clear that it would sell when it thought the price right.[130] Yet in the midst of the crisis, it made serious errors of judgement. For the sales it did make, Tobin & Pinney found itself justifying its decisions:

> During the whole of the last Season we never had a single offer for them ... owing to their very inferior Quality. ... better Sugars were selling at the same time, both in London and Liverpool, at some Shillings lower ... You must readily see that it is our Interest ... to procure high prices for Sugars consigned to us, tho' it may not always be in our power to do so ... We flatter ourselves however that taking the whole of our Sales of Mr Beckfords Sugars this Year together they will prove equal to the Sales of Sugars of the same Quality either in London or Liverpool

Finally, the firm told him, admitting what had become apparent in the crisis, that 'in times like the present we should be glad to act by the Judgement of our Principals rather than by our own as it would of course ease us of a great share of responsibility'—the responsibility for which it earned its

---

128 See Ryden, *West Indian Slavery*.
129 Ryden, *West Indian Slavery*, ch. 9; Ryden, 'Sugar', p. 52; Ragatz, *Planter Class*, pp. 331–32.
130 Tobin, Pinney & Tobin to Richard Samuel White, 18 January 1797, Tobin, Pinney & Tobin to Henry Wildman, 14 August 1798, and Tobin, Pinney & Tobin to Nicholas Williams, 30 January 1799, UoBSC, MS DM58/Letter Book/40.

commission.¹³¹ This allowed Tobin & Pinney to blame Beckford's agent, Williams: 'we have not had an offer for Mʳ Beckford's 20 hhds Sugar, and as you seem'd to think that Sugars would rise, we thought it imprudent to force a Sale'. It told Williams that 'our disappointment has been owing merely to an Error in Judgement, to which the wisest of us must sometimes be liable'. When the sugars did not sell for 'the price you [Williams] valued them at', Beckford's agents, displeased (whether with Tobin & Pinney or Bristol's market generally), arranged for them to be shipped to Holland.¹³² Tobin & Pinney thrust the responsibility back upon Beckford's agents, blamed the quality of Beckford's sugar, and did what it could to justify its decisions. Yet the firm knew that its ability to read the market had been impaired.

This is echoed in its correspondence with other clients. John Smith Budgen, for example, had little reason to complain when Tobin & Pinney, after the brief resurgence, 'thought it right to guard against a fresh depression, by selling a part of our Stock', because

> we expressed a desire when we had the pleasure of your Society in this Neighbourhood to be favored with your Sentiments, as to the disposal of the very Sugars, the Sales of which you appear so displeased at. If therefore you think, you have suffered by an Error in our Judgement, we have additional cause to regret, that you left us with a discretional power, when you might so easily have given us your explicit directions¹³³

The firm had given him the responsibility for authorising the sales so that it could be absolved of blame. Yet despite this, the firm was on the receiving end of planters' ire, as 'the proprietors have all found reason to complain'.¹³⁴ Tobin & Pinney had performed poorly, but what could it do? As they reflected, 'Merchants were obliged to act at hazard, more than on well grounded Speculations for the future', while 'no decisive reason appear'd to allow that Reduction' in prices which sugars suffered.¹³⁵ Its strategy relied on the market moving in a familiar way, as it had through both the 1780s and 1790s, and on the sustained high prices resulting from a scarcity that

---

131 Tobin, Pinney & Tobin to Nicholas Williams, 23 December 1799, UoBSC, MS DM58/Letter Book/40.
132 Tobin, Pinney & Tobin to Nicholas Williams, 7 and 13 March, 7 June and 2 July 1800, UoBSC, MS DM58/Letter Book/40.
133 Tobin, Pinney & Tobin to John Budgen, 31 January 1800, UoBSC, MS DM58/Letter Book/40.
134 Tobin, Pinney & Tobin to George Webbe Junior, 7 July 1800, UoBSC, MS DM58/Letter Book/40.
135 Tobin, Pinney & Tobin to Joseph Clarke, 30 September 1800, UoBSC, MS DM58/Letter Book/42.

reinforced the potency of withholding sugars from the market. All of this was undone in 1799, leading the merchants to abandon their judgement, relinquish their responsibility, and thrust the decision making back on their clients.

Over the next two years until the Peace of Amiens ended the French Revolutionary Wars, the market vacillated around its downward trend. Bristol's prices recovered over the summer of 1800, but few sales were made. Any rise in prices caused buyers to travel to London for sugars.[136] The markets in Liverpool remained 'much lower'—merchants in Bristol still held out for prices as high as 64s–82s while sugars were selling in Liverpool for 55s. There was 'no demand for the Exportation of West India Produce'.[137] The market remained 'heavy and depressed', and Tobin & Pinney continued to tell absentees that it would 'be very happy to receive your direction respecting the Sale of your consignment'. With its prices elevated above Liverpool's, the firm noted how 'The Buyers keep back and our plan is to avoid forcing any Sales, at the same time to accept such offers as we think ought not to be refused in a period of much uncertainty.' The market picked up in September 1801, but this did not last, and in October it was again 'miserably flat'. Tobin & Pinney reported to clients that the 'Preliminaries of Peace were signed' between Britain and France, but 'the opinions are very different as to the Effect it is likely to produce in the Sugar Market'. Unusually, it turned out that the 'Sugar Market has not experienced any material change since this event'—supply and demand continued to prove more powerful. The firm believed that 'Sugars will not be _much_ better for some Months', especially as the 'Purchasers hang back seeming confident of a considerable reduction in price'. By March 1802, the firm lamented that 'Our Sugar Market has been gradually declining for a long time past, and, from the immense quantity on hand, a reduction is rather expected than any material advance, even if a considerable export takes place.' The market continued to decline even after peace was made official, with prices at around 46s–72s over the summer, continuing 'flat and rather reduced in price' into the autumn.[138]

---

136 Tobin, Pinney & Tobin to George Webbe Junior, 20 August 1800 and 6 September 1800, Tobin, Pinney & Tobin to George Webbe, 15 September 1800, and Tobin, Pinney & Tobin to Joseph Clarke, 8 November 1800, UoBSC, MS DM58/Letter Book/42.

137 Tobin, Pinney & Tobin to John Colhoun Mills, 3 June 1801, and Tobin, Pinney & Tobin to John Garnett, 2 June 1801, UoBSC, MS DM58/Letter Book/42.

138 Tobin, Pinney & Tobin to John Lyons, 29 August 1801, Tobin, Pinney & Tobin to John Colhoun Mills, 19 September 1801, and 8 March and 29 July 1802, Tobin, Pinney & Tobin to Edward Brazier, 6 and 28 October 1801, Tobin, Pinney & Tobin to Francis Sherriff, 6 October 1801, Tobin, Pinney & Tobin to Woodbridge & Co.,

Conclusion

Warfare, commonly assumed by historians to have been the most potent threat to eighteenth-century merchants, was in this period less potent that the powers of supply and demand. Evidence from Bristol's market shows how periods of transition—from war to peace, with the threat of war, and from peace to war—affected the price of sugar. It was uncertainty over whether a transition would happen, rather than the effects of the new state, that led buyers to hang back from the market. Prices rose predictably with war; the uncertainty concerned whether or not war would happen. This was the case in 1782, 1787, and 1790.

It was transition to a new kind of sugar economy that made the most material change to the market in Bristol and Britain. This transition was caused by disruption to production following conflict of a very different kind—a rebellion driven by the enslaved people in Saint Domingue, rather than warfare driven by power struggles in Europe. This was conflict not between two European powers over the fate of territories in far-off lands (and the economic superiority they promised), but between slaver and enslaved. The revolutionaries of Saint Domingue, in their own bid for freedom, brought chaos, disruption, and opportunity to the British and European markets. Production in the British West Indies was increased, re-exports rose, and the government intervened, setting thresholds to block exports if prices rose too high. The transition into warfare with Revolutionary France firmed merchants' hands. War led to a predictable rise in prices, while high demand meant that merchants could easily wait out gluts from convoys, especially after the first few seasons following the declaration of war. The market paused only when peace was contemplated, given that peace threatened to lower the price of sugar, or when French advances threatened to cut off the continental market. In the end, such was the strength of demand, it was the British government that prevented exports to control prices, rather than the French army that prevented British imports. When production in the British West Indies was threatened by both insurrections of the enslaved people and the French forces present there, expeditionary forces were sent, at great cost of life for British soldiers, to protect these valuable colonies and expand British Caribbean holdings. The colonies were saved from scarcity by the reopening of trade with the United States, while sugar and rum prices experienced short-term boosts from the banning of grain distillation. In the end, profits remained high, if not becoming higher.

---

19 October 1801, and Tobin, Pinney & Tobin to Walter Maynard, 13 October 1802, UoBSC, MS DM58/Letter Book/42.

The great undoing of the sugar market was neither war nor peace, but the same mechanism that led to the boom of the 1790s: production. With the European market well supplied by the expansion of new sugar colonies, merchants in Britain finally began to suffer. Prices started to fall following a bumper British West India crop that could find no outlet in Europe. Bristol's place as the second city of sugar was ceded to Liverpool, where merchants were ruthless in lowering prices. With their ability to read the established patterns of the market taken away from them by the churn and uncertainty of this fresh crisis, merchants such as Tobin and Pinney thrust their responsibilities back on to their clients. They relinquished the judgement for which they were supposed to earn their commission. Resilience had its limits.

Merchants, interested in production, advised their clients on how best to grow sugar, and they organised the shipping and arranged its sale on the British markets. Yet there is one more element to their activity, among one of the most important: they acted as creditors, lending capital and leveraging credit to help planters and reap even more from the sugar trade. This meant that they operated in one more arena that exposed them to some of the most significant crises that they would face in this period.

5

Creditors, Debtors, and Caution in Times of Crisis

> In Trade you know a competency is absolutely necessary for the carrying it on here with Credit, & how is that to be obtain'd? Not by the present view you seem to have
>
> John Norton, writing to his son, 1769[1]

> The distress amongst the tradesmen is truly alarming. They are calling on me almost every day and begging for God's sake to spare them a little money, although their goods were delivered us only in June or July and not due till this time twelve months. Judge you the situation I am in and have compassion on me by enabling me to comply at the time agreed for these goods when the case may be altered to that of 'Sir, my bill is due and I insist on having my money'.
>
> Joshua Johnson, writing to his partners, 1772[2]

CREDIT WAS THE BACKBONE of the eighteenth-century economy. The merchants engaged in transatlantic commerce, as 'quasi-bankers', lent credit to planters and consumers in the Caribbean and the Americas to

---

1 John Norton to John Hatley Norton, 28 July 1769, in *John Norton and Sons: Merchants of London and Virginia*, ed. by Frances Norton Mason (Newton Abbot: David and Charles, 1968).
2 Joshua Johnson to Charles Wallace and John Davidson, 29 August 1772, in *Joshua Johnson's Letterbook, 1771–4*, ed. by Jacob M. Price (Chatham: London Record Society, 1979).

help them smooth their consumption and pay for production inputs. Such merchants, especially those involved in the sugar trade, came to be well acquainted with the needs of the plantations that they served. In this way, they were not just functioning cogs of the plantation machine, but investors and stakeholders who were profoundly interested in the success of the plantations and those who owned and operated them. This phenomenon has been well documented in the historiography.[3] A question less often asked, however, is how these merchants managed their credit during times of crisis.[4]

Here, I show that Tobin & Pinney, a successful sugar-importing firm, was able to withstand the pressure of crises by adopting a cautious approach to lending in which it attempted to keep advances small and tied closely to sugar consignments. This commitment to caution as a guiding principle was solidified during the late 1780s and throughout the 1790s by a succession of crises. While warfare was significant among these, the biggest crisis when it came to their investments was a challenge to the economic order: the movement to abolish the slave trade. Though unsuccessful at this time, it created an environment of uncertainty relating to sugar production. Ultimately, a period when sugar merchants perceived an existential threat to their trade conditioned their behaviour, so that by the time war was declared, they were already practising behaviours that other merchants in different trades were soon to follow.

Indeed, Tobin & Pinney's early attitude as a sugar-importing firm was optimistic, and its initial attempts at expansion from 1784 were successful. It was from 1787, following a series of poor harvests and threats of war with France and Spain, that the outlook began to worsen. The firm noticed that others in the community were lending less freely. The abolitionist movement in the late 1780s further compounded with these factors to create an environment of risk peculiar to the West Indies. Tobin & Pinney was, therefore, pressured to adopt a more cautious approach to lending. The war with France proved the value of this approach, and further reinforced it by presenting additional risks, as did the Hamburg Crisis towards the end of the century.

Tobin & Pinney's cautious behaviour was reinforced further through its experience with troublesome debtors. Because it operated within a framework that was not conducive to debt recovery, it had to develop a

---

3 See, among others, Price, 'What Did Merchants Do?', pp. 278–82; Morgan, *Bristol*, pp. 189–93; Haggerty, *Trading Community*, p. 143.

4 Significant exceptions include Pierre Gervais, 'Mercantile Credit and Trading Rings in the Eighteenth Century', *Annals. History, Social Sciences: English Edition*, 67:4 (2012), 693–730; Gervais, 'Surviving War'; Haggerty, *'Merely for Money'?*.

means of screening potential clients. This strategy—cautious lending and careful screening—was developed over time. It helped Tobin & Pinney get what it wanted: a good debt that was either paid quickly or that provided a steady income stream in the form of interest payments over several decades. It helped them manage its credit, firm its resilience, and remain operational into the nineteenth century.

The tools of the trade

Before delving into merchants' strategies for using credit, we need to understand the tools of credit that defined the business environment within which they operated. A good understanding of accounting methods and instruments such as bonds and mortgages helped West India merchants keep track of debts and the elements of credit. Most important to them, however, was the bill of exchange, which required both an explicit and tacit understanding of its functionalities. It was this knowledge that helped merchants navigate their lending environment, because it formed the basis for how credit itself was perceived and utilised.

Merchants kept a detailed series of account books, which were essential for recording and keeping track of credits and debts. These ranged from the waste books that recorded daily transactions to journals that recorded separate accounts for individuals, firms, and 'adventures'. A bank book was used to record specific dealings with their bankers. These were used to provide projections for accounts from expected sales, identify sources of profit and loss, and track the complex of debts.[5] Tobin & Pinney, similarly to other merchants, balanced its accounts yearly, on 1 May, after which the firm sent out copies to clients to confirm with their signature and return (or challenge).[6] As with the survey of the buyers in the sugar sales process, this offered the opportunity to raise and resolve disputes. The accounts were used to keep track of interest—typically 5%—as well as the time that payments

---

5 See Hart and Matson, 'Situating Merchants', p. 672; Gervais, 'Mercantile Credit', pp. 720–27; Pierre Gervais, 'A Merchant or a French Atlantic? Eighteenth-Century Account Books as Narratives of a Transnational Merchant Political Economy', *French History*, 25:1 (2011), 28–47 (pp. 35–36, 40–42, 45).

6 See numerous letters sent around May in UoBSC MS DM58/Letter Book/37–42. See also Emily Kadens, 'Pre-Modern Credit Networks and the Limits of Reputation', *Iowa Law Review*, 100:6 (2015), 2429–55 (p. 2436); B. L. Anderson, 'Money and the Structure of Credit in the Eighteenth Century', *Business History*, 12:2 (1970), 85–101 (pp. 91–92).

were due.[7] They were also used to keep track of payment due dates for items bought and sold. Tobin & Pinney usually bought manufactures at six months credit, though manufacturers could offer longer credit (specialist exporters usually took goods at 12 months, and this also varied for retailers, and for some manufacturers by region).[8] At Bristol's market, rum was 'generally sold at 3 months', and sugar 'much oftener at 2 months'. Tobin & Pinney noted, however, that purchasers of sugar 'deem themselves intitled to a few days additional indulgence in the date of their Bills', which the firm usually allowed.[9] Credit times were flexible. When prices were higher following the Saint Domingue Revolution, Tobin & Pinney found that 'We sometimes sell here at 2 Months but oftner lately at 3 Months and this year owing to the high price three Months has generally been expected and allowed.'[10] Account books were fundamental for keeping track of debts, credit times, interest, and for providing a mechanism for dispute resolution through sharing accounts. Knowledge of these elements was essential for any merchant.

Bonds and mortgages were used by merchants and lenders to secure long-term debts. For sugar merchants, these were detailed agreements that stipulated the amount to be borrowed, the interest rate, the means of repayment (including the number of sugar hogsheads and how much each should weigh), the amount from each consignment that would be directed towards the interest and the principal, and how much the planter could take to their credit on their book account thereafter.[11] The interest rate on bonds and mortgages was capped at 5% for domestic lending and was between 6% and 8% in the colonies, but this varied by colony. In Nevis, the rate was 8%. This gave merchants room to price risk into colonial lending, though not much.[12] It also gave them the flexibility to negotiate rates with

---

7 Tobin & Pinney to John Tobin Crosse, 1 October 1789, UoBSC, MS DM58/Letter Book/38; Haggerty, *Trading Community*, pp. 145–52; W. T. Baxter, 'Credit, Bills, and Bookkeeping in a Simple Economy', *The Accounting Review*, 21:2 (1946), 154–66 (p. 163).

8 Tobin & Pinney to Ulysses Lynch, 31 August, UoBSC, MS DM58/Letter Book/38; Price, 'What Did Merchants Do?', p. 273; John Smail, 'The Culture of Credit in Eighteenth-Century Commerce: The English Textile Industry', *Enterprise & Society*, 4:2 (2003), 299–325.

9 Pinney & Tobin to Charles Spooner, 30 January 1789, UoBSC, MS DM58/Letter Book/37.

10 Tobin & Pinney to Henry Jones, 13 June 1794, UoBSC, MS DM58/Letter Book/39.

11 Memorandum of Articles of Agreement between A. McKenzie and Lowbridge & Richard Bright, Letter 252, in Morgan, *Bright-Meyler Papers*.

12 Pares, *West-India Fortune*, pp. 258–59; Jacob M. Price, 'Transaction Costs: A Note on Merchant Credit and the Organisation of Private Trade', in *The Political Economy of Merchant Empires: State Power and World Trade, 1350–1750*, ed. by James D. Tracy

clients. When taking over a bond due from James and Edward Huggins, for example, Tobin & Pinney compounded the arrears of interest with the principal and lowered the interest rate from 7% to 5% to keep repayments effectively the same.[13] These were secured by the Colonial Debt Act of 1732, which made land, houses, chattel, and slaves liable to seizure for debts, and thus better supported creditors lending to the colonies. Other Acts followed that provided further security.[14] Bonds and mortgages were, thus, a further instrument at the disposal of merchant creditors that could be used to secure lending against various forms of property.

The bill of exchange, however, was the most important and widely used financial instrument at the time. This is because it helped overcome the scarcity of cash in Britain and the Atlantic world, which was a pressing issue in the eighteenth-century economy.[15] West India planters, through remittances of sugar, built up credits with merchants in Britain. These credits could be transferred using bills of exchange, which were paper instruments that indicated the transfer of a right to collect a payment from a mercantile house. Bills of exchange were versatile and widely used. They relied upon the reputation of the person drawing the bill and, once accepted, of the person upon whom it was drawn. They also provided a legal basis for proceeding against a debt.[16] However, the bill of exchange was a complicated instrument that had to be well understood by the people using it. These people included the 'drawer' (the one making a demand upon another for a particular sum), the 'drawee' (the person upon whom the demand was made), and the 'payee' (the person for whom the payment was intended). Upon accepting the bill, the 'drawee' became the 'acceptor' and, upon payment, the 'payer'. The payee

---

(Cambridge: Cambridge University Press, 1991), pp. 276–97 (p. 294); Smith, *Slavery*, pp. 168, 219–20.

13 Pinney & Tobin to James & Edward Huggins, 28 January 1788, UoBSC, MS DM58/Letter Book/37.

14 Jacob M. Price, 'The Imperial Economy, 1700–1776', in *The Oxford History of the British Empire, Vol. II: The Eighteenth Century*, ed. by P. J. Marshall (Oxford: Oxford University Press, 2001), pp. 78–104 (p. 96); Morgan, *Bright-Meyler Papers*, p. 101.

15 Craig Muldrew, *The Economy of Obligation: The Culture of Credit and Social Relations in Early Modern England* (London: Palgrave Macmillan, 1998), pp. 3–4; Craig Muldrew, 'Interpreting the Market: The Ethics of Credit and Community Relations in Early Modern England', *Social History*, 18:2 (1993), 163–83 (p. 171); McCusker, *Money*, p. 8.

16 Haggerty, *Trading Community*, pp. 152–59; Price, 'Transaction Costs', p. 285; Anderson, 'Money and the Structure of Credit', p. 90; Gervais, 'Mercantile Credit', pp. 713–15; Julian Hoppit, 'The Use and Abuse of Credit in Eighteenth-Century England', in *Business Life and Public Policy*, ed. by Neil McKendrick and R. B. Outhwaite (Cambridge: Cambridge University Press, 1986), pp. 64–78 (p. 66).

could transfer the right to collect the payment stipulated in the bill to another party: after signing the bill, the payee became the 'endorser', and the new recipient the 'endorsee'.[17] Bills of exchange, in this way, could be used to transfer funds between accounts to cover transactions that planters were making among themselves, or to transfer funds due from sales of sugar from the merchant who had sold the sugar to another merchant who had made a loan to the planter. To receive the payment on behalf of a client, Tobin & Pinney would have to be named as the endorsee. However, demonstrating that these were specialist tools, clients would often forget to sign their name on the bill and, thus, 'give it validity', meaning that Tobin & Pinney would have to return them.[18] Naming the parties, too, was important. Tobin & Pinney noted on one occasion that bills went missing in a mail robbery. The firm instructed its bankers not to pay the bills if they were presented, but, in the end, the thieves returned them (anonymously), finding them useless because they were made out to particular individuals.[19] Bills were also sent overseas in sets of three or four on different ships to guard against accidents. The bills would specify which of the four they were so that the house that they were drawn upon could make a note not to pay the others if they were later presented. Bill books were used to keep track.[20] With its transferability, and, given the difficulties with cash, its accessibility, the bill of exchange became the most important financial tool that merchants and planters used.

There were issues of timing that merchants and planters had to be aware of, however, as well as additional costs involved with using bills of exchange. Transfers were rarely instantaneous, and bills of exchange typically stipulated some future payment to be made. This could be flexible, with dates ranging from a week, to 30 or 60 days, or 3, 12, 18, or 24 months, if not longer. If the bill was drawn 'after sight', the time would start after the bill was presented and accepted. The time between acceptance and redemption was called the 'usance period', during which it could be transferred by endorsement.[21] Merchants charged a commission (Tobin & Pinney typically charged 0.25%,

---

17 Cuthbert W. Johnson, *The Law of Bills of Exchange, Promissory Notes, Checks, &c* (London: Richards, 1839), p. 6.
18 One example is John Pinney's son: Tobin, Pinney & Tobin to John Frederick Pinney, 11 April [1798], UoBSC, MS DM58/Letter Book/40.
19 Tobin & Pinney to Edward Parson, 13 and 31 October 1794, UoBSC, MS DM58/Letter Book/39.
20 Tobin & Pinney to Ladbroke, Rawlinson & Co., 22 July 1794, and Tobin & Pinney to George Webbe, 12 September 1794, UoBSC, MS DM58/Letter Book/39; McCusker, *Money*, p. 20.
21 Haggerty, *Trading Community*, p. 154; Price, 'Transaction Costs', p. 287; Morgan, 'Remittance Procedures', p. 724; McCusker, *Money*, p. 20.

which it considered 'the usual commission'), while other costs included postage and stamp duty.[22] The stamp duty was introduced in 1782, making bills of exchange worth under £50 subject to a 3d duty and those over £50 a 6d duty. This was later increased to 3d for under £10, 6d for under £50, and 1s for over £50. There were geographical conditions, including an exemption for bills drawn between houses within ten miles of one another, and differentiations made between foreign bills and domestic bills.[23] Tobin & Pinney also refer to an exemption on bills drawn at 30 days or lower, which was 'the customary time here when the Stamp is not charged'.[24] Merchants had to keep track of these timings, which could be recorded in their account books, especially if they wanted to endorse the bills to someone else. They further had to understand and keep track of the stamp duty, alongside commission and postage charges, especially when recommending a particular length and amount that a client draw.

Though complex, the bill of exchange was a versatile instrument. Because it could be endorsed to another party, it could also be discounted. Specialist discounters bought bills some time before they were due at less than face value and redeemed them at face value after the usance period was up. Discounting injected some much-needed liquidity into the market and allowed merchants to overcome the issues of timing payments, especially when the payment of one bill was dependent upon the acceptance of another.[25] Tobin & Pinney's frequent use of the discounting function demonstrates just how vital this service was. Bills of exchange were also used to transfer funds between London and Bristol. This was especially useful because, as we have seen, planters would send sugars to both ports. Tobin & Pinney made these kinds of transfers frequently, and had help from other houses, including merchants B. & T. Boddington & Co., banker Nathaniel Martin, and specialist banking houses Ladbroke, Rawlinson & Co. and Williams, Son, Drury & Co. Tobin & Pinney drew bills on these firms and endorsed bills over to them to keep

---

22 See Tobin, Pinney & Tobin to Cheap & Loughnan, 16 November 1796, and Tobin, Pinney & Tobin to Thomas Latham & Son, 4 January 1797, UoBSC, MS DM58/Letter Book/40.

23 Johnson, *Bills of Exchange*, pp. 99–100; *Stamp-Duty. Abstract of the last Act of Parliament, respecting the Stamp-Duty on Inland Bills of Exchange, Promissory Notes, &c* (London: Cornwell, [c. 1782]); *Laws for Regulating Bills of Exchange, Inland and Foreign; with Abstracts of the Several Acts Lately Passed* (London: Nicoll, 1783), pp. 3–6.

24 Tobin & Pinney to Worswick & Son, 5 December 1795, UoBSC, MS DM58/Letter Book/39; Tobin, Pinney & Tobin to Latham & Son, 11 May 1796, UoBSC, MS DM58/Letter Book/40.

25 Haggerty, *Trading Community*, pp. 156–57; Joseph Inikori, 'The Credit Needs of the African Trade and the Development of the Credit Economy in England', *Explorations in Economic History*, 27 (1990), 197–231 (pp. 214–17).

its accounts in credit.[26] It made use of local Bristol banks too, from which it could buy a bill drawn on London at 20 or 30 days for cash at 'par', or face value, meaning that it paid no credit premium.[27] Discounting and negotiability made bills of exchange a particularly flexible instrument.

However, there were times when the bills would not be accepted. If the drawer did not have adequate funds with the drawee and made no arrangements to cover it, the drawee might reject the bill. When presented, the drawee would 'note' the bill for non-acceptance and, once the bill was due, have it protested. Regulations, introduced in 1694, stipulated that, three days after the bill was due, it could be formally protested at a notary public and damages and interest could be charged. The bill would be returned to the drawer, and the disgruntled payee would demand some other form of payment; this also gave them a basis for litigation.[28] Charges or damages might be waived if, as Tobin & Pinney put it, the transaction was performed out of 'friendship' and not business.[29] Alternatively, a protested bill might be taken up by a guarantor. The technical name of such a guarantee was a 'case of need' endorsement, where the named guarantor would promise to pay the bill for the 'honour' of the drawer should the original drawee decline to pay.[30] Much to its alarm, Tobin & Pinney was often named as guarantor without its consent. The firm refused to pay bills for which it was unwittingly named as guarantor, to the embarrassment of its clients, who often made no arrangements to cover the costs.[31] The firm might have found itself protesting bills more often than not, given the poor reputation that West India planters had for drawing within their means.[32] A firm understanding of the protest procedures was essential for any merchant in order to help

---

26 For discounts and transfers, see numerous letters to B. & T. Boddington & Co., Boddingtons & Bettesworth, Samuel Boddington, Nathaniel Martin, Ladbroke, Rawlinson & Co., and Williams, Son & Co. in UoBSC, MS DM58/Letter Book/37–42.

27 See Tobin, Pinney & Tobin to R. S. White, 18 January 1797, UoBSC, MS DM58/Letter Book/40.

28 See numerous examples of Tobin & Pinney noting and protesting bills in UoBSC, MS DM58/Letter Book/37–42. See also Johnson, *Bills of Exchange*, pp. 87–89; Price, 'Transaction Costs', p. 286; Morgan, 'Remittance Procedures', p. 725; Haggerty, *Trading Community*, p. 158.

29 Tobin & Pinney to Nathaniel Martin, 15 October 1792, UoBSC, MS DM58/Letter Book/38.

30 Mary Poovey, *Genres of the Credit Economy: Mediating Value in Eighteenth- and Nineteenth-Century Britain* (Chicago: University of Chicago Press, 2008), p. 39.

31 See Tobin & Pinney to Josiah Maynard, 3 October 1790, UoBSC, MS DM58/Letter Book/38.

32 Haggerty, *'Merely for Money'?*, p. 125.

him prevent bills from being protested and to protest bills that he had no interest in paying.

Measures would also have to be taken to prevent the fraudulent use of bills. This was a growing problem, and the law was increasingly used to punish those who counterfeited bills or other forms of paper money.[33] However, merchants still needed their own approach to prevent fraud. Tobin & Pinney's methods are illustrative. The firm demanded that clients inform it of any bills that they intended to draw in advance (this also gave Tobin & Pinney time to make funds available, or else indicate its intention to refuse them and save the hassle of protesting). The wording of the bill was used to validate its identity—suspicions would be aroused if the bill was written to be paid 'after date' rather than 'after sight', for example, if correspondence or habit indicated the reverse. The handwriting would also be checked.[34] This represents the tacit side of what merchants needed to understand. From experience and knowledge of their clients (their habits and their handwriting) they built up an intuition about which bills should be accepted and which should be treated with suspicion.

Merchants thus had a range of tools at their disposal. Account books were used to record debts, credit times, and calculate interest. Sharing accounts provided an avenue for raising and resolving disputes. Bonds and mortgages provided merchants with a means of securing debts against property. The most important instrument was the bill of exchange, which helped overcome issues with cash scarcities. They were used to transfer the right to collect a payment or debt from a mercantile or banking house. The transfer was often stipulated for some point in the future, and timing could be flexible, though there were commonly used periods. Costs were involved that needed to be navigated and understood, including the stamp duty and postage and commission charges. The discounting feature was used frequently, and this maintained liquidity in the credit market. Further, transfers could be made across the country. If the drawee did not want to or could not pay, then the bill would be protested. There was a commonly understood, legally defined procedure for protesting bills that merchants and bankers were expected to follow. Merchants paid attention to the wording of the bill and its handwriting to prevent fraud. A firm understanding of this complex of mechanisms was fundamental for any

---

33 See Amy Milka, 'Feeling for Forgers: Character, Sympathy and Financial Crime in London during the Late Eighteenth Century', *Journal for Eighteenth-Century Studies*, 42:1 (2019), 7–25.

34 See Pinney & Tobin to George Webbe Junior, 3 July 1788, UoBSC, MS DM58/Letter Book/37; Tobin, Pinney & Tobin to George Webbe Junior, 2 July 1796, UoBSC, MS DM58/Letter Book/40.

merchant engaged in overseas trade, and especially for merchants who lent to West India planters and dealt with West India credit. This knowledge was foundational at any point, but especially so as the environment for lending in the West Indies became increasingly fraught with risk.

The hazards of lending

Tobin & Pinney operated in a high-risk environment. External pressures compounded to make lending an increasingly risky prospect. Furthermore, merchants operated within a framework that made debt collection difficult. As a result, Tobin & Pinney began operating with increasing caution. Indeed, Sheryllynne Haggerty has noted how periods of crises 'tended to lead to a contraction of credit as people "played safe"'; but what exactly did 'playing safe' mean for Tobin & Pinney?[35]

For Tobin & Pinney, a cautious approach to lending meant keeping advances small (if still frequent). The firm stressed that it was not keen on large advances, but would offer more 'trifling' ones—trifling meaning 'one, or two hundred pounds'.[36] It did not like to put a cap on lending, though this meant that accounts could swell, even if advances were small. The firm felt it 'rather indelicate on us to fix on any particular Sum', but would, for its 'friends ... go as far for their accommodation as Prudence will permit'; fixing a sum might well have sent its clients to a different house, though not fixing one pushed prudence to its limits. The firm took this approach with John Hendrickson, for example, but by 1800 his account was over £3,000 in debt, 'a Sum considerable larger than we ever undertook to advance'.[37] It found that a safer strategy was to wait until the sugars, or at least notice of their shipment (a request for insurance, or a bill of lading), were received before making an advance. With the sugars on hand and an idea of the market, Tobin & Pinney could advance their estimated value. The firm would also make an advance to the planter after the sale was agreed but two or three months before the buyer had paid.[38] In general, such caution was foundational to the company's business strategy. In 1789, as it informed a client,

---

35 Haggerty, *Trading Community*, p. 144.
36 Pinney & Tobin to James Tyson, 1 August 1786, UoBSC, MS DM58/Letter Book/37.
37 Tobin & Pinney to John Hendrickson, 15 August 1792, UoBSC, MS DM58/Letter Book/38; Tobin, Pinney & Tobin to John Hendrickson, 21 April 1800, UoBSC, MS DM58/Letter Book/40.
38 See Pinney & Tobin to William Colhoun, 9 December 1788, UoBSC, MS DM58/

> On the whole as we have observed those Merch.^t ... who have strictly adhered to a steady and regular course of business and have contented themselves with <u>moderate</u> profits on <u>moderate</u> risques, to have succeeded much better than such as have engaged in wild and unlimited schemes and Speculations in hopes of <u>larger profits</u>[39]

This, therefore, formed the bedrock of Tobin & Pinney's approach to lending, which was developed and reinforced over this period.

Caution in times of crisis

Because merchant firms such as Tobin & Pinney advanced credit to be reimbursed through sugar consignments, issues with sugar production and the shipment of sugar could prove to be a barrier to debt repayment. Goods were often sent out first and paid for in sugar.[40] Tobin & Pinney knew that 'there are few consignments to be procured without <u>some</u> advance', though the firm had to be careful, for 'consignments may be, and often are <u>bought too dear</u>'.[41] Sugar harvests could be hampered by a variety of factors, especially hurricanes, heavy rains, floods, and droughts. Nevis experienced a series of poor harvests in 1787 and 1788 thanks to the borer worm, while the threat of war, which merchants experienced in 1787 and 1790, compounded with these natural hazards to further affect the lending environment. The Dutch Crisis in 1787 made Tobin & Pinney hesitate due to the 'gloomy and unsettled appearance of the Political Hemisphere', with the anticipation of war leading to a 'critical situation of public and private credit'. This, as the firm informed its clients, made everyone more cautious, with West India credit difficult to procure owing to the uncertainty.[42] Tobin & Pinney rejected some requests for money because, even in November, the partners could not 'consider the storm as entirely blown over'.[43] The Nootka Sound Crisis was similar. Though the firm received proposals from 'Gentlemen' of 'good Character', owing to

---

Letter Book/37; Tobin & Pinney to John Garnett, 3 August 1795, UoBSC, MS DM58/Letter Book/39.
39 Tobin & Pinney to Ulysses Lynch, 31 August 1789, UoBSC, MS DM58/Letter Book/38.
40 Pares, *West-India Fortune*, pp. 253–55; Ragatz, *Planter Class*, p. 101.
41 Tobin & Pinney to Ulysses Lynch, 31 August 1789, UoBSC, MS DM58/Letter Book/38.
42 Pinney & Tobin to Edward Brazier, and Joseph Pemberton, 28 September 1787, and Pinney & Tobin to Webbe Hobson, 13 and 29 October 1787, UoBSC, MS DM58/Letter Book/37; Thomas Lamb to William Dickinson, 18 October 1787, SHC, MS DD/DN/4/2/22(2).
43 Pinney & Tobin to Henry Dench, 3 November 1787, UoBSC, MS DM58/Letter Book/37.

the 'critical situation of the times with respect to W. India property', given that Britain was 'probably on the eve of a war with Spain', the firm was 'under the necessity of declining' some proposals.[44] Poor harvests, in combination with the uncertain geopolitical situation, made the lending environment from 1787 particularly risky. Tobin and Pinney followed their peers in behaving with caution.

However, there was a further factor that compounded with these that seemed certain at the time to be an existential threat to the West India sugar trade: the abolitionist movement. The abolition of the slave trade threatened to deprive the plantations of their source of labour, and thus their source of value. Indeed, as Christer Petley summarises, 'the British Atlantic slave system was profoundly shaken' by the abolitionists.[45] In the early stages of the abolitionist movement, Tobin & Pinney worried that 'such restrictions may be laid upon [the slave trade] as will render any further improvement of our Estates too expensive to be pursued'. Planters were advised to be careful in 'raising and seasoning' the enslaved Africans on their estates, given that abolition was a 'Cloud' that was 'hanging over all kind of West India property'.[46] Sugar merchants doubled down on their cautious behaviour. As Tobin & Pinney informed a client, 'We are sorry to say that the Question respecting the abolition of the Slave Trade has had a very considerable effect on West India Credit and has prevented many advances which would otherwise have been entered into.' This influenced the firm's own approach, for 'Merchants of the Utmost sagacity ... are occasionally taken in ... we ought to be very cautious as to what engagements we enter into particularly in times like these so unfavourable to West India Credit'.[47] Others, too, such as Lowbridge Bright, demonstrated caution by abstaining from participating in the slave trade during this time.[48] Their caution was seemingly vindicated as the motion for abolition was passed in 1792. Tobin & Pinney was doubtful that it would 'be effectively opposed in the Lords'. It seemed that, 'After much altercation, and most vehement speechifying, the Abolition of the Slave Trade is it seems to take place on the 1st of Janu^y 1796 – It's fate remains still to be decided in the Lords, but from the complexion of the popular opinions,

---

44 Tobin & Pinney to Joseph Powell Senior, 1 November 1790, UoBSC, MS DM58/Letter Book/38.
45 Petley, *White Fury*, p. 147.
46 Pinney & Tobin to George Webbe Junior and to John Hendrickson, 3 July 1788, UoBSC, MS DM58/Letter Book/37; Tobin & Pinney to William Coker, 30 May 1789, UoBSC, MS DM58/Letter Book/38.
47 Tobin & Pinney to Ulysses Lynch, 31 March 1790 and 21 December 1789, UoBSC, MS DM58/Letter Book/38.
48 Morgan, *Bright-Meyler Papers*, p. 123.

we apprehend the Die is cast.'⁴⁹ Because, as these merchants and planters saw it, the abolitionist movement posed an existential threat to sugar production, West India merchants were forced to consider the ability of planters to make consistent payments. Caution, already an established principle, now reigned supreme.

With a bill for abolition passed through the House of Commons, and the sight of oncoming war with France, the pessimistic outlook seemed set to continue. However, the Terrors of the French Revolution and the war against France gave the House of Lords the reasons it had sought to delay and reject the bill.⁵⁰ The abolitionists, already associated with the French revolutionaries, became tarnished by their excesses; meanwhile, the introduction of the term 'gradual' to the 1792 bill by Henry Dundas had given Parliament a mechanism by which to enact further delay.⁵¹ This relieved the West India merchants from one threat, though they faced another—still impactful, but less existential. The transition into war led to a wave of bankruptcies across Britain as credit became tighter and the commercial world expected the worst.⁵² The scale of the failures had 'given an <u>unprecedented</u> check to credit of every kind and more particularly to the circulation of paper'.⁵³ Some of the failures were substantial. James Rogers, a Bristol slave trader, failed with debts of around £100,000. The reckless expansion of his slave trading activities before 1793 led to his precipitous decline. He was never considered to have been a particularly competent trader by Tobin and Pinney who, in 1790, commented that his behaviour was so bad that he needed to 'clear up his conduct'.⁵⁴ Rogers's connections suffered too: Richard Fydell reportedly hanged himself over a debt of £120,000, while Blake & Powell failed with £60,000 in bills in circulation. Others failed through the endorsement of various bills of exchange, which, when called upon, made them unable to honour their own debts.⁵⁵ While the beginning of the war had removed the threat of the abolitionists, who would have to wait over a decade before

---

49 Tobin & Pinney to Edward Brazier, 28 April 1792, and Tobin & Pinney to William Jones, 26 April 1792, UoBSC, MS DM58/Letter Book/38.
50 Morgan, *Bright-Meyler Papers*, p. 123; Ryden, *West Indian Slavery*, p. 179; Petley, *White Fury*, pp. 169–71.
51 Scanlan, *Slave Empire*, pp. 169–72.
52 Hoppit, *Risk and Failure*, pp. 122–39.
53 Tobin & Pinney to Edward Brazier & Thomas Pym Weekes, 18 March 1793, UoBSC, MS DM58/Letter Book/39.
54 Morgan, 'James Rogers'; Tobin & Pinney to B. & T. Boddington, 28 September 1790, UoBSC, MS DM58/Letter Book/38.
55 Edward Shiercliff to William Dickinson, 7 and 27 March, and 22 April 1793, SHC, MS DD/DN/4/2/1(2), 41(2).

making up the same ground, it had led to an unprecedented scale of failures and made credit particularly hard to obtain.

Tobin & Pinney looked on unsympathetically. The firm believed that the wave of bankruptcies had brought only the 'incautious, and adventurous Speculators' to a standstill. These 'disagreeable accidents' would eventually strengthen, rather than weaken, the credit in the city.[56] The large circulation of bills of exchange had become an 'enormous evil', and the war was of 'infinite service … by giving a check to a very ruinous circulation of Bills of mere accommodation'.[57] This attitude was not unusual for the time.[58] The firm, along with the other West India merchants who had restricted their lending during the height of the abolitionist movement, must have felt particularly vindicated. However, the community was not immune to the bankruptcies experienced in this wave. Of 34 known bankrupts in Bristol in 1793, 12 were significant importers of sugar, and of these, four carried on importing sugar after 1793. Yet the community of sugar importers actually grew after 1793, showing remarkable resilience: the members of the West India community appear to have been less affected than one might have anticipated.[59] This is perhaps due to the scale of their operations. Many of the prominent West India men were also the wealthiest men in Bristol, meaning that they were well connected and had good access to credit, which others were less likely to have had. The high price of sugar that followed the Saint Domingue Revolution almost certainly helped. However, they also benefited from a strategy guided by caution, which was conditioned in previous years by the experience of threats particular to the West India trade.

As the war continued, the outlook remained pessimistic. Tobin & Pinney's approach to the market had helped it withstand the pressures of war and make the most of the high price of sugar. However, although the market continued to function much as it had before, the firm still retained its cautious approach to lending. War brought with it price certainty, but it also brought threats to the West Indies, as we have seen. While these threats did not necessarily materialise in the ways merchants feared, this still affected their approach to long-term lending, based as it was on issues that affected production more

---

56 Tobin & Pinney to Mr Thomas, 18 March 1793, UoBSC, MS DM58/Letter Book/39.

57 Tobin & Pinney to Edward Brazier & Thomas Pym Weekes, 18 March 1793, and Tobin & Pinney to William Jones, 1 May 1793, UoBSC, MS DM58/Letter Book/39.

58 Haggerty, *'Merely for Money'?*, pp. 205–06.

59 This analysis is based on Thornton's estimates in Leslie Pressnell, *Country Banking in the Industrial Revolution* (Oxford: Clarendon Press, 1956), pp. 546–47, and W. Bailey's in Minchinton, *The Trade of Bristol*, pp. 190–91, alongside a database constructed from BA, MS SMV/7/1/1/72–83 WB.

so than the short-term performance of the sugar market. Tobin & Pinney described the situation as 'unsettled', 'gloomy', and 'unpromising', and at its worst 'precarious', 'hazardous', and 'perilous'. This was influenced by reports from the war, just as the sugar market was unsettled at times by such rumours.[60] French successes in Germany and Italy, the threat of invasion (and the attempted French invasion of Ireland), the prospect of Spain being dragged into the war on the French side, and failed attempts at finding peace all filled traders' minds with negativity and induced caution.[61] Throughout the war, at the heart of the West India merchants' worries was the threat of a French capture of the British colonial possessions. Tobin & Pinney understood that 'it is clear, beyond a doubt, that the French still aim at a total subversion of our Colonies, the entire destruction of our Trade, and in short at our complete annihilation as a Nation'.[62] The reality, as it appeared in retrospect, was better than the outlook as it seemed at the time—British forces kept the islands relatively secure, as we have seen. The threat did not materialise into anything as catastrophic as anticipated, but it was this anticipation that guided lending behaviour.

Tobin & Pinney became increasingly conscious of the advances it made. The firm emphasised to clients that it would be prudent, but accommodating. It was in this vein that bills of exchange and drafts were still accepted, though, with an eye on the extent of advances, not always.[63] The more outlandish requests were dismissed out of hand. Edward Huggins made a request for £15,000–20,000 to purchase lands 'in the Carib Country of St. Vincent' following the slave insurrection in 1795, which would be in addition to the possessions he already had in Nevis. Tobin & Pinney rejected this proposition, given 'the alarming situation to which Money concerns of every kind are, at present, reduced to in this Country', adding 'God only knows what turn things may ultimately take'. The firm promised Huggins that it would review his proposal again with the return of peace.[64] On occasion, a proposal from a new client would be accepted with the right guarantee, but

---

60 There are several examples of such comments in UoBSC MS DM58/Letter Book/39–40, such as Tobin & Pinney to Martin & William Krause, 18 February 1795, UoBSC, MS DM58/Letter Book/39.
61 One example of such anxiety is Tobin, Pinney & Tobin to Joseph Chabert, 4 September 1796, UoBSC, MS DM58/Letter Book/40.
62 Tobin, Pinney & Tobin to Joseph Chabert, 30 July 1796, UoBSC, MS DM58/Letter Book/40.
63 One example is Tobin & Pinney to Edward Huggins, 3 August 1795, UoBSC, MS DM58/Letter Book/39.
64 Tobin, Pinney & Tobin to Edward Huggins, 6 April, 20 September and 4 October 1797, UoBSC, MS DM58/Letter Book/40.

on the whole, new advances were rejected. The firm gave up on the idea of investing in a ship to Tortola, which would have been a significant capital investment in itself, and which would undoubtedly have entailed further lending in order to induce planters to ship their produce to Tobin & Pinney in Bristol.[65] Already cautious before 1793, the firm's approach to lending was vindicated and reinforced by the war.

The fall in price in 1799 dented the prospects of good returns and, thus, limited the willingness of Tobin & Pinney to lend. Furthermore, with the market at a standstill, liquidity issues made new advances unlikely. Planters, largely oblivious to the situation, were requesting large advances to buy land in Trinidad or St Vincent, seeking to take advantage of Britain's colonial expansion. These were rejected by Tobin & Pinney.[66] The sugar merchant's place as both seller of sugar and investor in production put him in a good position to respond quickly to the fall in prices. Planters were informed that the firm's 'Engagements at present are very heavy considering the little assistance we have derived from Remittance of this Year'. Moreover, a bad crop in Nevis and St Kitts had compounded to make matters worse: Tobin & Pinney reported that this situation had 'put it out of our power to accommodate even our oldest, and best established friends'.[67] Absentees were told to 'draw as little as possible upon us, until matters take a more favourable turn', with Tobin & Pinney planning to reject all but the most pressing payments.[68] Some bills due to the firm, which depended on the high price of sugar, failed to cover debts when the market fell.[69] To safeguard its own solvency, Tobin & Pinney arranged to have £8,000 in bills discounted with its bankers to ensure that it had enough cash on hand to meet immediate demands.[70] Furthermore, the Bank of England stepped in to provide liquidity with a loan of £1.5m to the West India community via the Society of West India Merchants of London, alongside a £500,000 loan from the Treasury for merchants in Liverpool and Lancaster, intervening just as it had done in 1795

---

65 See Tobin & Pinney to John G. Krause, 8 February 1796, and Tobin & Pinney to Martin & William Krause, 13 May 1795, UoBSC, MS DM58/Letter Book/39.
66 Tobin, Pinney & Tobin to William Hendrickson, 2 October 1799, and Tobin, Pinney & Tobin to John Hendrickson, 21 April 1800, UoBSC, MS DM58/Letter Book/40.
67 Tobin, Pinney & Tobin to John Hendrickson, 30 September 1800, and Tobin, Pinney & Tobin to Mrs MacEvoy, 18 October 1800, UoBSC, MS DM58/Letter Book/42.
68 Tobin, Pinney & Tobin to William Colhoun, 19 November 1799, and 19 June 1800, and Tobin, Pinney & Tobin to John Colhoun Mills, 29 November 1799, UoBSC, MS DM58/Letter Book/40.
69 Tobin, Pinney & Tobin to Martin & William Krause, 23 November 1799 and 11 July 1800, UoBSC, MS DM58/Letter Book/40.
70 Tobin, Pinney & Tobin to Williams, Son & Co., 23 June 1800, UoBSC, MS DM58/Letter Book/40.

after the slave uprising in St Vincent and Grenada.[71] In the end, Tobin & Pinney did not need to take advantage of any state aid. The tools at the firm's disposal, alongside its cautious approach to lending, ensured its liquidity.

Over time, Tobin & Pinney began to develop an approach to lending that was continually conditioned and reinforced by the environment in which the firm operated. It preferred to keep advances small and linked as much as possible to remittances. The need for caution became more pressing after a series of poor harvests limited the planters' ability to make remittances. At the same time, the threat of war induced caution in the community. This caution was reinforced by the threat of the abolitionist movement. Though it proved unsuccessful at this stage, the caution that the movement had forced upon the West India community appears to have benefited them as Britain entered the war against France. Tobin & Pinney, alongside many of their peers, seems to have weathered the credit crisis well. The outlook remained gloomy, however, influenced by news from the war. Tobin & Pinney, for the most part, stuck with its cautious approach to lending. Large advances were typically rejected. This was, again, reinforced by the collapse of sugar prices, which lowered the returns from the sugar shipments. By using the discounting services of London banks, Tobin & Pinney was able to remain liquid enough to ensure that it continued operations into the nineteenth century. Yet it was not just the external environment that conditioned the firm's approach. Its experience with recalcitrant debtors, alongside the inadequacies of the framework for debt collection, further reinforced Tobin & Pinney's belief that the firm should proceed with caution.

The problems of debt recovery

One of the most pressing issues with lending money was getting it back; some debtors were less reliable than others, and, in the context of the West Indies, where plantation owners had developed a poor reputation as debtors (for good reason), debt recovery was a particular challenge for transatlantic money lenders such as the sugar merchants examined here.[72] Problems particular to the trade, such as a poor harvest, were endemic, and frequent causes of late payments, muddying the waters and making it hard to distinguish between a dishonest or incompetent debtor and an honest debtor who was down on their luck. As a rule, given that bad weather would affect 'every one connected with the Island', a planter would 'in common, with [their] neighbours' make a bad crop.[73] The incompetent planters could, therefore, be identified as those

---

71 Ragatz, *Planter Class*, pp. 221, 289; Checkland, 'Finance', p. 468.
72 Haggerty, *'Merely for Money'?*, p. 125.
73 Pinney & Tobin to Archbald & Williamson, 30 August 1788, UoBSC, MS DM58/

whose crops continued to suffer when others prospered, and the planters less suited to their profession were revealed over time. Further complicating matters was the volatile nature of the market; hogsheads of sugar were promised in repayment for debt, but should the market take a downward turn, and should the planter have too rosy a view of their product's quality, then the debt was less likely to be repaid.[74] Furthermore, planters did not necessarily see debt repayment as their most pressing concern. Richard Pares does not believe that planters were overly duplicitous. Rather, he argues that few planters 'were intentionally guilty of anything worse than concealing their previous encumbrances when they took up with a new merchant, and resisting to the best of their ability their creditors' attempts to interfere with their comfort or their control of the plantations'.[75] As Tobin & Pinney's experience shows, coaxing planters into making debt repayments could be problematic, and, despite its best efforts, the firm found its strategies for debt recovery to be highly flawed.

Tobin & Pinney's first step in attempting to reclaim debts was to chase the proceeds from sugar sales for consignments that were sent to other merchants. Planters would divide their shipments between, say, Bristol and London, and so merchants in one port became accustomed to the merchants in the other who also served their clients, sending and receiving payments to one another. More irksome was when a planter promised payment (in the form of a consignment) to one merchant and then sent the consignment to another. When Tobin & Pinney found out that James Tyson, a Nevis planter, had been sending his sugars to James Akers, another Bristol merchant, it reprimanded Tyson, feeling it 'a little singular ... that you should draw on us and send him the remittance'. This revealed to the firm that Tyson had become 'engaged in a variety of extensive concerns, and different correspondences'. He had debts in several places, and this meant he could not prioritise payment to Tobin & Pinney. The firm therefore regretted that 'a permanent intercourse of mutual convenience ... does not seem likely to take place' and refused to honour his bills.[76] The partners were particularly incensed when long-standing client Edward Huggins had 'no less a Quantity than 120hhds consigned to another House'. They remarked that 'we think you would have found no

---

Letter Book/37; Tobin, Pinney & Tobin to John Garnett, and John Hendrickson, 18 September 1800, UoBSC, MS DM58/Letter Book/42.

74 See Inikori, 'Credit Needs', p. 212; Price, 'Transaction Costs', p. 290; Morgan, 'Remittance Procedures', pp. 721–23.

75 Pares, *West-India Fortune*, p. 266.

76 Pinney & Tobin to James Tyson, 30 October 1788 and 21 January 1789, UoBSC, MS DM58/Letter Book/37.

difficulty in consigning part of the above Sugars to our address'.[77] Chasing down these shipments and finding out where planters were sending their consignments—and then making it clear to the client that proceeds should be transferred or that their firm should be prioritised in future—was a key part of debt recovery; however, this strategy could only be pursued if planters were actually sending shipments back.

If nothing was being remitted at all, then the firm would send frequent prompts to its debtors. In its letters, Tobin & Pinney would feign surprise at not receiving anything from its more problematic clients, such as John Hendrickson. The partners told him that they were 'relying on your making proper remittances' (and, eventually, a 'substantial remittance'). They frequently reminded these planters that their debts were still active.[78] On occasion, Tobin & Pinney had to prompt sugar buyers to pay, though this was unusual, at least in writing (the partners may have prompted them in person).[79] Letters, of course, could be ignored; promises could be made with all the optimism that a wealth of distance between creditor and debtor allowed. When responses were not forthcoming, however, and promises unfulfilled, then other pressures were needed.

Planters still relied on having regular orders to keep their plantations running. If little was being remitted, then merchants could restrict orders to all but the necessities until they received a substantial consignment. When the firm received drafts totalling over £900 in value from James Tyson on a proposed advance of £200, Tobin & Pinney selected a few to honour and rejected others. The partners kept his advance in line with this until he made adequate remittances.[80] When Ulysses Lynch, a planter on St Kitts, kept sending orders for goods, Tobin & Pinney expressed its surprise that, 'although most of your Letters contained fresh additional Orders for Goods, (which would have amounted to a considerable Sum) no mention was ever made of any intended specific remittances on your part, for what we had already advanced'. The partners therefore informed Lynch that they would

---

77 Tobin, Pinney & Tobin to Edward Huggins, 3 July 1801, UoBSC, MS DM58/Letter Book/42.
78 See numerous letters to John Hendrickson, John Tobin Crosse, Martin & William Krause, Andrew Moore Crosse, Josiah Webbe Hendrickson, William Ruan, Archibald Washington, Charles Ellery, among others in UoBSC MS DM58/Letter Book/37–42.
79 Tobin & Pinney to Adam Prattinton, 29 March and 1 April 1791, UoBSC, MS DM58/Letter Book/38.
80 See Pinney & Tobin to James Tyson, 4 September, and numerous others in UoBSC, MS DM58/Letter Book/37.

be confining his shipment to only the orders that they had already placed.[81] Care had to be taken, however, to ensure that they did not scare the debtor away. By restricting orders, they risked upsetting the planter and losing their cooperation. Tyson was particularly difficult to manage; when Tobin & Pinney restricted his advances, he accused the firm of 'indifference' and 'inattention' and of treating him as 'unworthy'.[82] Again, restricting advances was not always effective. Indeed, as Richard Pares argues, 'the Pinneys usually found that they had about as much power as King Canute to lay down an arbitrary highwater mark for the tide of debt'.[83] When a debtor failed to make payments, it put the firm in a difficult situation. Merchants could either restrict advances and risk losing the good will of the debtor (or worse, risk negatively affecting the operations of the plantation), or they could keep advancing—and risk more money.

The next step, therefore, was to force a more formal arrangement. In the case of Lynch, Tobin & Pinney identified his other London creditors, Davis, McKenzie & Strachan, and came to an agreement with them. Tobin & Pinney wanted Lynch to sign a deed of trust to properly secure his debt to the firm, which had, by this stage, reached £2,113 8d. To keep him placated (and, thus, willing to sign it), the firm continued with his orders. Thomas Daniel & Son, Lynch's other creditors in Bristol, did not take part in the agreement, but promised not to make a move against Lynch that would disturb it.[84] By May 1792, his debt stood at £1,880 9s 8d. Tobin & Pinney had kept its shipments, as far as possible, within the limits of what remittance he made, though this slowed the pace with which his debt was repaid.[85] Eventually, Lynch made £800 available to his creditors, which Tobin & Pinney sought its share of. After prompting Davis, McKenzie & Strachan, the firm was able to secure £178 for itself.[86] Yet Tobin & Pinney fell out with Davis, McKenzie & Strachan in a dispute over the division of the money and was asked to send some back. Fearing that the firm would receive nothing further from

---

81 Tobin & Pinney to Ulysses Lynch, 30 September 1790, Tobin & Pinney to Nicholas Richards, 29 September 1790, UoBSC, MS DM58/Letter Book/38.
82 Tobin & Pinney to James Tyson, 25 September 1789, UoBSC, MS DM58/Letter Book/38.
83 Pares, *West-India Fortune*, p. 293.
84 Tobin & Pinney to Ulysses Lynch, 25 October, 1 November 1790, and 24 January and 14 March 1791, Tobin & Pinney to Nicholas Richards, 1 November 1790, UoBSC, MS DM58/Letter Book/38.
85 Tobin & Pinney to Ulysses Lynch, 24 October 1791, and 5 May 1792, UoBSC, MS DM58/Letter Book/38.
86 Tobin, Pinney & Tobin to Strachan, McKenzie & Co., 3 February, and 3 and 20 October 1798, Tobin, Pinney & Tobin to Ulysses Lynch, 3 February 1798, UoBSC, MS DM58/Letter Book/40.

Davis, McKenzie & Strachan, Tobin & Pinney told Lynch to send whatever was to be divided between his creditors to them instead.[87] A rift had formed between Lynch's creditors, making cooperation between the parties difficult as they argued over what paucity of a remittance Lynch could make. All the while, Lynch was able to get away with not paying.

In the meantime, Tobin & Pinney had exercised its other option: having its attorneys on the islands move against the debtor. A key responsibility of attorneys included collecting debts and chasing down debtors on behalf of the firms they served, or having bills redrawn and secured against property or produce. When John Tobin Crosse and Archibald Washington repeatedly failed to make a remittance, for example, Tobin & Pinney wrote to inform them that the firm had asked its attorney 'to proceed to a Settlement of your Account with us'. Attorneys had to be careful, however: when Charles Ellery indicated his intention to pay his debt in rum, James Williams, the manager of Pinney's plantation and attorney to the firm, was warned 'not to give Rum at a high price, and convert Currency into Sterling at an unreasonable Exchange'.[88] With 'the greatest reliance on' their attorneys' 'knowledge of West India transactions', the firm therefore pressed its attorneys to come to an agreement with Lynch. Tobin & Pinney told Nicholas Richards, its St Kitts attorney, to 'insist on an immediate settlement of our demand'. The partners moved to have Lynch's account 'properly proved under our City Seal', which would give them the legal basis for a suit, and directed Lynch to either settle outright or provide some security to Richards for the payment. Richards was given instructions the following year to negotiate 'whatever arrangement you may think adviseable to make'. Richards therefore wrote the debt down to £1,000 and had it secured by bond.[89] However, this only seemed to open up for Lynch the opportunity of reducing his obligation further: he offered his creditors 2s in the £1, to be paid over ten years and free of interest. Tobin & Pinney objected to the lack of security, and further to Lynch, who 'has

---

[87] Tobin, Pinney & Tobin to McKenzie & Glennie, 6 and 15 November 1800, 10 and 14 January 1801, and Tobin, Pinney & Tobin to Ulysses Lynch, 5 February 1801, UoBSC, MS DM58/Letter Book/42.

[88] Tobin, Pinney & Tobin to John Tobin Crosse, and Archibald Washington, 4 November 1797, UoBSC, MS DM58/Letter Book/40; Tobin, Pinney & Tobin to James Williams, 30 September 1800, UoBSC, MS DM58/Letter Book/42.

[89] Tobin & Pinney to Nicholas Richards, 14 March 1791, UoBSC, MS DM58/Letter Book/38; Tobin & Pinney to Nicholas Richards, and to Ulysses Lynch, 3 August and 12 October 1795, UoBSC, MS DM58/Letter Book/39; Tobin, Pinney & Tobin to Nicholas Richards, 18 May 1796, to Henry Berkeley, 26 January 1797, to Strachan, McKenzie & Co., 4 June 1796, to Ulysses Lynch, 31 July 1797, and to Berkeley & Whitehall, 12 February 1798, UoBSC, MS DM58/Letter Book/40.

made us so many fair promises, and has so often deceived us, that we have no reason whatever to suppose he will be inclined to attend more rigidly to the arrangement he now proposes, than to any of his former agreements'. However, the firm finally acquiesced to five annual payments of £100 and security for the same. Upon repayment, Tobin & Pinney agreed to discharge the whole debt.[90] The firm did not seem to recover even this, however; it had written the debt down to make it easier to pay back—but in writing it down, it was left with little to recover.

Tobin & Pinney did not litigate against Lynch and, alongside others in their community, showed an aversion to litigation more generally. According to the firm, it was out of 'regard to his family' that Tobin & Pinney had its attorneys 'refrain from enforcing the Judgements'. Lynch was given this leeway to enable him to remain productive, and, as long as he made regular repayments, the firm asserted that it would not move against his property.[91] The fact that his debt had been formally written down so much probably meant that it was no longer worth the firm's time or money to proceed against him. The partners' attitude to litigation appears to have been to avoid it if possible: they expressed their desire to Lynch 'to avoid extremities', and they similarly commented that fellow merchants John Cave & Co. 'do not wish to proceed to extremities if it can be prevented' when they were chasing a debt in St Croix.[92] Albane Forestier, in her assessment of the use of the courts in Nevis, similarly finds that Tobin & Pinney only sued for debt once in the islands (though John Pinney, perhaps acting as planter rather than merchant, was a more active litigator). With planters sitting in the courts, the balance was rarely in the favour of metropolitan firms. The one case that Tobin & Pinney did litigate was against William Jones, for a debt of £8,000.[93] The firm's reluctance to litigate might be reflective of David Hancock's assessment that merchants were loath to use the courts lest they threaten the 'harmony of the community'; chasing down debts through the courts risked making merchants appear greedy or aggressive.[94] It might be, further, that the courts were simply too costly and time-consuming to bother with, especially when

---

90 Tobin, Pinney & Tobin to James Stephens, 17 and 26 April 1799, UoBSC, MS DM58/Letter Book/40.

91 Tobin, Pinney & Tobin to James Stephens, 3 February 1798, and Tobin, Pinney & Tobin to Berkeley & Whitehall, 12 February 1798, UoBSC, MS DM58/Letter Book/40.

92 Tobin & Pinney to Nicholas Richards, 10 March 1793, and to Ulysses Lynch, 16 March and 14 May 1793, UoBSC, MS DM58/Letter Book/39; Tobin, Pinney & Tobin to Joseph Chabert, 2 October 1800, UoBSC, MS DM58/Letter Book/42.

93 Forestier, 'Commercial Organisation', pp. 163–70.

94 Hancock, *Citizens*, p. 249.

the action would be taken by a firm on the other side of the Atlantic to the debtor. Creditors therefore seemingly preferred to use the threat of litigation, which would embroil both parties in costly and time-consuming court cases, to push planters.[95] Tobin & Pinney appeared to prefer to write the debt down and let small debts lie rather than litigate; the firm would rather risk losing the debt than force a settlement through the courts.

Indeed, other cases show Tobin & Pinney's preference for letting debts lie over the years, while simply putting pressure on debtors to pay up. This was the firm's approach to the debts of Joseph Blake and Henry Keyworth. For Blake's debt, the partners took it upon themselves to recover the amount of £9,700 due to Charles Chabert, resident in St Croix, from Joseph Blake in Ireland. Tobin & Pinney was to be compensated with the interest due. However, Blake was far from cooperative, and though the entire saga of this debt is too long to recount in any detail, the length of time that it lingered, and the amount of communication and negotiation Tobin & Pinney went through in an attempt to recover the debt before even considering litigation (and they certainly considered it, though only threatened it), shows their preference for this approach over the courts. They originally took up this obligation in 1789, and the saga of recovery extended long into the 1800s and involved numerous parties, including family members, attorneys, and agents in Ireland.[96] The Keyworth debt was similar, with Henry Keyworth contracting thousands of pounds of debt for the settlement of a new estate in St Vincent in 1794, which he failed to establish himself in. Tobin & Pinney negotiated with Keyworth's father and others in an attempt to cajole Keyworth to work his estate and pay the firm back. This again lasted into the 1800s.[97] As well as showing a preference for writing debts down, Tobin & Pinney further demonstrated that it would rather let the debts lie for years than go to the courts.

Yet long debts were fairly normal. As Peter Mathias points out, it was common for firms to let short-term debts roll over into long-term debts.[98]

---

95 Peter Mathias, 'Risk, Credit and Kinship in Early Modern Enterprise', in *The Early Modern Atlantic Economy*, ed. by John J. McCusker and Kenneth Morgan (Cambridge: Cambridge University Press, 2001), pp. 15–35 (p. 27); John Smail, 'Credit, Risk, and Honor in Eighteenth-Century Commerce', *Journal of British Studies*, 44 (2005), 439–56 (p. 445); Hoppit, *Risk and Failure*, pp. 37–40; Christian R. Burset, 'Merchant Courts, Arbitration, and the Politics of Commercial Litigation in the Eighteenth-Century British Empire', *Law & History Review*, 34:3 (2016), 615–47 (pp. 618–20); Pares, *West-India Fortune*, pp. 269–70.

96 See numerous letters to Charles Chabert, Joseph Chabert, Joseph Blake, William Furlong and James Fitzgerald in UoBSC, MS DM58/Letter Book/38–42.

97 See numerous letters to Henry Keyworth Jr, Henry Keyworth Sr, William John Struth, and Azariah Pinney in UoBSC, MS DM58/Letter Book/39–42.

98 Mathias, 'Risk', p. 27.

The firm's floating debt from planters was often around £20,000–30,000. This was not always the intention—that it made frequent requests to planters for 'considerable remittances' that could be put 'towards the reduction of our Debt, and which will prevent us from taking any unpleasant Steps to recover the Sum due to us' shows that the firm still wanted debts, especially those drawn on book accounts, to be paid down.[99] However, Tobin & Pinney, and John Pinney personally, allowed debts to linger sometimes for decades, constantly reframing them and adding additional security. Arrears could be, and were, recontracted into new mortgages on the threat of litigation. Even when Tobin & Pinney told clients upfront that the advance was 'a temporary loan', the partners still added that, if it somehow manifested into a 'standing Loan' to be paid over several years, then they expected, for example, 'Security bearing an Interest of 6 pC'.[100]

As long as there were remittances of sugar that could be used to pay the interest, or even the legitimate promise of future remittances, a lingering debt could be tolerated; it was rare for a planter to make his (or her) way out of debt, and this was something the firm was aware of. Commenting on John Hendrickson's debt, for example, Pinney informed the firm that 'I shall have no objection to let my demand remain, so [long] as the Interest is regularly kept down.' Debts such as his might increase, and the firm would 'of course expect a Mortgage' on its clients' property. Edward Brazier's debt was similarly recontracted into mortgage debt: in September 1800, he was offered a fresh advance of £3,000 in return for a 'second mortgage of your Estate'.[101] Indeed, mortgages were often held in perpetuity, with the interest payments acting as a form of annuity. In this way, a lump sum was lent to a planter in return for what could, theoretically, function as a source of income over several lifetimes. Many of John Pinney's mortgages were held until his death, and it was his sons in the 1820s who moved against most of the mortgaged property in an effort to liquidate these assets. Pares calculates that John Pinney earned £12,000 a year in interest payments.[102] It was not necessarily the case that mortgage debt followed a build-up of debt on current accounts, but this is reflective of Tobin & Pinney's experience.[103] A

---

99 Tobin, Pinney & Tobin to James Huggins, 10 July 1801, UoBSC, MS DM58/Letter Book/42.

100 Tobin, Pinney & Tobin to John George Goldfrap, 19 December 1800, UoBSC, MS DM58/Letter Book/42.

101 Tobin, Pinney & Tobin to John Hendrickson, 10 July 1801, and Tobin, Pinney & Tobin to Edward Brazier, 30 September 1800, UoBSC, MS DM58/Letter Book/42.

102 Pares, *West-India Fortune*, p. 177, and chs 11 and 12. See also Morgan, *Bright-Meyler Papers*, pp. 100–05.

103 Smith, *Slavery*, pp. 139–50.

good debt, therefore, could last a lifetime. This is why Tobin & Pinney was reluctant to move against debts that had lingered for a decade: the debt was still thought to be in its infancy.

Tobin & Pinney's experience shows that some debts could be painful to recover. The partners attempted to recover shipments from other merchants and pressured planters into sending all their shipments to them. If shipments were not forthcoming, they sent frequent prompts to planters and restricted their future orders to all but essentials. If this proved ineffective, the firm could make a formal agreement with the planter's other creditors and have its attorneys pressure the debtors into repayment. This was all executed under the threat of the courts, though these were used infrequently, given their cost and the stigma against their use. Ultimately, however, because it was normal for debts to last a lifetime (or more), the firm preferred to let them linger on its accounts for as long as interest payments remained possible. Significantly, the inadequacies of debt collection coupled with the length of time that debts could acceptably last meant that merchants had to be very particular about who they lent to. This, in addition to the high-risk environment in which they operated, meant that having a set of effective screening criteria was of the utmost importance.

An effective screening process

Merchants were pressured into lending cautiously by both their environment and the difficulties of debt collection. Cautious lending meant restricting advances in size and keeping credit linked as near as possible to the value of sugar consignments. However, given the length of time that debts lasted, it also meant developing effective criteria for screening potential debtors. Having a process for evaluating requests from new planters helped Tobin & Pinney manage its credit effectively. How did this work, given that, as Peter Mathias argues, 'very little knowledge was available: no credit ratings, no published accounts and no professional auditing, while bank dealings were a highly personal affair'?[104] At the beginning of the business, Tobin & Pinney emphasised the values of 'friendship' and developing a 'personal intimacy' with its clients. After a series of poor harvests, and under pressure from the abolitionist movement, the firm began to develop a stricter set of standards that helped it effectively reject planters who were less likely to make repayments. This involved considering the reputation of planters and using recommendations. Yet this, in itself, was inadequate. Subsequently, Tobin & Pinney began extending its network of attorneys, who could be trusted to provide information about potential debtors' assets and productive

---

104 Mathias, 'Risk', p. 28.

capabilities. These strategies together helped the firm navigate the increasingly risky environment within which it operated.

Early on, Tobin & Pinney relied on personal relationships as the foundation for lending.[105] This was driven, at least in part, by the partners' previous residence in the islands and the plantations that they still had there. They had relied on 'old friends' to help them establish their firm. However, Tobin & Pinney's experience shows that attempts to create personal relationships, which were intended to support and prompt repayment, could backfire. The partners expressed to several clients, at a point of particular distress and exasperation during the early stages of the abolitionist movement, that they believed that they had 'been applied to for loans of money, more as <u>friends</u> than as <u>Merchants</u>'. They told their attorney that 'our <u>personal</u> intimacy with our acquaintance in the W Indies has operated directly opposite to what <u>might</u> have been expected by subjecting us to <u>applications</u> which would not ever had been made to <u>Strangers</u>'.[106] The increased risks that they faced had revealed the flaws in their approach, as the personalisation of their relationships made implementing a strategy based on principles of cautious lending more difficult. The clients, expecting treatment as 'friends', would not abide by the more restrictive lending that a policy of caution entailed.

Tobin & Pinney found it more effective to assess planters by their reputations. As historians have widely observed, a good reputation was a valuable asset, and it became a useful shorthand in the increasingly multifarious business environment, where it was impossible to know everyone personally.[107] The firm indicated that it would 'feel a particular pleasure in obliging any Gentleman whom we know and have a good opinion of'. Tobin & Pinney considered '<u>punctuality</u> even in <u>trifles</u> as a strong mark of ... <u>Steadiness</u>'. Planters should send substantial remittances and be polite to their creditors. They were expected to live within their means.[108] In the case

---

105 Pinney & Tobin to James Tyson, 11 February 1789, UoBSC, MS DM58/Letter Book/37.

106 Pinney & Tobin to William Coker, 10 February 1789, and Pinney & Tobin to Lucretia Pemberton, 23 February 1789, UoBSC, MS DM58/Letter Book/37. See also Forestier, 'Commercial Organisation', pp. 134–35; Haggerty, *'Merely for Money'?*, pp. 66–67, 73.

107 A recent survey is Emily Buchnea, 'Networks and Clusters in Business History', in *The Routledge Companion to Business History*, ed. by John F. Wilson, Steven Toms, and Emily Buchnea (Abingdon: Routledge, 2017), pp. 259–73 (pp. 262–63).

108 Pinney & Tobin to Edward Huggins, 3 July 1787, UoBSC, MS DM58/Letter Book/37; Tobin & Pinney to Ulysses Lynch, 21 December 1789, UoBSC, MS DM58/Letter Book/38; Tobin & Pinney to John Scarbrough, 11 September 1793, and to Charles Chabert, 8 January 1795, UoBSC, MS DM58/Letter Book/39.

of planters such as John Smith Budgen and Edward Huggins, then, the firm informed them that, if they 'should find it convenient to increase your Drafts on us, we beg you will use no ceremony, as the experience we have had of your punctuality will encourage us to pay them due honour'.[109] As with other businesspeople in a range of occupations, Tobin & Pinney valued traits such as sobriety, honesty, neatness, steadiness, industriousness, and knowledge of business.[110] The firm, therefore, used a common metric for assessing others, and what the partners valued conformed to standards common for the time.

Reputations were remembered and communicated through conversation and correspondence. For example, Tobin & Pinney was asked about Samuel Allen, who was in partnership with a stationer, Mr Evans. The enquiry regarded some alleged insolvency. Tobin & Pinney reported that Allen never publicly stopped payment, though he might have made some private compromise with his creditors. The partners knew little of his circumstances, but had heard nothing negative against his character.[111] This shows how common understandings of reputations lingered in people's minds. This is further demonstrated by instances where past acquaintances of Tobin & Pinney contacted the firm again with new business opportunities. Thomas, Samuel & Miers Fisher, for example, sent an order for glass to Tobin & Pinney to be shipped to America, remembering Pinney from when he was a planter and used to order goods from them in Philadelphia.[112] Merchants sought information in coffee shops, at the local Exchange, and from their own personal networks, tapping into the 'network memory' to find out how others were perceived.[113] Tobin and Pinney, as members of Bristol's West India Association, could use the dinners as an opportunity to share gossip.[114] These enquiries formed the basis for how reputations were communicated.

---

109 Tobin & Pinney to John Budgen, 11 May 1793, Tobin & Pinney to Edward Huggins, 25 September 1794, UoBSC, MS DM58/Letter Book/39.
110 See especially Haggerty, *'Merely for Money'?*, pp. 98, 109–12; Jon Stobart, 'Information, Trust and Reputation: Shaping a Merchant Elite in Early 18th-century England', *Scandinavian Journal of History*, 30:3–4 (2005), 298–307 (pp. 303–04); Toby L. Ditz, 'Shipwrecked; or, Masculinity Imperiled: Mercantile Representations of Failure and the Gendered Self in Eighteenth-Century Philadelphia', *The Journal of American History*, 81 (1994), 51–80 (p. 61).
111 Tobin & Pinney to Alexander Douglas, 12 February 1795, UoBSC, MS DM58/Letter Book/39.
112 Tobin & Pinney to Thomas, Samuel & Miers Fisher, 6 August 1789, UoBSC, MS DM58/Letter Book/38.
113 Hancock, 'Trouble', p. 479; Nuala Zahedieh, 'Making Mercantilism Work: London Merchants and Atlantic Trade in the Seventeenth Century', *Transactions of the Royal Historical Society*, 9 (1999), 143–58 (p. 153); Haggerty, *Trading Community*, p. 128.
114 BA, MS SMV/8/3/2/1 WIA.

Tobin & Pinney also relied on reputations being communicated through recommendations from respected planters. Jens Friedenreich Hage was recommended both by Charles Chabert and Nicholas Strode, and though Tobin & Pinney had no real interest in sending goods out to be sold by planters in the West Indies, this recommendation persuaded them. It was, perhaps, out of politeness to Chabert and Strode—or based on the power of *their* reputations—that Tobin & Pinney deviated from its general rule about not sending goods in return for bills.[115] Chabert similarly recommended Martin and William Krause, who also wanted goods in return for bills, which the firm obliged. The Krauses themselves recommended William Ruan to Tobin & Pinney, though the firm was less interested in this case, showing that it was Chabert's opinion they privileged (though they did, in the end, promise to send goods, as long as Ruan sent the bills first).[116] The firm likewise received a letter of introduction from William Jones for Archibald Washington, wherein Tobin & Pinney was recommended to advance him £200 or £300 (though it had already advanced him £500).[117] Recommendations were, then, another means of communicating reputations, which relied on the reputability of the person making the recommendation.

However, reputation was limited as a predictor of future performance. Tobin & Pinney realised this on a number of occasions, though the firm's experience with Lynch was especially revealing. Their correspondence began initially with letters containing 'entertaining intelligence' that went beyond 'mere business'. Lynch's letters gave Tobin & Pinney 'much pleasure in hearing how the West India world wags'. The firm was close to Lynch's wife, too, and reported on her well-being. The partners were anxious to secure Lynch as a 'permanent correspondent', informing him that they were 'willing and ready to enter into any connection with a Gent^n of your established character'. Tobin & Pinney sent him orders totalling £1,691 11s 10d, a considerable advance that demonstrated the firm's appreciation of his reputation. However, Lynch was not easily pleased when it came to his orders. The partners were pressed, on several occasions, to answer 'the whole of the different remarks you have been pleased to make on the different prices, and qualities, of the few articles which did not entirely meet with your approbation'.[118] Lynch's orders became increasingly impractical. Some he wanted delivered sooner than was feasible.

---

115 Tobin & Pinney to Jens Freidenreich Hage, 4 August 1790, and Tobin & Pinney to Charles Chabert, 1 November 1790, UoBSC, MS DM58/Letter Book/38.
116 Tobin & Pinney to Martin & William Krause, 12 October 1793, and to William Ruan, 3 and 18 August 1795, UoBSC, MS DM58/Letter Book/39.
117 Tobin & Pinney to Archibald Washington and William Jones, 19 February 1793, UoBSC, MS DM58/Letter Book/39.
118 Pinney & Tobin to Ulysses Lynch, 23 April 1788 and 10 February 1789, UoBSC,

Others were too vague to make sense of. Fatally, the firm found out that Lynch was 'so much in arrears with your other Correspondents, particularly the House in London'.[119]

Tobin & Pinney had been misled by Lynch's reputation, on the basis of which the partners had expected a more fulfilling relationship than could be delivered. Efforts were therefore made, as we have seen, to limit further advances and recover his debts, but in vain. They bemoaned how they had been taken in by their impression of Lynch as a 'man of affluence', and had, thus, failed to 'inquire into particulars' regarding his estate and circumstances. There was a 'long acquaintance between Mr Pinney and our JT and Mr Lynch & his family' which encouraged this negligence. Through their business relationship, Tobin & Pinney's idea of Lynch's reputation completely changed. Experience revealed the 'disagreeable traits in his character'. He was 'unpleasant', with 'an inclination to be easily dissatisfied' and—egregiously—'somewhat willing to deceive himself, & to wish to represent his affairs in a more flourishing situation than we fear is really the case'. Though the partners still believed he was 'industrious & œconomical', he appeared completely ignorant as to the limits of credit and the care with which merchants should advance it. The firm would 'be well pleased to be released' from its engagement with him 'on terms of inconvenience or at even some loss'.[120] This resulted, as shown, in a troubled saga of debt recovery. This experience supports the arguments made by other historians, who similarly point out the limits of reputation.[121] It shows how reputations could be misleading, and demonstrated the importance to Tobin & Pinney of having other means of screening potential clients.

To screen clients more effectively, Tobin & Pinney built up and relied upon a network of attorneys in the islands. These were people of whom they had a good opinion, people who were close to their own plantation operations, or planters with whom the firm had a long-standing trading relationship. Tobin & Pinney understood the power of a good network of attorneys and informants.

MS DM58/Letter Book/37; Tobin & Pinney to Ulysses Lynch, 15 June, 8 July, and 1 October 1789, and 5 May 1790, UoBSC, MS DM58/Letter Book/38.
119 Tobin & Pinney to Ulysses Lynch, 10 June, 4 August, and 30 September 1790, and to Nicholas Richards, 29 September 1790, UoBSC, MS DM58/Letter Book/38.
120 Tobin & Pinney to Nicholas Richards and Edward Parson, 16 May 1791, and to Nicholas Richards, 24 October 1791, UoBSC, MS DM58/Letter Book/38.
121 See especially Kadens, 'Pre-Modern Credit Networks', pp. 2430-51; Ana Sofia Ribeiro, 'The Evolution of Norms in Trade and Financial Networks in the First Global Age: The Case of Simon Ruiz's Network', in *Beyond Empires: Global, Self-Organising, Cross-imperial Networks, 1500–1800*, ed. by Catia Antunes and Amelia Polonia (Leiden: Brill, 2016), pp. 12-40 (pp. 29-31).

Speaking of another West India financier, the partners admired his 'long personal intercourse and connection' with St Kitts, his acquaintance 'with the situation of most individuals in it', and, especially, his access to 'confidential Correspondents on the Spot even better informed than himself'. He was, therefore, 'much less likely to get on the wrong side of the Post, than others with an inferior knowledge'.[122] Indeed, information sharing was one of the key benefits to having a broad and diverse network.[123] This motivated Tobin & Pinney to expand its connections and sources of information. The firm sent powers of attorney (or instructions to act as agents) to William Coker, Thomas Pym Weekes, James Williams (all managers of John Pinney's plantation), John Taylor, John Colhoun Mills, Edward Brazier, and Cossley Saunders. These individuals acted as attorneys or agents at various points on Nevis. Nicholas Richards, Edward Parson, and Henry Berkeley were together on St Kitts, Charles and Joseph Chabert were based on St Croix, and George Lowman and James French were on St Vincent.[124] Figure 5.1 shows the extensive network that all these individuals, together with their contacts, formed, representing the network of knowledge that Tobin & Pinney had access to. Remember that these networks are based on transacting relationships; the network of more minor interactions will have extended much further than even this.

One of the most important responsibilities of these attorneys was to perform background checks on potential clients. Tobin and Pinney might be impressed by reports of a planter's character, and they might have a good experience of his politeness and punctuality, but they realised that they needed more if they were to make any significant advances. For a prospective client, the firm wanted to know from its attorney 'the Situation & value of his Estate; & whether he has stock & Negroes to work it; & whether he is supposed to owe money in the W. Indies, and to what amount'. The partners asked William Coker to investigate James Carroll, who was unwittingly nominated as a guarantor for a £500 loan by Samuel Croker. Carroll stated candidly to Coker that 'I am surprised Mr Pinney can expect any such thing from me when I cannot pay him the money I already owe him.'[125] The firm understandably rejected this advance. The merchants also requested that Edward Brazier investigate Archibald Washington, to whom they

---

122 Tobin & Pinney to Ulysses Lynch, 21 December 1789, UoBSC, MS DM58/Letter Book/38.
123 See, among others, Haggerty, *Trading Community*, pp. 110–13.
124 See numerous letters to these individuals in UoBSC, MS DM58/Letter Book/37–42. See also Forestier, 'Commercial Organisation', pp. 90–97.
125 Pinney & Tobin to William Coker, 27 September 1787, and to William Coker and John Tobin Crosse, 11 March 1789, UoBSC, MS DM58/Letter Book/37; Pinney & Tobin to William Coker, 30 May 1789, UoBSC, MS DM58/Letter Book/38.

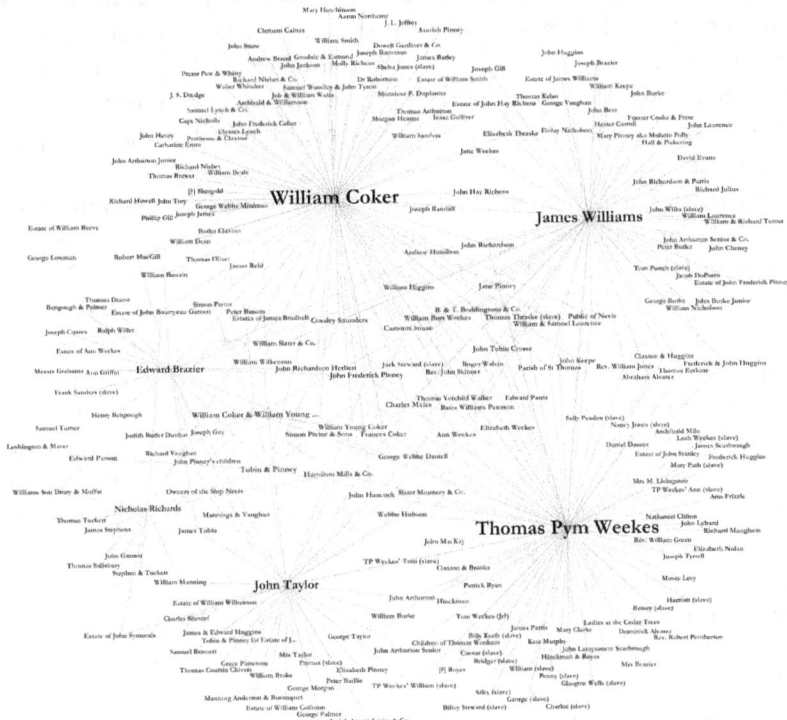

Figure 5.1: Network of Attorneys within John Pinney's Nevis–Bristol Network, 1783–1803
Note: John Pinney removed. Rendered in Gephi <https://gephi.org/>.

Source: UoBSC, DM58 Pinney Family Papers, 1538–1948, Account Books 30, 31, 33, 34, 35, 36, 39, 41, 43, 45, 47, 52, 54, 57, and 59.

https://liverpooluniversitypress.manifoldapp.org/projects/crisis-and-resilience/resource/crisis-and-resilience-figure-5-1

had extended a small amount, to see if his estates could support increased borrowing. They had a positive impression from his remittances up to that point, but needed more information on his state of indebtedness and the productive capacity of his estates.[126] They rejected a request for £1,200 from

---

126 Tobin & Pinney to Archibald Washington and William Jones, 29 October 1792, UoBSC, MS DM58/Letter Book/38.

John Tyson because, though they had 'little doubt of your intention to ship early next year' that amount in sugar, they were 'totally unacquainted with the situation of your resources'.[127] With an understanding of the limits of character and reputation, Tobin & Pinney relied increasingly on having attorneys who could provide estimates for the value and productive capacity of planters' estates.

By relying on a network of attorneys in the islands that the firm served, Tobin & Pinney's business became geographically concentrated. Significantly, the firm had no interest in making loans to Jamaican planters. Tobin & Pinney declined Thomas Hughan's request for provisions and stores, though the partners had shipped him goods on behalf of some London merchants, stating that 'Our present connexions are entirely with the Windward & Leeward Islands; and we have not a single correspondent in Jamaica.' The crux of their refusal was their being 'totally unacquainted with the situation of Gentlemen there'. Their inability to send someone to the estates in Jamaica meant that they could not ascertain the 'situation' of planters whom they would otherwise have 'no objection' to serving, or they would only send out goods if they received a sugar shipment or payment first.[128] The heightened risk environment only served to reinforce this approach. The partners repeated this concern in 1793, especially considering that the 'commencement of a War likely to prove very obstinate and destructive' would make that time 'the most improper one to form any few connections' with planters in Jamaica.[129] They had no interest in forming a connection with Jamaica because they had no attorneys there who could report on the Jamaican planters. They were not unusual among their peers in having a geographical focus.[130] Their emphasis on lending only in islands where they had a network of attorneys represented a trade-off. The firm became specialised in operating on particular islands, which reduced the risks of exposure to the more incompetent planters, but heightened its exposure to the impact of hurricanes and other weather on particular islands. Tobin & Pinney would rather be exposed to the natural hazards that came from geographical specialisation than the moral hazards that came from geographical diversification.

---

127 Pinney & Tobin to John Tyson, 4 September 1786, UoBSC, MS DM58/Letter Book/37.
128 See Pinney & Tobin to Thomas Hughan, 9 July 1787, to Wildman & Smith, 30 August and 23 October 1786, and to Hughan & Harding, 19 February 1787, UoBSC, MS DM58/Letter Book/37.
129 Tobin & Pinney to William Delaroche, 14 February 1793, UoBSC, MS DM58/Letter Book/39.
130 See Forestier, 'Commercial Organisation', p. 110.

Conclusion

With knowledge of accounting methods and with instruments such as bonds, mortgages, and bills of exchange, Tobin and Pinney were well positioned to keep track of their credits and debts. The tools of their trade helped them record debts, credit times, and interest, and their yearly balancing of accounts helped them resolve disputes. They knew how to secure debts to property. Fundamentally, they understood how to use the bill of exchange to their advantage. Its transferability gave them, and their firm's clients, flexibility and liquidity.

However, these tools had to be used ever more wisely in an environment that was increasingly fraught with risk. To cope, the firm developed a cautious approach to lending. This meant keeping advances to planters small and tied closely to consignments of sugar. This approach was both conditioned and reaffirmed by issues with harvests, the threat of war, and the abolitionist movement. Tobin & Pinney's exposure to the abolitionist movement, in particular, proved the value of caution as a guiding principle, and this helped the partners navigate the credit crisis in 1793. Yet throughout the war the outlook remained dim, and this again reaffirmed the value of caution and small advances. When the price of sugar fell in 1799, Tobin & Pinney was well placed to survive, using the tools at the firm's disposal to remain liquid while further restricting advances. This cautious attitude was not just conditioned by exogenous pressures, but through exposure to incompetent planters and recalcitrant debtors. The partners' strategies for debt recovery, from obtaining transfers from other merchants to sending prompts and making threats, were not the most effective. The insufficient support from the courts, coupled with their own philosophy that interest from debts should be a long-lasting source of income, meant that debts lingered long on their accounts.

Both the environment within which they operated and their experience with debtors proved to Tobin and Pinney that cautious lending needed to be coupled with careful screening. Their early experiences with treating clients as 'friends' proved incompatible with a more restrictive lending policy. They therefore began using reputation and recommendations, rather than 'personal intimacy', as the basis for lending. While this was a broadly useful (and widely used) strategy, it had its limitations. Reputations were imperfect, and a planter who worked hard to cultivate a good reputation could be masking other undesirable traits. It was, therefore, important for merchants in the West India trade to have a strong network of attorneys in the islands who could provide information about the indebtedness and productive capacity of potential clients and their plantations. The use of this strategy led Tobin

& Pinney, like other merchant firms, to specialise on particular islands. It was the partners' connections to others that helped solidify and secure their business, and provided resilience in the face of financial crises and challenges to credit.

Conclusion

> But Mr. Tobin's Rejoinder is calculated for readers who wish to be persuaded into the belief, that nothing is necessary, or can be done for the relief of oppressed slaves. By all my accounts from the W. Indies, my Essay has already had the happiest effects, in rendering insensibly the treatment of slaves less oppressive. But such is the natural indolence of man, so easily is he flattered into what favours sloth, or pretends to be for his interest, that if I allow Mr. Tobin uncontradicted to tell them, that they have all along behaved irreprehensibly to their slaves, and that it is not necessary or not possible to improve their condition, they will readily believe him, and be more apt to resume their former unfeeling behaviour.
>
> Revd James Ramsay, *A Letter to James Tobin*, 1787[1]

A KEY UNDERCURRENT OF THIS BOOK has been that, while any individual crisis is something unusual that challenges or threatens the status quo, crises are normal, even frequent. This is certainly true for this period, as demonstrated by the range of crises that merchants faced. The transition into the peace that followed the American Revolution was significant for the West Indies, especially as problems with food shortages experienced during the war were compounded by a series of devastating hurricanes. The threat of war in 1787 and 1790 threatened disruption through a transition back into a wartime period. The abolitionist movement, which began again in earnest in the late 1780s, threatened to up-end the system of slavery upon which the

---

1 Ramsay, *Letter to James Tobin*, p. v.

prosperity of the West Indies was built. The Saint Domingue Revolution showed the potentially distressing effects that slave revolts could have for the white Europeans who benefited from the violent system of slavery. And this was all before the war with France in 1793. From 1793, these merchants endured a transition into warfare, a credit crisis, conflict in Europe and the West Indies, and a crisis in the markets in Hamburg that followed the severe overproduction of sugar.

Yet these merchants were, for the most part, resilient. Their knowledge of West India affairs and the sugar production process, supported by their networks, helped merchants overcome the subsistence crisis that followed the American Revolution. Moreover, their knowledge of the system of slavery and subsequent claim to expertise was weaponised against the abolitionist movement. When it came to their control of shipping, the West India men were able to ensure that their shipping routes were stable, even as tonnage entering Bristol from Europe and North America fell during the war. This was achieved because merchants lobbied for convoys—these were not imposed upon them, but requested by them—which they used to safeguard their ships and obtain cheaper insurance. When merchants experienced price uncertainty in the sugar market because of the threat of war, the Saint Domingue Revolution, and the transition from peace to war, they were able to weather the changes in the market using established practices. Indeed, their strategy to overcome uncertainty was the same as their strategy for overcoming gluts: they withheld their sugar from the market until the price was right. In addition to this, the crises they faced, especially warfare and the threat posed by the abolitionist movement, induced a culture of caution in the West India community. This caution, further realised by Tobin and Pinney from their experience in dealing with recalcitrant debtors, was expressed by them in their reluctance to advance large amounts, especially to planters who could provide limited consignments. In this way, these Bristol merchants overcame many of the challenges they faced.

Resilience was further bolstered by the other actors along the sugar commodity chain, who secured the business not just against crises, but against the everyday hazards inherent in the trade. This success was founded on violence: stability relied on the managers, overseers, enslaved people, and free people of colour in the West Indies who were involved in the production process. The trade also included the captains, first mates, and crew in the ships, whose responsibilities concerned not merely shipping: captains acted as agents for mercantile firms; the first mates and crew looked after the sugar; and the first mates had a hand in the sampling process. It further involved insurance brokers and underwriters: as problematic as they might sometimes have been, they were important in the market for insurance that safeguarded the profits from shipping. It included sugar brokers and coopers, who were involved in the sampling and taring process. They determined quality, constructed prices, and cared for the sugar in the warehouse. It included networks of attorneys, who were important in generating information about the creditworthiness of planters. These people managed various aspects of the business on behalf of principals and proprietors, reducing natural hazards, moral hazards, overcoming information asymmetries, and securing the business against a range of challenges. Merchants, as high-profile and important as they were, were not alone. This speaks to the character of the trading community as it was built around this particular trade; this character is part of what strengthened the community against crises.

Yet resilience had its limits. The collapse of sugar prices in 1799 brought about a new era for the sugar trade, one that involved the dominance of Cuba, the surpassing of Bristol by Liverpool, and the renewed threat of the abolitionist movement.[2] This is of major significance. The abolition of the slave trade was a profound development during one of the fiercest wars of Britain's history thus far. Indeed, balancing humanitarian and economic concerns was a complex arithmetic for a country that was increasingly reliant on the tax contributions of sugar for its war effort; for a country whose burgeoning industry, until the eastward shift in its perspective, relied significantly for its development on markets in the West Indies.[3] But so it was that sugar lost its place as 'king'. And with the slow decline of sugar's importance came, too, changes in the economy of Bristol. Among other developments, in the nineteenth century the city's economy experienced a shift away from its port, along with a movement away from sugar to other commodities and products, such as chocolate.[4]

But where British sugar was dethroned, another king emerged: American cotton. And with cotton came the indefatigable persistence of plantation capitalism, the building block around which contemporary capitalism was built.[5] This is as much a story of continuation as change. The cotton plantations were influenced by the sugar plantations developed in the previous century: the slave-based plantation system that facilitated the production of sugar provided a model for cotton planters. As Caitlin Rosenthal has shown, West India planters migrated, bringing accounting methods and practices

---

2 See Ryden, *West Indian Slavery*.
3 See Williams, *Capitalism & Slavery*; Inikori, *Africans*.
4 Harvey and Press, 'Industrial Change'.
5 Of recent works, see Calvin Schermerhorn, *The Business of Slavery and the Rise of American Capitalism, 1815–1860* (New Haven, CT: Yale University Press, 2015); Sven Beckert and Seth Rockman, eds, *Slavery's Capitalism: A New History of American Economic Development* (Philadelphia: University of Pennsylvania Press, 2016).

developed in the West Indies with them to the Antebellum South.⁶ The parallels (as well as the differences) between the two systems are made clear in Richard Dunn's extensive work on the Mesopotamia and Mount Airy plantations in Jamaica and Virginia, respectively.⁷ Further, early investors in American cotton had links to the West India trades.⁸ And, as this book has shown, sugar merchants, as investors in plantations, intervened in plantation operations, just as cotton merchants did.⁹ There were similarities, too, between the sugar markets of the late eighteenth century and the early nineteenth-century cotton markets.¹⁰ If 'the empire of cotton ushered in the modern world', as Sven Beckert argues, it might not be too much of a stretch to suggest that the empire of sugar ushered in the empire of cotton.¹¹

The story of sugar, and the role merchants played in supporting this trade against crises, is therefore part of the broader story of slavery and the impact this had on the emergence of modern capitalism; the merchants examined in this book are a key part of this story. In Bristol, merchants did all they could to ensure the continuation of their trade and the preservation of a way of living that had made them exceedingly wealthy—far wealthier than most men and women at the time could have dreamed. It was their persistence, their business acumen, and the organisation and defence of their trade that contributed to their resilience to crises in this period. In many ways the Revd Ramsay is too charitable to the planters he describes in the passage above. It was not indolence or sloth that rendered the planters and merchants who benefited from plantation slavery unable or unwilling to change; these were not lazy men. They profited directly and greatly from the trade in enslaved people and the sugar that slave labour produced. And they worked hard, as cogs in this plantation machine, to ensure that nothing—revolution, natural disaster, war—would interrupt the flow of that sickly sweet substance.

---

6 Rosenthal, *Accounting*, pp. 71–79.
7 Richard S. Dunn, *A Tale of Two Plantations: Slave Life and Labor in Jamaica and Virginia* (Cambridge, MA: Harvard University Press, 2014).
8 Sven Beckert, *Empire of Cotton: A New History of Global Capitalism* (New York: Vintage, 2014), p. 147.
9 See Chapter 1.
10 Cf. Chapter 3 and Haggerty, 'What's in a Price?'.
11 Beckert, *Empire*, p. xii.

Bibliography

Manuscript sources

University of Bristol Special Collections
DM58 Pinney Family Papers, 1538–1948
    DM58/Account Books/30 Pinney Account Book 30, 8 March 1783–1 August 1790
    DM58/Account Books/31 Pinney Account Book 31, 29 June 1783–25 March 1786
    DM58/Account Books/32 Pinney Account Book 32, 5 July 1783–1 May 1800
    DM58/Account Books/33 Pinney Account Book 33, 15 August 1783–31 July 1790
    DM58/Account Books/34 Pinney Account Book 34, 15 August 1783–31 March 1802
    DM58/Account Books/35 Pinney Account Book 35, 30 April 1784–31 December 1788
    DM58/Account Books/36 Pinney Account Book 36, 24 June 1784–31 December 1787
    DM58/Account Books/37 Pinney Account Book 37, 15 October 1785–31 December 1801
    DM58/Account Books/39 Pinney Account Book 39, 1 January 1789–1 January 1795
    DM58/Account Books/40 Pinney Account Book 40, 1 May 1789–31 October 1793
    DM58/Account Books/41 Pinney Account Book 41, 1 May 1789–31 December 1800

DM58/Account Books/43   Pinney Account Book 43, 1 January 1790–31 January 1791
DM58/Account Books/45   Pinney Account Book 45, 1 May 1790–30 July 1794
DM58/Account Books/47   Pinney Account Book 47, 21 November 1792–1 January 1802
DM58/Account Books/52   Pinney Account Book 52, 1795–1802
DM58/Account Books/54   Pinney Account Book 54, 1 January–31 December 1797
DM58/Account Books/57   Pinney Account Book 57, 1 January 1798–31 December 1803
DM58/Account Books/59   Pinney Account Book 59, 28 December 1798–31 December 1801
DM58/Letter Book/37   Pinney Letter Book 37, 31 May 1784–1 May 1789
DM58/Letter Book/38   Pinney Letter Book 38, 2 May 1789–30 November 1792
DM58/Letter Book/39   Pinney Letter Book 39, 26 December 1792–10 May 1796
DM58/Letter Book/40   Pinney Letter Book 40, 1 May 1796–18 August 1800
DM58/Letter Book/42   Pinney Letter Book 42, 20 August 1800–12 June 1803

Bristol Archives
SMV Records of the Society of Merchant Venturers, 1493–2003
   SMV/7/1/1/72   Wharfage Book, 1784–1785
   SMV/7/1/1/73   Wharfage Book, 1785–1786
   SMV/7/1/1/74   Wharfage Book, 1787–1788
   SMV/7/1/1/75   Wharfage Book, 1788–1789
   SMV/7/1/1/76   Wharfage Book, 1791–1792
   SMV/7/1/1/77   Wharfage Book, 1792–1793
   SMV/7/1/1/78   Wharfage Book, 1796–1797
   SMV/7/1/1/79   Wharfage Book, 1797–1798
   SMV/7/1/1/80   Wharfage Book, 1799–1800
   SMV/7/1/1/81   Wharfage Book, 1800–1801
   SMV/7/1/1/82   Wharfage Book, 1801–1802
   SMV/7/1/1/83   Wharfage Book, 1802–1803
   SMV/7/2/1/15   Papers against Abolition of the Slave Trade, 1788–1789
   SMV/8/3/2/1   West India Association Minute Book, 1782–1804
   SMV/8/3/2/5   Slave Trade – 1789
39654 Volumes of accounts for managing voyages of Bristol ships
   39654/3   Voyage Accounts for the *Triton*, 1770–1790
   39654/4   Voyage Accounts for the *Druid*, 1790–1792

Somerset Heritage Centre
DD/DN Papers of the Dickinson Family of Kingweston, 1545–2004
- DD/DN/4/2/1   Correspondence received mainly by William Dickinson (mainly at London and Kingweston), concerning business and family matters, 1709–1889
- DD/DN/4/2/15   Correspondence received by William Dickinson (mainly in London), from various authors, mainly concerning business matters, 1781
- DD/DN/4/2/16   Correspondence received by William Dickinson (mainly in London), from various authors, mainly concerning business matters, 1782
- DD/DN/4/2/17   Correspondence received by William Dickinson (mainly in London), from various authors, mainly concerning business and estate matters, 1783
- DD/DN/4/2/20   Correspondence received by William Dickinson (at London and Kingweston), concerning business and family matters, 1786
- DD/DN/4/2/22   Correspondence received by William Dickinson (at London and Kingweston), concerning business and family matters, 1787
- DD/DN/4/2/24   Correspondence received by William Dickinson (at London and Kingweston), concerning business and family matters, 1787–1788
- DD/DN/4/2/25   Correspondence received by William Dickinson (at London and Kingweston), concerning business and family matters, 1787–1806
- DD/DN/4/2/26   Correspondence received by William Dickinson (at London and Kingweston), concerning business and family matters, 1788
- DD/DN/4/2/28   Correspondence received by William Dickinson (at London and Kingweston), concerning business and family matters, 1789
- DD/DN/4/2/29   Correspondence received by William Dickinson (at London and Kingweston), concerning business and family matters, 1789
- DD/DN/4/2/30   Correspondence received by William Dickinson (at London and Kingweston), concerning business and family matters, 1789–1790
- DD/DN/4/2/32   Correspondence received by William Dickinson (at London, Kingweston and Brighton), concerning business and family matters, 1790
- DD/DN/4/2/33   Correspondence received by William Dickinson (at London, Kingweston and Bath), concerning business and family matters, 1790
- DD/DN/4/2/35   Correspondence received by William Dickinson (mainly

at London and Kingweston), concerning business and family matters, 1791

DD/DN/4/2/36 Correspondence received by William Dickinson (mainly at London), concerning business and family matters, 1791

DD/DN/4/2/37 Correspondence received by William Dickinson (mainly at London and Kingweston), concerning business and family matters, 1791–1793

DD/DN/4/2/38 Correspondence received by William Dickinson (mainly at London and Kingweston), concerning business and family matters, 1792

DD/DN/4/2/39 Correspondence received by William Dickinson (mainly at London and Kingweston), concerning business and family matters, 1792

DD/DN/4/2/40 Jamaica letter book of William Dickinson, 1792–1801

DD/DN/4/2/41 Correspondence received by William Dickinson (mainly at London and Kingweston), concerning business and family matters, 1793–1803

DD/DN/4/2/42 Correspondence received by William Dickinson (at London and Weymouth), concerning business and family matters, 1794

Printed primary sources

Anon., *The Art of Making Sugar* (London: Willock, 1752)

Edwards, Bryan, 'History of the British West-Indies, 1819', in *Papers Respecting the Culture and Manufacture of Sugar in British India* (London: Cox, 1822), Third Appendix, pp. 106–19

John Norton and Sons: Merchants of London and Virginia, ed. by Frances Norton Mason (Newton Abbot: David and Charles, 1968)

Johnson, Cuthbert W., *The Law of Bills of Exchange, Promissory Notes, Checks, &c* (London: Richards, 1839)

Joshua Johnson's Letterbook, 1771–4, ed. by Jacob M. Price (Chatham: London Record Society, 1979)

Laws for Regulating Bills of Exchange, Inland and Foreign; with Abstracts of the Several Acts Lately Passed (London: Nicoll, 1783)

Long, Edward, *The History of Jamaica; Or, General Survey of the Antient and Modern State of That Island, With Reflections on Its Situation, Settlements, Inhabitants, Climate, Products, Commerce, Laws, and Government*, Vol. II (London: T. Lowndes, 1774)

Minchinton, Walter E., ed., *Politics and the Port of Bristol in the Eighteenth Century: The Petitions of the Society of Merchant Venturers, 1698–1803* (Bristol: Bristol Records Society, 1963)

Morgan, Kenneth, ed., 'Calendar of Correspondence from William Miles to John Tharp, 1770–1789', in *A Bristol Miscellany*, ed. by Patrick McGrath (Bristol: Bristol Records Society, 1985), pp. 79–122

Morgan, Kenneth, ed., *The Bright-Meyler Papers: A Bristol–West India Connection, 1732–1837* (Oxford: Oxford University Press, 2007)

Ramsay, James, *A Letter to James Tobin, Esq., Late Member of His Majesty's Council in the Island of Nevis* (London: James Phillips, 1787)
Rogers, Nicholas, ed., *Manning the Royal Navy in Bristol: Liberty, Impressment and the State, 1739–1815* (Bristol: Bristol Records Society, 2014)
Shiercliff, Edward, *The Bristol and Hotwell Guide* (Bristol: Bulgin and Rosser, 1789)
Sketchley, James, *Sketchley's Bristol Directory, 1775* (Bath: Kingsmead Reprints, 1971 [1775])
Smith, Adam, *An Inquiry into the Nature and Causes of the Wealth of Nations*, Vol. I (London: Cadell and Davies, 1812 [1776])
Stamp-Duty. Abstract of the last Act of Parliament, respecting the Stamp-Duty on Inland Bills of Exchange, Promissory Notes, &c (London: Cornwell, [c. 1782])
Tobin, James, *Cursory Remarks upon the Reverend Mr Ramsay's Essay on the Treatment and Conversion of African Slaves in the Sugar Colonies* (London: G. and T. Wilkie, 1785)
Tooke, Thomas, *A History of Prices and of the State of Circulation from 1793 to 1837*, Vol. II (London: Longman and others, 1838)
Waterston, W., *A Manual of Commerce* (Edinburgh: Oliver and Boyd, 1865)

Online sources

Bank of England, *Inflation Calculator* (2023) <https://www.bankofengland.co.uk/monetary-policy/inflation/inflation-calculator> [accessed 1 February 2023]
Eickelmann, Christine, *The Mountravers Plantation Community, 1734–1834* (2020) <https://seis.bristol.ac.uk/~emceee/mountraversplantationcommunity.html> [accessed 23 September 2020]
'HNR Bibliography', *Historical Network Research: Network Analysis in the Historical Disciplines* <http://historicalnetworkresearch.org/bibliography/> [accessed 12 February 2023]
'Mail coaches', *The Post Museum* <https://www.postalmuseum.org/collections/mail-coaches/> [accessed 29 January 2023]
Shariatmadari, David, 'A year of "permacrisis"', *Collins Language Lovers Blog* (1 November 2022) <https://blog.collinsdictionary.com/language-lovers/a-year-of-permacrisis/> [accessed 22 February 2023]
Small, David, 'Tobin, George (1768–1838), naval officer and artist', *Oxford Dictionary of National Biography* (2004) <https://doi.org/10.1093/ref:odnb/27484>
Small, David, 'Tobin, James Webbe (1767–1814), slavery abolitionist', *Oxford Dictionary of National Biography* (2004) <https://doi.org/10.1093/ref:odnb/58446>
Small, David, 'Tobin, John (1770–1804), playwright', *Oxford Dictionary of National Biography* (2004) <https://doi.org/10.1093/ref:odnb/27485>
The Trans-Atlantic Slave Trade Database <https://www.slavevoyages.org/> [accessed 1 March 2023]
US Department of Justice and the Federal Trade Commission, 'Horizontal Merger Guidelines' (2010) <https://www.justice.gov/atr/horizontal-merger-guidelines-08192010> [accessed 12 February 2023]

Articles and chapters

Anderson, B. L., 'Money and the Structure of Credit in the Eighteenth Century', *Business History*, 12:2 (1970), 85–101

Atkinson, Brian J., 'An Early Example of the Decline of the Industrial Spirit? Bristol Enterprise in the First Half of the Nineteenth Century', *Southern History*, 9 (1987), 71–89

Basdeo, S., and H. Robertson, 'The Nova Scotia–British West Indies Commercial Experiment in the Aftermath of the American Revolution, 1783–1802', in *Canada and the Commonwealth Caribbean*, ed. by Brian Douglas Tennyson (Lanham, MD: University Press of America, 1987), pp. 25–49

Baxter, W. T., 'Credit, Bills, and Bookkeeping in a Simple Economy', *The Accounting Review*, 21:2 (1946), 154–66

Bell, Herbert C., 'British Commercial Policy in the West Indies, 1783–93', *The English Historical Review*, 31:123 (1916), 429–41

Bos, Jaap W. B., and others, 'Competition, Concentration and Critical Mass: Why the Herfindahl–Hirschman Index is a Biased Competition Measure', in *Handbook of Competition in Banking and Finance*, ed. by Jacob A. Bikker and Laura Spierdijk (Cheltenham: Edward Elgar, 2019), pp. 58–88

Bradburn, Douglas, 'The Visible Fist: The Chesapeake Tobacco Trade in War and the Purpose of Empire, 1690–1715', *The William and Mary Quarterly*, 68:3 (2011), 361–86

Buchnea, Emily, 'Networks and Clusters in Business History', in *The Routledge Companion to Business History*, ed. by John F. Wilson, Steven Toms, and Emily Buchnea (Abingdon: Routledge, 2017)

Buckles, Peter, 'Spreading Information in Eighteenth-Century Mercantile Networks: Experiments in Historical Social Network Analysis', in *Business News in the Early Modern Atlantic World*, ed. by Sophie Jones and Siobhan Talbott (Leiden: Brill, forthcoming)

Buckles, Peter, 'A Historical Social Network Analysis of John Pinney's Nevis–Bristol Network: Change over Time, the "Network Memory," and Reading Against the Grain of Historical Sources', *Enterprise & Society* (2022) <doi:10.1017/eso.2022.19>

Burset, Christian R., 'Merchant Courts, Arbitration, and the Politics of Commercial Litigation in the Eighteenth-Century British Empire', *Law & History Review*, 34:3 (2016), 615–47

Carrington, Selwyn H. H., 'The United States and the British West Indian Trade, 1783–1807', in *West Indies Accounts: Essays on the History of the British Caribbean and the Atlantic Economy in Honour of Richard Sheridan*, ed. by Roderick A. McDonald (Kingston, Jamaica: University of West India Press, 1996), pp. 149–68

Checkland, Sydney G., 'American versus West Indian Traders in Liverpool, 1793–1815', *The Journal of Economic History*, 18:2 (1958), 141–60

Checkland, Sydney G., 'Finance for the West Indies, 1780–1815', *The Economic History Review*, 10:3 (1958), 461–69

Crouzet, Francois, 'America and the Crisis of the British Imperial Economy, 1803–1807', in *The Early Modern Atlantic Economy*, ed. by John J. McCusker and Kenneth Morgan (Cambridge: Cambridge University Press, 2000), pp. 278–318

Crouzet, Francois, 'Wars, Blockade, and Economic Change in Europe, 1792–1815', *Journal of Economic History*, 24:4 (1964), 567–88

Cutterham, Tom, 'The Revolutionary Transformation of American Merchant Networks: Carter and Wadsworth and their World, 1775–1800', *Enterprise & Society*, 18:1 (2017), 1–31

Davison, Kate, 'Early Modern Social Networks: Antecedents, Opportunities, and Challenges', *The American Historical Review*, 124:2 (2019), 456–82

Ditz, Toby L., 'Shipwrecked; or, Masculinity Imperiled: Mercantile Representations of Failure and the Gendered Self in Eighteenth-Century Philadelphia', *The Journal of American History*, 81 (1994), 51–80

Evans, Chris, 'The Plantation Hoe: The Rise and Fall of an Atlantic Commodity, 1650–1850', *The William and Mary Quarterly*, 69:1 (2012), 71–100

Farber, Hannah, 'Sailing on Paper: The Embellished Bill of Lading in the Material Atlantic, 1720–1864', *Early American Studies*, 17:1 (2019), 37–83

Forestier, Albane, 'Risk, Kinship and Personal Relationships in Late Eighteenth-Century West Indian Trade: The Commercial Network of Tobin & Pinney', *Business History*, 52:6 (2010), 912–31

Foyle, C. Ernest, 'The Employment of British Shipping', in *The Trade Winds: A Study of British Overseas Trade during the French Wars, 1793–1815*, ed. by C. Northcote Parkinson (London: George Allen and Unwin, 1948), pp. 72–86

Galloway, J. H., 'Tradition and Innovation in the American Sugar Industry, c. 1500–1800: An Explanation', *Annals of the Association of American Geographers*, 75:3 (1985), 334–51

Gervais, Pierre, 'Facing and Surviving War: Merchant Strategies, Market Management and Transnational Merchant Rings', in *Merchants in Times of Crisis (16th to Mid-19th Century)*, ed. by Andrea Bonoldi and others (Stuttgart: Franz Steiner, 2015), pp. 79–95

Gervais, Pierre, 'Mercantile Credit and Trading Rings in the Eighteenth Century', *Annals. History, Social Sciences: English Edition*, 67:4 (2012), 693–730

Gervais, Pierre, 'A Merchant or a French Atlantic? Eighteenth-Century Account Books as Narratives of a Transnational Merchant Political Economy', *French History*, 25:1 (2011), 28–47

Haggerty, Sheryllynne, 'What's in a Price? The American Raw Cotton Market in Liverpool and the Anglo-American War', *Business History*, 61:6 (2019), 942–70

Hamilton, Douglas, 'Local Connections, Global Ambitions: Creating a Transoceanic Network in the Eighteenth-Century British Atlantic Empire', *The International Journal of Maritime History*, 23:2 (2011), 283–300

Hancock, David, 'The Trouble with Networks: Managing the Scots' Early-Modern Madeira Trade', *The Business History Review*, 79:3 (2005), 467–91

Hart, Emma, and Cathy Matson, 'Situating Merchants in Late Eighteenth-Century British Atlantic Port Cities', *Early American Studies*, 15:4 (2017), 660–82

Harvey, Charles, and Jon Press, 'Industrial Change and the Economic Life of Bristol Since 1800', in *Studies in the Business History of Bristol*, ed. by Charles Harvey and Jon Press (Bristol: Bristol Academic Press, 1988), pp. 1–32

Heaton, Herbert, 'The American Trade', in *The Trade Winds: A Study of British Overseas Trade during the French Wars, 1793–1815*, ed. by C. Northcote Parkinson (London: George Allen and Unwin, 1948), pp. 194–226

Hillmann, Henning, and Christina Gathmann, 'Overseas Trade and the Decline of Privateering', *The Journal of Economic History*, 71:3 (2011), 730–61

Hoppit, Julian, 'The Use and Abuse of Credit in Eighteenth-Century England', in *Business Life and Public Policy*, ed. by Neil McKendrick and R. B. Outhwaite (Cambridge: Cambridge University Press, 1986), pp. 64–78

Horsfall, Lucy Frances, 'The West Indian Trade', in *The Trade Winds: A Study of British Overseas Trade during the French Wars, 1793–1815*, ed. by C. Northcote Parkinson (London: George Allen and Unwin, 1948), pp. 157–93

Hume, Robert D., 'The Value of Money in Eighteenth-Century England: Incomes, Prices, Buying Power—and Some Problems in Cultural Economics', *Huntington Library Quarterly*, 77:4 (2015), 373–416

Inikori, Joseph, 'The Credit Needs of the African Trade and the Development of the Credit Economy in England', *Explorations in Economic History*, 27 (1990), 197–231

Kadens, Emily, 'Pre-Modern Credit Networks and the Limits of Reputation', *Iowa Law Review*, 100:6 (2015), 2429–55

Keith, Alice B., 'Relaxations in the British Restrictions on the American Trade with the British West Indies, 1783–1802', *The Journal of Modern History*, 20:1 (1948), 1–18

Kingston, Christopher, 'Marine Insurance in Britain and America, 1720–1844: A Comparative Institutional Analysis', *The Journal of Economic History*, 67:2 (2007), 379–409

Knight, Roger, and Martin Wilcox, 'War, Government and the Market: The Direction of the Debate on the British Contractor State, c. 1740–1815', in *The Contractor State and Its Implications, 1659–1815*, ed. by Richard Harding and Sergio Solbes Ferri (Las Palmas: Universidad de Las Palmas de Gran Canaria, 2012), pp. 169–92

Leonard, Adrian B., 'From Local to Transatlantic: Insuring Trade in the Caribbean', in *The Caribbean and the Atlantic World Economy: Circuits of Trade, Money and Knowledge, 1650–1914*, ed. by Adrian B. Leonard and D. Pretel (London: Palgrave Macmillan, 2015), pp. 137–60

Leonard, Adrian B., 'Underwriting Marine Warfare: Insurance and Conflict in the Eighteenth Century', *International Journal of Maritime History*, 25:2 (2013), 173–85

Marshall, P. J., 'A Polite and Commercial People in the Caribbean', in *Revisiting the Polite and Commercial People: Essays in Georgian Politics, Society, and Culture in Honour of Professor Paul Langford*, ed. by Elaine Chalus and Perry Gauci (Oxford: Oxford University Press, 2019), pp. 173–90

Marzagalli, Silvia, 'Establishing Transatlantic Trade Networks in Time of War: Bordeaux and the United States, 1793–1815', *Business History Review*, 79:4 (2005), 811–44

Marzagalli, Silvia, 'Was Warfare Necessary for the Functioning of Eighteenth-Century Colonial Systems? Some Reflections of the Necessity of Cross-Imperial and Foreign Trade in the French Case', in *Beyond Empires: Global, Self-Organising, Cross-imperial Networks, 1500–1800*, ed. by Catia Antunes and Amelia Polonia (Leiden: Brill, 2016), pp. 253–77

Mathias, Peter, 'Risk, Credit and Kinship in Early Modern Enterprise', in *The Early Modern Atlantic Economy*, ed. by John J. McCusker and Kenneth Morgan (Cambridge: Cambridge University Press, 2001), pp. 15–35

Milka, Amy, 'Feeling for Forgers: Character, Sympathy and Financial Crime in London during the Late Eighteenth Century', *Journal for Eighteenth-Century Studies*, 42:1 (2019), 7–25

Minchinton, Walter E., 'Abolition and Emancipation: Williams, Drescher and the Continuing Debate', in *West Indies Accounts: Essays on the History of the British Caribbean and the Atlantic Economy in Honour of Richard Sheridan*, ed. by Roderick A. McDonald (Kingston, Jamaica: University of West India Press, 1996), pp. 253–73.

Minchinton, Walter E., 'The Port of Bristol in the Eighteenth Century', in *Bristol in the Eighteenth Century*, ed. by Patrick McGrath (Newton Abbot: David and Charles, 1972), pp. 127–60

Morgan, Kenneth, 'Bristol West India Merchants in the Eighteenth Century', *Transactions of the Royal Historical Society*, 3 (1993), 185–208

Morgan, Kenneth, 'The Economic Development of Bristol, 1700–1850', in *The Making of Modern Bristol*, ed. by Madge Dresser and Philip Ollerenshaw (Tiverton: Redcliffe, 1996), pp. 48–75

Morgan, Kenneth, 'James Rogers and the Bristol Slave Trade', *Historical Research*, 76:192 (2003), 189–216

Morgan, Kenneth, 'Merchant Networks, the Guarantee System and the British Slave Trade to Jamaica in the 1790s', *Slavery & Abolition*, 37:2 (2016), 334–52

Morgan, Kenneth, 'Remittance Procedures in the Eighteenth-Century British Slave Trade', *The Business History Review*, 79:4 (2005), 715–49

Muldrew, Craig, 'Interpreting the Market: The Ethics of Credit and Community Relations in Early Modern England', *Social History*, 18:2 (1993), 163–83

O'Brien, Patrick K., 'The Political Economy of Taxation, 1660–1815', *Economic History Review*, 41:1 (1988), 1–32

Pearson, Robin, and David Richardson, 'Insuring the Transatlantic Slave Trade', *The Journal of Economic History*, 79:2 (2019), 417–46

Price, Jacob M., 'The Imperial Economy, 1700–1776', in *The Oxford History of the British Empire: Volume II: The Eighteenth Century*, ed. by P. J. Marshall (Oxford: Oxford University Press, 1998), pp. 78–104

Price, Jacob M., 'Transaction Costs: A Note on Merchant Credit and the Organisation of Private Trade', in *The Political Economy of Merchant Empires: State Power and World Trade, 1350–1750*, ed. by James D. Tracy (Cambridge: Cambridge University Press, 1991), pp. 276–97

Price, Jacob M., 'What Did Merchants Do? Reflections on British Overseas Trade, 1660–1790', *The Journal of Economic History*, 49:2 (1989), 267–84

Price, Jacob M., and Paul G. E. Clemens, 'A Revolution of Scale in Overseas Trade: British Firms in the Chesapeake Trade, 1675–1775', *The Journal of Economic History*, 47:1 (1987), 1–43

Reid, Ahmed, 'Sugar, Slavery and Productivity in Jamaica, 1750–1807', *Slavery & Abolition*, 37:1 (2016), 159–82

Ribeiro, Ana Sofia, 'The Evolution of Norms in Trade and Financial Networks in the First Global Age: The Case of Simon Ruiz's Network', in *Beyond Empires: Global, Self-Organising, Cross-imperial Networks, 1500–1800*, ed. by Catia Antunes and Amelia Polonia (Leiden: Brill, 2016), pp. 12–40

Richardson, David, 'The British Empire and the Atlantic Slave Trade, 1660–1807', in *The Oxford History of the British Empire, Vol. II: The Eighteenth Century*, ed. by P. J. Marshall (Oxford: Oxford University Press, 2001), pp. 440–64

Rönnbäck, Klas, 'Sweet Business: Quantifying the Value Added in the British Colonial Sugar Trade in the 18th Century', *Journal of Iberian and Latin American Economic History*, 32:2 (2014), 223–45

Ryden, David Beck, 'Sugar, Spirits, and Fodder: The London West India Interest and the Glut of 1807–15', *Atlantic Studies*, 9:1 (2012), 41–64

Sharp, Paul, and Jacob Weisdorf, 'Globalization Revisited: Market Integration and the Wheat Trade between North America and Britain from the Eighteenth Century', *Explorations in Economic History*, 50:1 (2013), 88–98

Sheridan, Richard B., 'The Formation of Caribbean Plantation Society, 1689–1748', in *The Oxford History of the British Empire: Volume II: The Eighteenth Century*, ed. by P. J. Marshall (Oxford: Oxford University Press, 1998), pp. 394–414

Singerman, David Roth, 'The Limits of Chemical Control in the Caribbean Sugar Factory', *Radical History Review*, 127 (2017), 39–61

Smail, John, 'Credit, Risk, and Honor in Eighteenth-Century Commerce', *Journal of British Studies*, 44 (2005), 439–56

Smail, John, 'The Culture of Credit in Eighteenth-Century Commerce: The English Textile Industry', *Enterprise & Society*, 4:2 (2003), 299–325

Stobart, Jon, 'Information, Trust and Reputation: Shaping a Merchant Elite in Early 18th-century England', *Scandinavian Journal of History*, 30:3–4 (2005), 298–307

Tomich, Dale, 'Commodity Frontiers, Spatial Economy, and Technological Innovation in the Caribbean Sugar Industry, 1783–1878', in *The Caribbean and the Atlantic World Economy: Circuits of Trade, Money and Knowledge, 1650–1914*, ed. by Adrian B. Leonard and D. Pretel (London: Palgrave Macmillan, 2015), pp. 184–216

Ward, J. R., 'The Profitability of Sugar Planting in the British West Indies, 1650–1834', *The Economic History Review*, n.s., 31:2 (1978), 197–213

Ward, Owen, 'The House of Pinney and Garnett's Patent Rollers', *Transactions of the Bristol and Gloucestershire Archaeological Society*, 128 (2010), 189–205

Wardle, A. C., 'The Post Office Packets', in *The Trade Winds: A Study of British Overseas Trade during the French Wars, 1793–1815*, ed. by C. Northcote Parkinson (London: George Allen and Unwin, 1948), pp. 278–90

Williams, Alan F., 'Bristol Port Plans and Improvement Schemes of the Eighteenth Century', *Transactions of the Bristol and Gloucestershire Archaeological Society*, 81 (1962), 138–88

Zahedieh, Nuala, 'Making Mercantilism Work: London Merchants and Atlantic Trade in the Seventeenth Century', *Transactions of the Royal Historical Society*, 9 (1999), 143–58

Books

Baskes, Jeremy, *Staying Afloat: Risk and Uncertainty in Spanish Atlantic World Trade, 1760–1820* (Stanford, CA: Stanford University Press, 2013)

Beckert, Sven, and Seth Rockman, eds, *Slavery's Capitalism: A New History of American Economic Development* (Philadelphia: University of Pennsylvania Press, 2016)

Beckert, Sven, *Empire of Cotton: A New History of Global Capitalism* (New York: Vintage, 2014)

Burnard, Trevor, and John Garrigus, *The Plantation Machine: Atlantic Capitalism in French Saint-Domingue and British Jamaica* (Philadelphia: University of Pennsylvania Press, 2016)

Colley, Linda, *The Gun, the Ship and the Pen: Warfare, Constitutions and the Making of the Modern World* (London: Profile Books, 2021)

Crowhurst, Patrick, *The French War on Trade: Privateering 1793–1815* (Aldershot: Scholar Press, 1989)

Davey, James, *In Nelson's Wake: How the Royal Navy Ruled the Waves after Trafalgar* (New Haven, CT: Yale University Press, 2017)

Duffy, Michael, *Soldiers, Sugar, and Seapower: The British Expeditions to the West Indies and the War against Revolutionary France* (Oxford: Clarendon Press, 1987)

Dunn, Richard S., *A Tale of Two Plantations: Slave Life and Labor in Jamaica and Virginia* (Cambridge, MA: Harvard University Press, 2014)

Eickelmann, Christine, and David Small, *Pero: The Life of a Slave in Eighteenth-Century Bristol* (Bristol: Redcliffe, 2004)

Emsley, Clive, *British Society and the French Wars, 1793–1815* (London: Macmillan, 1979)

Everill, Bronwen, *Not Made by Slaves: Ethical Capitalism in the Age of Abolition* (Cambridge, MA: Harvard University Press, 2020)

Haggerty, Sheryllynne, *The British-Atlantic Trading Community, 1760–1810: Men, Women, and the Distribution of Goods* (Leiden: Brill, 2006)

Haggerty, Sheryllynne, *'Merely for Money'? Business Culture in the British Atlantic, 1750–1815* (Liverpool: Liverpool University Press, 2012)
Hancock, David, *Citizens of the World: London Merchants and the Integration of the British Atlantic Community, 1735–1785* (Cambridge: Cambridge University Press, 1997)
Hoppit, Julian, *Risk and Failure in English Business, 1700–1800* (Cambridge: Cambridge University Press, 1987)
Inikori, Joseph, *Africans and the Industrial Revolution in England: A Study in International Trade and Economic Development* (Cambridge: Cambridge University Press, 2002)
Knight, Roger, *Britain Against Napoleon: The Organization of Victory, 1793–1815* (London: Penguin, 2014)
Knight, Roger, *Convoys: The British Struggle Against Napoleonic Europe and America* (New Haven, CT: Yale University Press, 2022)
Lincoln, Margarette, *Trading in War: London's Maritime World in the Age of Cook and Nelson* (New Haven, CT: Yale University Press, 2018)
MacInnes, C. M., *A Gateway of Empire* (Bristol: Arrowsmith, 1939)
McCusker, John J., *Money and Exchange in Europe and America, 1600–1775: A Handbook* (London: Macmillan, 1978)
McCusker, John J., *Essays in the Economic History of the Atlantic World* (London: Routledge, 1997)
Meniketti, Marco G., *Sugar Cane Capitalism and Environmental Transformation: An Archaeology of Colonial Nevis, West Indies* (Tuscaloosa: University of Alabama Press, 2015)
Minchinton, Walter E., *Jamaica Plantation Records from the Dickinson Papers 1675–1849 in Somerset Record Office and Wiltshire & Swindon Record Office: Introduction to the Microfilm Collection* (Wakefield: Microform Academic Publishers, 1978)
Mintz, Sidney, *Sweetness and Power: The Place of Sugar in Modern History* (New York: Penguin, 1985)
Morgan, Kenneth, *Bristol and the Atlantic Trade in the Eighteenth Century* (Cambridge: Cambridge University Press, 1993)
Morgan, Kenneth, *Slavery, Atlantic Trade and the British Economy, 1660–1800* (Cambridge: Cambridge University Press, 2000)
Morgan, Kenneth, *Slavery and the British Empire: From Africa to America* (Oxford: Oxford University Press, 2007)
Mulcahy, Matthew, *Hubs of Empire: The Southeastern Lowcountry and British Caribbean* (Baltimore, MD: Johns Hopkins University Press, 2014)
Muldrew, Craig, *The Economy of Obligation: The Culture of Credit and Social Relations in Early Modern England* (London: Palgrave Macmillan, 1998)
O'Shaughnessy, Andrew Jackson, *An Empire Divided: The American Revolution and the British Caribbean* (Philadelphia: University of Pennsylvania Press, 2000)
Pares, Richard, *A West-India Fortune* (Bristol: Longmans, Green, 1950)

Petley, Christer, *White Fury: A Jamaican Slaveholder and the Age of Revolution* (Oxford: Oxford University Press, 2018)

Poovey, Mary, *Genres of the Credit Economy: Mediating Value in Eighteenth- and Nineteenth-Century Britain* (Chicago: University of Chicago Press, 2008)

Pressnell, Leslie, *Country Banking in the Industrial Revolution* (Oxford: Clarendon Press, 1956)

Quinn, William, and John D. Turner, *Boom and Bust: A Global History of Financial Bubbles* (Cambridge: Cambridge University Press, 2020)

Ragatz, Lowell Joseph, *The Fall of the Planter Class in the British Caribbean, 1763–1833* (New York: Octagon Books, 1971)

Robinson, Howard, *Carrying British Mail Overseas* (London: George Allen and Unwin, 1964)

Rodger, N. A. M., *The Command of the Ocean: A Naval History of Britain, 1649–1815* (London: Penguin, 2004)

Rosenthal, Caitlin, *Accounting for Slavery: Masters and Management* (Cambridge, MA: Harvard University Press, 2018)

Ryden, David Beck, *West Indian Slavery and British Abolition, 1783–1807* (Cambridge: Cambridge University Press, 2010)

Scanlan, Padraic X., *Slave Empire: How Slavery Built Modern Britain* (London: Robinson, 2020)

Schermerhorn, Calvin, *The Business of Slavery and the Rise of American Capitalism, 1815–1860* (New Haven, CT: Yale University Press, 2015)

Schumpeter, Elizabeth, *English Overseas Trade Statistics, 1697–1808* (Oxford: Clarendon Press, 1960)

Sheridan, Richard B., *Sugar and Slavery: An Economic History of the British West Indies, 1623–1775* (Barbados: Caribbean Universities Press, 1974)

Smith, Edmond, *Merchants: The Community That Shaped England's Trade and Empire* (New Haven, CT: Yale University Press, 2021)

Smith, S. D., *Slavery, Family, and Gentry Capitalism in the British Atlantic: The World of the Lascelles, 1648–1834* (Cambridge: Cambridge University Press, 2006)

Talbott, Siobhan, *Conflict, Commerce and Franco-Scottish Relations, 1560–1713* (London: Pickering and Chatto, 2014)

Taylor, Michael, *The Interest: How the British Establishment Resisted the Abolition of Slavery* (London: Bodley Head, 2020)

Walvin, James, *Sugar: The World Corrupted, from Slavery to Obesity* (London: Robinson, 2017)

Williams, Eric, *Capitalism & Slavery* (Chapel Hill: University of South Carolina Press, 1994)

Zahedieh, Nuala, *The Capital and the Colonies: London and the Atlantic Economy, 1660–1700* (Cambridge: Cambridge University Press, 2012)

Theses

Forestier, Albane, 'Commercial Organisation in the late Eighteenth Century Atlantic World: A Comparative Analysis of the British and French West Indian Trades', unpublished PhD thesis, London School of Economics, 2009

MacMillan, John Gilbert, 'The Port of Bristol in the Second Half of the Eighteenth Century: An Examination of the Organisational Structure of the Port Pertaining to the Management and Operation of its Shipping with Special Reference to Ships Trading with the West Indies and America', unpublished PhD thesis, University of Exeter, 2015

Index

abolition of the slave trade 14, 20–21, 33–37, 43, 124n5, 133–34, 152, 168–70, 182
accounting 21, 27, 42–44, 53, 58–60, 67, 104–05, 159–61, 166
  see also credit
accounts of sale 102, 104–05
Akers, James 174
Almond (enslaved person) 55–56
American Revolution 3–4, 9, 18–20, 34, 43, 125, 128, 143
  see also United States of America
Antigua 71, 73, 111, 142
attorneys 27, 29, 177–78, 185–88

Baillie, Evan 10–11, 31, 61, 91–92, 97
  see also Bright, Baillie & Bright
Baillie, Peter 10
Bank of England 172
Barbados 20, 39, 45, 68, 72–73, 99, 108
Beckford, William 97, 152–53
Berbice 43, 130, 148
Berkeley, Henry 186
Bettesworth, Thomas 114
bills of exchange 33, 54, 161–65, 169–72

bills of lading 58, 96–97, 104, 117, 166
Blake, Joseph 179
Blake & Powell 169
Boddington, B. & T. 114, 117, 163
Bonbonous, James 92, 100
book-keeping
  see accounting
Booth, Thomas 100
Brazier, Edward 106, 115, 180, 186
Brazil 148
breakage 101–02, 118
Bright, Baillie & Bright 91, 97
Bright, Lowbridge 168
Bright, Lowbridge & Richard 11, 13, 91–92
Bristol
  decline 3, 8–9, 89, 151–52
  port congestion 10, 66, 69
  sugar imports 86–91
brokers xiii
  insurance 57–58, 114, 127
  sugar 40, 58, 96, 98–101, 103, 105, 136
Budgen, John Smith 153, 183

Canada 144–45
  see also North America

captains 52–56, 58, 62, 71–72, 96–98, 103
  see also crew
  see also ships
Carroll, James 186
cartelisation 95
Cave, John & Co. 178
Chabert, Charles 179, 184, 186
Chabert, Joseph 186
clerks 98, 102–03
clough
  see breakage
Codando 55
Coker, John Frederick 27
Coker, William 25–29, 186
Colhoun, William 135
commission system 53, 80, 96–97, 104–06, 117–18, 152–53, 162–63, 165
communications
  see information
Compulsory Convoy Act (1798) 64
convoys 3, 58, 63, 69
  benefits and drawbacks of 65–80
  impact on sugar market 136–40, 149
  timings of 64–65, 70–71
coopers 55, 58, 98, 101–03, 106
cotton 9, 15, 41, 110, 123, 131, 193–94
courts
  see litigation
credit
  bonds and mortgages 160–61
  credit crisis (1793) 95, 138, 169–70
  credit lengths 160, 179–80
  lending strategies 166–67, 171–72
  see also accounting
  see also bills of exchange
  see also investment
  see also networks
crew
  role in sugar market 97–98, 100, 103
  wages 62, 75
Croker, Samuel 186

Crosse, John Tobin 177
Cuba 43, 130, 148, 150, 152
Customs 53, 60, 85, 98, 102n60, 118, 145

Daniel (enslaved person) 55
Daniel, Thomas (& Son) 11, 92, 130, 176
Davis, McKenzie & Strachan 176–77
Demerara 43, 130, 144, 148
Dickinson, William 12–13, 40–42, 85, 91, 102–03, 106, 108, 115, 117, 131, 145
droghers 78
Dutch Crisis (1787) 61, 125–27, 167
duties
  see taxes

East Indies 133, 134n51
Ellery, Charles 177
enslaved people
  clothing 30
  death rates 19–20, 23–24, 31, 34, 168
  labour 12, 18, 24, 38–39, 41, 54–56, 78
  punishment 24–25, 27, 37
  stereotypes of 32, 34
  terminology xiii, xiiin3
  uprisings 6, 130, 139, 142–43, 173
  see also plantations
  see also slave trade
Essequibo 130, 144, 148
exchange rates 25n18

factors xiii, 7–8, 37, 91, 97, 105–06
first mate
  see crew
Fisher, Samuel & Miers 183
Fisher, William 55
food
  see provisions
freight 3, 42, 52–54, 56, 61–62, 104, 146–47
French, James 186
French Revolution 5, 129, 169

Fuller, Stephen 12
Fuller, Stephen & Rose 13, 98, 100, 106, 126, 131
Fydell, Richard 92, 169

Gill, Joseph 10, 25–29
Glasgow (city) 18, 79, 118
Glasgow (enslaved person) 55
government
    contracts with merchants 3–4
    and convoys 64–65
    regulation of trade 30, 131–33, 140, 142, 145–46, 150
    shipbuilding 61–62
    support of slave trade 35–36
Graph Theory
    see social network analysis
Grenada 139, 142–43, 173
Guadeloupe 63, 143

Hage, Jens Friedenreich 184
Haiti
    see Saint Domingue
Hamburg Crisis (1799) 149–54
Harris, Thomas 11, 13, 85, 91–92, 98–100, 103, 110, 118
hazards
    see moral hazards
    see natural hazards
Hendrickson, John 166, 175, 180
Hendrickson, Josiah Webbe 104
Herfindahl–Hirschman Index xvi, 94
hogsheads, size of 84–86, 97
Huggins, Edward 161, 171, 174, 183
Huggins, James 161
Hughan, Thomas 188
hurricanes 20–21, 23, 29, 31, 40–41, 57, 79n108, 167, 188
    hurricane season 66, 68, 71, 77
    see also natural hazards

impressment
    see press gangs
information 21–22, 39–43, 66, 71–73, 84, 95, 97, 103–04, 114, 117, 131, 136, 138, 140, 183–87

insurance 3, 51, 57–61, 66, 76–80, 98–99, 166
    premiums 77–79, 147
    underwriters 57–61, 76–77
    see also brokers
investment 3
    in plantations 23, 35, 41, 158, 167, 170–72, 175–76
    in shipping 52
    in slave trade 32
    see also credit
Ireland 20, 30, 118, 140, 145, 149, 171, 179

Jamaica 12, 20, 39, 41, 63, 65, 68, 71–72, 76, 97, 99, 110–12, 126–27, 129, 131, 138–40, 142, 147, 152, 188
Jay Treaty 145
Jones, Billy 55
Jones, Pero 12
Jones, William 70, 104, 178, 184

Keyworth, Henry 179
Krause, Martin and William 184

Ladbroke, Rawlinson & Co. 163
lime
    see temper lime
litigation 164, 178–80
Liverpool
    and Bristol 3, 8–9, 72, 118, 124, 150–52, 156
    and cotton 110
    and slavery 24, 31, 31n36, 33–35
    sugar market 88, 118, 148–52, 154
    and the West Indies 18, 34, 172
London
    and credit 163–64, 173, 176, 185
    merchants 7–8, 13, 18, 97–98, 100, 104, 188
    and shipping 51, 56, 61–62, 78–79, 174
    and slavery 24, 33–35
    sugar market 8, 88, 101, 109, 112–19, 126–28, 127n20, 131,

135–36, 138–40, 144, 150–52, 154
West India Society 36, 132, 144, 150, 172
Long, Edward 1, 8
Lovell, Robert 106
Lowman, George 104, 186
Lynch, Ulysses 44, 175–78, 184–85

Maies, Charles 53–56
manufactures 8–9, 30, 33–35, 41–42, 45–46, 71, 133, 160
Martin, Nathaniel 163
Martinique 43, 143–44
Maxse, John 85, 92, 97, 102
McGill, Tom 55–56
Miles, William 11, 32–33, 91–92, 125
Mills, John Colhoun 186
molasses 19, 39–40, 58, 83, 97, 99, 106, 146
Montserrat 111, 142
moral hazards 53–61, 96–99, 173–81, 188

natural hazards 40–41, 50, 53, 57, 73, 74–76, 78–79, 96–99, 167, 188
  see also hurricanes
networks 6–7, 25–28, 53, 55
  of credit 2, 22–23, 54–55, 117
  of knowledge 21–23, 41–42, 183–88
  see also social network analysis
Nevis 10–11, 19, 27, 39–41, 45, 54, 63, 67, 70, 99, 110, 142, 146, 160, 167, 171–72, 174, 178, 186
Noble & Hunt 58
Nootka Sound Crisis (1790) 61, 77–78, 127–28, 130, 167–68
North America 19–20, 66–67, 119, 144–45, 183
  see also United States of America

oligopoly 94–95, 105

packet ships 21, 72–73
Parson, Edward 186

perils of the sea
  see natural hazards
petitions 13, 33–37, 64, 86
pilferage 54, 97–98, 104
Pinney, Azariah 10
Pinney, Jane 10, 27, 30–31
Pinney, John
  background of 10–11, 13
  personal finances 180
  plantation of 25, 27, 143
Pinney, John Frederick 10, 12
plantation machine 17–18, 37, 81, 158
plantations
  absenteeism 12, 24, 33, 41–42, 97, 118–19
  animal labour 18, 38, 43–44
  enslaved labour 24, 38–39, 41
  innovation 43
  managers 24–27
  ownership 25
  violence 24–25, 37
  see also enslaved people
plunderage
  see pilferage
press gangs 34, 49, 61–62, 127
Prince (enslaved person) 55–56
privateering 3, 62–63, 65, 73–74, 79, 143, 145
Protheroe & Claxton 11, 52, 60, 91–92
provisions 4, 19–20, 23, 27, 29–30, 61, 75, 77, 125, 135, 144–45, 147, 188

Ramsay, Revd James 11, 17, 36–37, 191, 194
reputation 2, 8, 53–54, 56–57, 106, 114, 161, 164, 173, 181–85, 188
revolution
  see American Revolution
  see French Revolution
  see Saint Domingue
Richards, Nicholas 177, 186
Rogers, James 31, 76, 92, 169
Ruan, William 184
rum 19, 27, 33, 39, 83, 106, 117–19, 135, 143, 146, 160, 177

Saint Domingue 63
  Saint Domingue Revolution 7,
    88, 94, 124, 124n5, 129–35,
    140–42, 146–48, 150, 160, 170
  sugar production in 119, 124,
    129
Saunders, Cossley 186
Shiercliff, Edward 13
ship-ownership 11, 51–52
  and wages 53, 62, 75, 147
  see also captains
  see also crew
ships
  Albion 63
  Duke of Clarence 75
  Edward 52, 63, 68
  Fame 52, 63
  Guiana Planter 76
  Hebe 75
  Hector 52
  Industry 52
  King David 52, 75
  Mercury 63
  Nevis 52–53, 56, 58, 61–62, 67–68,
    74–75, 106
  Pilgrim 67
  Rachel 52, 67
  Russia Merchant 63
  Tobago Planter 52
  Trio 52
  Union Island 52, 61
  Venus 67
  see also captains
  see also crew
slaked lime
  see temper lime
slave trade 31–32
  defence of 33–37
  guarantee system 32–33
  and insurance 76
  see also abolition of the slave trade
  see also enslaved people
slaves
  see enslaved people
Smith, Adam 7–8, 83
social network analysis xv, 21–23

Society for Effecting the Abolition of
  the Slave Trade 21
  see also abolition of the slave trade
Society of Merchant Venturers 13,
  33, 35
Span, Samuel 52–53, 61, 92
St Croix 63, 141, 178–79, 186
St Kitts 41, 67, 172, 175, 177, 186
St Lucia 143
St Martin 143
St Vincent 139, 142–43, 171–73, 179,
  186
Strode, Nicholas 184
sugar
  bakers/refiners 33–35, 101, 107–11,
    113, 116, 118, 128, 131, 133,
    139–42, 146, 149, 151–52, 175
  European markets 119–20, 129,
    141–42, 149–51
  grocers 107–09, 131, 136
  imports 86–91, 111–12
  plantation production 18, 38–39,
    103–04, 129
  quality 27, 39–40, 43, 99–100,
    103–04, 106, 174
  refinement 108
  sales strategies 95, 105–06, 109,
    136, 138, 140–41, 152–54
  sampling 100–01, 103, 136
  see also plantation machine
Sutton, James 13, 128

tare 101–03, 102n60
Taylor, John 186
Taylor, Simon 76
taxes 3, 8, 35, 64, 104, 125, 132–33,
  147, 163
temper lime 38–39, 44
Tobago 36, 143
Tobin, Elizabeth 10, 30–31
Tobin, Henry Hope 10
  background of 10, 13
  debate with Revd James Ramsay
    17, 36–37
Tobin, James Webbe 10
Tortola 60, 63, 172

trade winds 67–68
Trans-Atlantic Slave Trade Database 31
Trinidad 144, 172
Tyson, James 174–76
Tyson, John 188

underwriters
see insurance
United States of America 7, 20, 27, 29–30, 34, 66–67, 135, 144–46
see also American Revolution
see also North America

warfare
costs imposed by 146–48
impact on shipping 61–63, 68–69
merchants' familiarity with 4–6
threat of 125–28, 170–71
transition into 135–36
transition out of 125
Warren, John 57, 60, 114, 127, 131
Washington, Archibald 177, 184, 186
Weare, John Fisher 11, 13, 52, 91–92, 108, 115, 136, 138
weather
see natural hazards
see also hurricanes
Webbe, George 44, 97, 145
Weekes, Thomas Pym 25–29, 186
West India Association (Bristol) 11, 13, 29, 33, 50, 62, 64–65, 71, 74, 86, 91, 98, 101–02, 125, 183
Wilks, John 56
William, Dr Weekes' (enslaved person) 56
Williams, James 26, 28, 177, 186
Williams, Nicholas 153
Williams, Son, Drury & Co. 163

www.ingramcontent.com/pod-product-compliance
Lightning Source LLC
Chambersburg PA
CBHW071408300426
44114CB00016B/2232